Hockey
In Search of Excellence

CORE VALUES

Ron Johnson BSC., MSC

Hockey - In Search of Excellence
Copyright © 2018 by Ronald S Johnson, BSc, MSc

All rights reserved. No part of this publication may be reproduced, distributed, or transmitted in any form or by any means, including photocopying, recording, or other electronic or mechanical methods, without the prior written permission of the author, except in the case of brief quotations embodied in critical reviews and certain other non-commercial uses permitted by copyright law.

Tellwell Talent
www.tellwell.ca

ISBN
978-0-22880-945-6 (Paperback)
978-0-22880-946-3 (eBook)

TABLE OF CONTENTS

DEDICATION vii
PREFACE... ix
FOREWORD xiii
INTRODUCTION xvii
FOR THE LOVE OF THE GAME.. 1
PLAYER CONTRIBUTIONS 7
    BILL FORDY 9
    GARRY TOOR..14
    STEVE WICKLUM 21
    CAM STEWART 26
    MIKE VALLEY 30
    PETER HARROLD 36
    ADAM BURISH 44
    SHAWN HORCOFF 50
    ETHAN WOLTHERS 57
    BEN ISRAEL 62
    CHRIS CONNER 68
    KALEIGH FRATKIN 73
    MATHEW BARZAL 78
    ANDREW COPP 85
    DYLAN LARKIN 92

BRENDEN DILLON	97
JOE PAVELSKI	101
RYAN KESLER	108
PATRICK MARLEAU	114
RANDALL JOHANSEN	120
JEREMY RUPKE	125
IAN GALLAGHER	132
JOE OLIVER	142
MIKE JOHNSTON	151
TROY WARD	156
KURT OVERHARDT	163

LIFE EXPERIENCES 167

RESPECT	169
WORK ETHIC	171
COMPETITIVENESS	174
MENTAL TOUGHNESS	177
HUMILITY	181
SACRIFICE	183
DISCIPLINE	190
DISCIPLINE - TRAINING	193
ACCOUNTABILITY	197
CONFIDENCE	202
TEAMWORK	208
POLITENESS	216
HONESTY	218

ADDITIONAL LIFE LESSONS 229

THE MIRROR	231
THE EMPTY CUP	236

THE SENSEI AND THE MASTER 239
　　　THE HANDSHAKE 244
　　　RIDDLE A DAY 246

LAST STORY – SPECIAL FORCES 250
SYNOPSIS 256
REFERENCES 261
TESTIMONIALS 265
BIOGRAPHY 267
CLOSING COMMENTS 269

DEDICATION

First and foremost, I would like to dedicate this book to my mother and father. Without their guidance and love, and their making the ultimate sacrifice of time to take me in, I would not be the man I am today.

While I am most certainly not without my flaws, I try my best to navigate this, at times, confusing construct of life. Many other people have also assisted me along my journey and for them I am grateful:

Bud McNabb – The native Indian father of a dear friend, now deceased, who allowed me to bounce many of my life's concerns off him as I grew up. He managed the ice rink where I was allowed to pursue my passion and saw value in my work ethic and focus, and employed me through some tough financial times.

Dick Doyle – A man who took the time to find little jobs for me after my father passed away, when I was alone and trying to pay my way. He supported my hockey through my teenage years, and gave me encouragement along the way.

My wife Catherine – She has been a best friend for over forty years and always encouraged and understood my passion for the game. She supported me through this process and provided some helpful insights.

Peter Harrold – A former hockey professional who shared his passion for the sport with me. I appreciate his guidance, wonderful editing suggestions and many hours of great hockey conversation. He frequently encouraged me to keep at it and to complete this book.

Shaylun Young – A dear friend, who supported me when others wouldn't and who believes in the process. He has renewed my faith in character and his outstanding values are enriching others in Reston, Virginia, where he teaches.

Lastly – to the many wonderful people, both amateur and professional, that I have met along my life journey. They have enriched me beyond measure and without them this book would not be possible.

To all, thank you.

Ron Johnson, BSc. MSc.

PREFACE

Why this book? Why a series of books?

Writing about hockey has been on my mind for a long time. For far too many years, I have observed the trials and tribulations of youth, aspiring to reach the NHL, with many failing, and few succeeding.

I have seen the incredible sacrifices of families; committing countless hours and finance to their son or daughter's dream. I have seen players quit from frustration or emotional pain. They put their skates away in storage for many years before they find the courage to venture back. There have been devastating injuries that have ended careers and left players wondering what could have been. There have been stories of courage where the passion to play has overcome all odds.

With over forty years of teaching and coaching under my belt, I have been witness to both wonderful and heart-wrenching stories of success and loss. At times, witnessing such events has been a vexation on my spirit while others have provided sheer elation. The dream to acquire excellence is a long and at times unforgiving road.

What I endeavor to provide in this book are stories of hope, some lessons on life, and stories of successes on the journey from the amateurs and professionals that have enriched my life through their experiences.

There are many reasons why players succeed or fail. Poor skills' habits, parent intervention, improper coaching, freak injuries, and the intangibles, to name but a few. The real determining factor is an elite skill that separates and the attitude behind the desire to acquire them. While an elite skill may determine who makes the NHL and who doesn't, that elite skill is the product of something deeper. The acquisition of elite skill requires deep desire and a determined attitude to excel.

I have had many discussions with players, parents and hockey personnel over the years with the sole objective of isolating the character traits and skills that push players forward. As a current skills and former Junior hockey coach, I felt it was imperative to provide answers to these issues for both students and their parents. During my late twenties and early thirties, I embarked on a quest for answers, to help shape my developmental objectives. The initial answers I got from these interviews didn't sit well with me. There appeared to be a lot of subjectivity and speculation, without much fact.

A growing suspicion that these answers were incorrect served as the driving force behind my co-founding a research company in 1993 called Excel Hockey. The primary objective of this was to put to bed the long held premise that forward skating speed was the most important skating skill for offensive production. Working in partnership with the BCHL, which is touted as the premier Junior A Tier 2 league in Canada, and after analyzing the data on twenty-one skating skills, with and without a puck, I found that short game skating skills were the most predominant contributors to offense. Short game skating skills are defined as those performed in small areas such as forward tight turns, stop/starts, and crossovers.

Coaches were surprised at this data and even more surprising was the fact that many of the players whom they thought were the fastest on the team, were not. In fact, most times, the tall lanky kids won the time trial. I then took that 1996 study and applied all the research into developing a training program for a Bantam AAA team that I was coaching out of North Delta. We won the provincial and Western Canadian Bantam Championship in 1999, the first time in seventeen years that a lower mainland team had done so. From our roster of seventeen players, fifteen went on to junior, college and pro careers.

I then made the jump to junior hockey again, applying the same developmental program. We won the PIJHL (Pacific International Junior Hockey League – now known as the PJHL) provincial championships, as well as bronze and silver medals at the Junior Hockey Nationals in the 2003-04 and 2004-05 seasons respectively. We did all of this with the youngest teams in junior hockey history (we rostered six fifteen-year-olds).

It became absolutely clear to me that research can pay huge dividends in performance training and yet, I felt that some information was still missing.

In 2005 I again co-founded a hockey research company, this time called Next Testing with Mike Valley, former goaltending coach for the Dallas Stars. While the data that I found, during the 1996 research project had proved fruitful, I still felt that off-ice testing needed some quantifiable data in order to isolate those discriminating performance variables. We conducted a study with the 2008 NHL prospects camp, in Edmonton, which produced more evidence that short game skills were the most important for elite performance, and certain muscular attributes were more desirable for the performance of said skills.

While I had already researched skating mechanics relative to speed, as well as their physiological contributors, I still needed to understand how to use them in game play, to complete the final picture.

In 2010, I founded a research company called Elite Hockey Science. The aim was to isolate the skills and tactics that had the highest rate of occurrence or ROO in offensive success. This included over fifth data points including shot type, skating skills utilized, shot location, direction of attack, zone origin, zone entry, offensive tactics used, passing sequences, visual system, defensive error and many more.

Over the past year, I sat down and discussed my experiences and findings with a former professional player. His suggestion "maybe a book is in order; so, throw your findings and experiences at the wall and see what sticks" has now grown wings.

At times over the years, and especially after scouring mounds of data, I have felt a little like Chicken Little running around yelling, "*The sky is falling, the sky is falling!*" or that freeway driver, yelling to John Candy in the movie "Planes, Trains and Automobiles"; "*You're going the wrong way*". It seemed to me as if current training models were going in the wrong direction because they did not fit the game skills "rate of occurrence" (ROO) model.

Finally, with the advice and some pushing of my hockey friends, I acquiesced and decided to write it all down. The idea was to put together a series of books that could lead a player/parent, through a sort of development progression, if you will. In other words, I am trying to provide a logical, chronological set of commentary and training guidelines that lead a player down a better path in their search for excellence.

Of course this means that there had to be a beginning and an end to the series, which took some thought. I have always looked at development as a series of chronological steps that moved a student from A to Z. In the beginning it is the desire to play hockey that pushes one to put on skates. Where that comes from varies from person to person, but it is unquestionable that the next step is to acquire skill. We then move on to learning skill, then using skill, working with others and finally, keeping skill.

Based on the above logic, the first book in the series covers the core values or character requirements that players need, in order to both maximize the learning process and to achieve their dream result.

This book is a combination of my discoveries and lessons (as a son, player, hockey coach, parent, researcher and academic) and those of the players that are either on their way to, playing in or have formerly played in the NHL. It is about what made them and what they discovered about themselves and others on their journey.

When I discussed my intentions with the player, they all told me that they felt that the youth of today needed more guidance and they hoped that their experiences and advice could help enlighten you, the reader, in your Search for Excellence.

There will be several books in this series and this is the first: "Core Values". I hope that you can glean some valuable insights that will help to you or your son/daughter on their journey.

FOREWORD

So what are core values?

One could say that they are the underlying belief system that carries us forward each day. They speak of honor, integrity, pride, respect, discipline or just simply, one's attitude. They are not a given in our life. They have to be taught and reinforced along our journey by those that are assigned as our mentors and guides, some through direct contact and others observationally. These could be our parents, coaches, teachers, bosses or even our friends or idols.

I had been taught many such principles in my life and while I have struggled with some, I have embraced others more readily. Such is the conflict in our life's journey. It is a road, paved with good intentions and along the journey we learn the easy way and, at times, the hard way hits us upside the head, knocks us down and forces us to change. My mother and father were great administrators of these lessons as were others I encountered along my own road.

In the world of hockey, there is a kind of unwritten code of conduct. It is what is expected of you every day, when you show up to the rink to practice or play. It is how you treat your teammates and how your treat your fans. It is how your respond to new ideas and concepts. It is how you approach training, your commitment to excellence, and your willingness to compete.

Over the years, I have been blessed to know and work with many talented players. When I was a young coach, I thought that systems and skills were the key to winning. While I won my fair share of championships, I was working harder than necessary on issues outside the game itself. It became evident that I was spending unnecessary amounts of energy trying to instill some of the missing, basic core values in my players that were essential to becoming a champion. In tryouts, I tended to pick skill over attitude. I finally won my first national championship in 1999 with a Bantam A1 team out of Delta, BC. They were an amazing group of young men who had an incredible work ethic and urge to compete.

When I moved into junior hockey several years later, I realized that picking a team of players who exhibited strong core values, such as work ethic, accountability, team work, and discipline, led to far greater coaching success. However, whereas I had worked with younger players, who moved up the ladder to the NHL, I had not really worked with a concentrated group of professional athletes, where I could really see how core values impacted on success or failure.

Years ago, Adam Burish, a player with the Chicago Blackhawks and a Stanley Cup Champion, invited me to teach a camp in Madison Wisconsin. I was to instruct him and several other NHL players in shooting mechanics. This is where I got my first real glimpse of the men who drive the future of the game. Included in this group were Joe Pavelski, Tom Gilbert, Blake Geoffrion and Adam, plus several others. It was during this first ice session that I truly came to appreciate the Core Values of the Professional Player.

Since that time, the list has grown substantially to include players such as Joe Pavelski, Ryan Kesler, Patrick Marleau, Dylan Larkin, Andrew Copp, Travis Zajac, Bryce Salvador, Kevin Bieksa, Andrew Cogliano, Shawn Horcoff, Matt Barzal, Ryan Nugent-Hopkins, Kyle Connor, and Ben Street as well as many, many others. I have also had the pleasure of meeting many people that are involved directly or indirectly in those players' lives; trainers, agents, scouts, and media personnel.

This book will be a combination of life stories. It will include some of my life experiences; those which have allowed me to see and appreciate core values in others. It will also include the stories of others, both amateur and professional. They are currently on the path, have acquired the ultimate goal, or have left the road to use the lessons that they learned on their journey to create other successes in their life. It's all about how core values came into being and how all learned to be

CORE VALUES

the high character people that they are. It will be about the lessons and observations that helped guide them on their journey, either to support or to become the players that grace our television screens. In sharing these stories, I hope to help guide you on your hockey quest.

I hope that you enjoy this book and look forward to reading the ones that follow.

Yours in hockey,

Ron Johnson, BSc. MSc.

INTRODUCTION

I have been asked many times; "With all the hockey knowledge that you've gathered over your life, through your research and personal experience, why start the '*In Search of Excellence*' series with Core Values?"

It's a simple question, however, putting the reasons into simple words may prove to be more difficult. Often, during my journey through life, I have looked at my failures and successes with an objective eye and tried to figure out why each event turned out the way it did. What I have noticed is that there is always some underlying habit or repeated action that contributed to the outcome. Whether positive or negative, outcomes are greatly influenced by our habits and patterns of behavior, many of which we are unaware of. I have found that becoming aware of our habits and behaviors is sometimes very difficult, and it helps to study others and to ask ourselves if we have some of the same habits that other people do.

I have read many books that discuss the habits of highly successful people and I realized that some of these habits were missing in my every day actions. Reading these books pointed out some habits others had that I did not. I came to realize that having very successful operational habits can lead to better results in production. However, I had neglected some interpersonal habits were also necessary to success. We live in a world that sometimes overvalues results at the expense of the process, and individual success at the expense of the team. The quality of the process is built on a foundation, of deeper values and habits, which makes success sustainable. Qualities such as humility, respect, forgiveness, and accountability are the foundation of sustained individual and team success in business, sports, and life.

While ambition, focus, and productivity are all necessary parts of success in anything, the outsized importance that society puts on them does not necessarily lead to lasting success in business or a sense of meaning in life. If those motivations are all that matter, then results will eventually suffer and so too will personal relationships.

I have worked my whole life in the service industry and as an educator, so ambition and career climbing were not primary motivations for me. I was able to learn from my failures because I was humble enough to admit mistakes, and determined enough to find out what went wrong, so I could improve as a teacher and coach.

I have been a skill, tactical and team coach for over forty years. I have failed many times, but each time I failed at something new. Success in any domain is determined by who learns from their mistakes the fastest. Very successful people are those who can also learn from the mistakes of others. I understand how important mistakes are to the process of learning and to our lives in general.

Each hockey season is a microcosm of the course of life. We follow a passion, we establish some goals, we work at the skills necessary to achieve our goals, we have to work with others to make it happen, we have to commit to a process, we learn to take direction and criticism, we evaluate our efforts and make adjustments - all while being part of something bigger than ourselves. After a season of play, we have either achieved our desired objectives or we have not. The lessons happen quickly and we have to adapt to the process. The process very much resembles a condensed version of life. We learn, we change, and we move on to the next season to start the process all over again.

However, what are the foundations of our actions that push players towards success in the game?

The cycle of learning starts with intent. Kids play sports because they have a desire to play the game. This is the mental driving factor behind putting their skates on for the first time. This does not mean that, at this stage, the player has discovered a passion for the game, but they are motivated by some urge to engage in the process.

CORE VALUES

The player moves into the next phase of participation and now has to learn skill. This process requires that two opposite philosophies materialize, in order for development to take place. There has to be a teacher and the young player now has to become a student. The student acquires knowledge and accepts guidance from the teacher and the teacher evaluates the student's performance and improvement.

Successes and failures are often measured against the particular values put on them by peers, parents, coaches or even the media. These may represent; goals, assists, plays made, blocked shots, shots taken, and pucks through, etc. While these surface level results are useful, they do not always measure the true success of the process, which is continual improvement. However, more on that later…

The player moves up division-by-division by competing and with speed of play, size and strength of players and the pressures to win and contribute to offense becoming the great filters. The player either continues to improve or they fall out of the competition. This cycle continues over and over through their career.

Given this, "What defines a *Great Teacher* and what defines a *Great Student?*"

We may all have different views on this but most people will agree that a great teacher should have the following:

1. Subject knowledge
2. Experience
3. The ability to communicate ideas quickly and efficiently
4. Patience
5. Adaptability
6. The ability to correct positively
7. The ability to recognize effort and improvements and reward them accordingly
8. The ability to guide and direct but not to control

I'm sure that you could add to this list but I thought that these hit the main points.

What is the make-up a great student? They should be:

1. Able to pay attention – look and listen
2. Aware of their own bodies
3. Able to concentrate
4. Able to remember teaching points verbally, visually and physically
5. Able to take correction
6. Willing to improve
7. Self-motivated enough to practice
8. Disciplined to do things correctly
9. Persevering when the going gets tough
10. Humble in that one can always get better

Again, one can add to the list, but in my opinion the real question then becomes; *"Is it the skill that the player possesses that makes them great or is it the desire to acquire skill that makes them great?"*

It is my belief that it is the latter that makes the difference. We have all heard the saying; *"One can take a horse to water but one can't make him drink"*. My view on this is quite simple; *"Why take a horse to water if it isn't thirsty?"* Ultimately it is the desire to learn, or awareness of thirst, that drives a student to seek knowledge or allows a horse to be guided to the watering hole.

An Eastern philosophy says; *"When the student is ready the master will appear!"* This begs the question; *"How does the student know when they are ready?"* The answer of course is; *"When they are ready to ask a question?"*

This is why I chose to make the first book about Core Values. It is all about how we deal with the questions and the answers, how we adapt and grow, and how we assimilate and apply. It is core values that create an attitude which helps guide us and which keeps us on track.

FOR THE LOVE OF THE GAME

Isn't this what drives us all? The push, the drive, the sacrifice, the competition, the learning and the being a part of a team. People in this book either carry what lessons the game has taught them or are still engaged in the fight.

I'm someone that is caught between both worlds; every day I carry what the game has taught me, but I am still engaged in the fight to be the best hockey instructor that I can be. My story, which I am sure is a mere drop of water in a vast sea of young aspiring hockey minds, begins over fifty years ago.

I was born in March of 1958 in a small northern Canadian town called Ft. Nelson British Columbia, and yes, that makes me an old timer. Then, we all played hockey on outdoor rinks until it got too cold in the mid-winter months.

We were a poor family and while there was never any shortage of food on the table, and there was a warm place to sleep and an abundance of love, we couldn't afford hockey gear or even a new pair of skates. Our next-door neighbor had an old pair of figure skates, which I remember borrowing, which were four or five sizes too big. My father built a small outdoor rink that the neighbor kids skated on. The only way that I could try skating with them was to stuff the toes of my borrowed skates with grey wool work socks so that my feet fit tight enough. I was determined to skate and it didn't matter whether or not they were hockey or figure skates, I took whatever I was offered.

The first pair of skates that I fell in love with was called Black Panthers. They were proudly displayed at the local Hudson Bay Company outlet. I remember walking into the store one busy day, several weeks before Christmas and seeing them for the first time. I felt my heart race at the possibility of somehow buying them and then sadly realized that this was never going to happen. I was about to turn away when I noticed that below the skates was a sign stating that there was a color Santa contest going on and the winner would receive the skates for free.

I quickly picked up several entry forms, on the way out, and left determined to win the skates, no matter how many coloring attempts it took. As fate would have it, I managed to win those skates and again by buying a pair a couple of sizes too big, I was on my passionate journey to make some kind to hockey player out of myself. I was ten-years-old and my minor hockey career was born, out of a color Santa contest.

Minor hockey was played inside an old army heavy equipment repair hangar. The rink was small. There was no glass at that time, just chain link fencing on each end to stop the puck from going over the boards. The locals used to go down to watch hockey games on the weekends with everyone standing around the boards excitedly watching the game unfold. Goaltenders wore no masks and players wore no helmets.

Our practices where held at the same rink and my father would pick up a friend and then drop us off a couple hours early, before our Saturday morning practice. As long as we helped sweep the walkways and the dressing rooms, we were welcome to use the ice. It was a wonderful crazy time.

My first recollection of a professional hockey game was sitting in front of an old tube radio listening to Foster Hewitt call a game between the Montreal Canadians and the Boston Bruins. I was seven-years-old. Foster Hewitt had an amazing ability to draw you into his magic circle. His voice was captivatingly different and his ability to create pictures in one's mind's eye was legendary. He made it seem as if you were actually sitting at the game watching the legends of hockey traversing the ice with their power and grace.

A young player's mind created wonderful images, when no picture was available, and I'm sure that this is where I began to fantasize about the possibility of playing hockey at a professional level. My father was an avid Boston Bruins' fan and I remember him saying; "Wouldn't it be a great honor to play for the Bruins?" With my Black Panther skates, and an outdoor rink in my backyard, I was determined to make that happen.

Financially, playing minor hockey was a challenge and the only way that I could afford it was to come up with a plan to earn the money to pay for my equipment and league fees. My mother, an amazing frontiers woman, was never short of ideas and knew that pop cans and beer bottles were worth money at the local depot. Ft. Nelson was an oil and lumber town, and it had residents that lived hard and fast, so there was never a shortage of collectables. With that in mind, we set about walking the Alaska Highway on the evenings and weekends, looking for those discarded pennies that people had thrown into the ditch during their travels. I would stack the empties in my father's garage and in the fall, just before hockey season, I would trade them in for just enough dollars to allow me to buy the necessary equipment.

In 1972, the town built a new indoor regulation-sized ice rink and while there was now a beautiful rink available, there was no Zamboni. Instead they looked for what was affectionately called "Rink Rats", who would operate the metal hand shovels between periods or games to clean the ice. At that time, the ice was flooded by a large forty-five-gallon barrel of hot water, mounted on a sled of sorts. The local iceman would pull the contraption around the ice, very much as Zambonis do it today, with hot water streaming out the back and falling onto a cotton towel attached to a bar behind, to smooth out the ripples.

Pay was nominal at $1.25 per hour, if my memory serves me correctly. Looking for any way to make money to pay my way, I applied at the office and was accepted.

Anyone who has ever cleaned ice with a four-foot wide sharpened metal shovel would certainly remember the definite strain on the legs. It was imperative that the ice was cleaned properly and that meant as much downward force as possible. This was to remove most of the surface snow to ensure that the hockey game or practice to follow would have the smoothest playing surface possible.

The rink went through many "Rink Rats" during this time until the town purchased its first paddle Zamboni, a couple of years later. It was strenuous work and after four or five cleans a day, ones legs would be completely fatigued. However, I could not afford to lose the job and no matter how tired I was, I still had to practice and play games. My father was a former cowboy who had ridden horses and Brahman bulls at the Calgary Stampede in his younger days and when I tried to complain about how exhausted my legs were, he would just tell me to suck it up.

There were many times I wanted to quit but somehow a passion had been ignited within me and during the summers on the farm, where work was hard, and the winters shoveling snow at the local rink, I was completely focused on my goal of doing what I could to play at the highest level.

In my second year of bantam hockey, I moved up to play rep. I loved being with my friends but realized that I was becoming more competitive; I needed a little more of a challenge. I matured early and by the time I was twelve, I had stopped growing at five foot nine inches. Facial hair started to grow at thirteen and my skills coach at the time suggested that I get on the weights; since, as he put it, there was no way I was going to be six-foot-tall.

That Christmas, I received a Weider weight set. For those that can still remember these, they were blue plastic and filled with a powder substance to make up the weight. Every day after that, I trained and by the time I was sixteen, I had a head start on most of the other kids. I had put on some muscle, weighed a hundred and ninety pounds and had no trouble competing physically.

Our head coach at the time, Don Mako, moved me up to forward winger position to play with two very talented players; Brent Doyle and Tim Roberts. Tim was a great play maker, Brent had great speed and I was supposed to be the physical guy with the shot. It worked out with us gelling as a line.

The community was home to a senior team that was made up of former NHL, IHL and Junior players and they would play weekend games for the town's entertainment. They were short a line, resulting in our line being called up to play games with them. For the first time, I experienced what it was like to compete with players who had real hockey sense. While one can fantasize about playing professional hockey, it can't truly be appreciated unless you actually play a game with that caliber of talent. After my first game, I realized that playing with elite players was something that I really wanted to do.

During the summer of my seventeenth year, my dream of playing professional hockey came to an end. My father, who was eighty-one, died of a heart attack while I was traveling south on a quick holiday. It was the end of my grade eleven summer and I had decided to travel south with a friend, after a busy summer of hard work in the local oil-drilling camp. I came back to school to finish my grade twelve year, and tried to play with the local rep team, but found that the passion had diminished. All I had ever wanted to do was to make my father proud.

During this time I had been recruited to coach some ten to eleven-year-old players with another hockey friend of mine. While my hockey journey seemed lost, I found that helping youth rekindled my love of the game. That season came and went. Hockey politics reared its' ugly head and my card was conveniently lost by the local rep team manager, leaving me out of hockey on January 10th. Following the death of my father, who had been very well-respected in the community, I was now the kid on the outside looking in.

I finished my eighteen and nineteen-year-old seasons playing on the local Juvenile rep team, since there was no junior team that far north. I had to focus on paying the bills. I still laugh at the fact that during some of the games, I would throw on my skate guards, drive the Zamboni and then jump back into the game. Work priorities had taken over and my life as a hockey player had taken a back seat.

From the day that my father passed away onwards, I had to grow up fast. My mother was retired and had moved away to live with my sister, leaving me on my own to fend for myself. I had to work full-time to put gas in the tank, food on the table and pay the other bills. I met and fell in love with a girl from the south and having a daughter, by the time I was nineteen, put into motion other celestial plans which included much responsibility.

My love of giving back to the game was ignited again when I moved to Vancouver, B.C., where I have coached, for the past thirty-eight years, now. I only recently retired from coaching, in 2017, to focus on my developmental business.

It has been a journey and while dreams come and go, the path somehow seems to find its own way. As has been said; "When a door closes, a window opens". This has been the story of my life. I have been blessed to work with amazing ambassadors of this sport. Hockey is a culture in Canada, and a way of life, especially for those who are smitten once they have truly felt its embrace. I was such a lad with dreams in my eyes and a passion that burned strong in my heart.

Funnily enough, my path has brought me full circle and while I never played in the NHL, over the forty-plus years I have had the privilege of coaching/teaching many amazing amateur players as well as many of the NHL's finest.

PLAYER CONTRIBUTIONS

BILL FORDY

FORMER PRO HOCKEY PLAYER, DEPUTY POLICE CHIEF NIAGRA FALLS

I had the pleasure of getting to know Bill many years ago when I was the head coach for the Senior AAA Bellingham Flyers of the West Coast Hockey League. Senior AAA hockey has been a long-time contributor to hockey in Canada, going back as far as 1909, when the Allan Cup was donated by Sir Montagu Allan of Ravenscrag, Montreal. From 1920 to the 1960s, the winner of the Allan Cup represented Canada in amateur play at the Olympics and World Championships. This was hockey that I grew up watching, and it featured ex-NHL, IHL and WHL players. With the prestigious history of the league, I was honored to be named as head coach.

Our game circuit included the Anchorage Aces, the Fairbanks Gold Kings, the Powell River Paper Kings, and the Seattle Indians. The team was based out of Abbotsford and then moved to Bellingham, where I coached them for a couple years. I got to know Bill when he joined our roster as a skilled power forward.

As for Bill, he was born in Oshawa, Ontario and made the jump to junior hockey in 1982, playing for the Ontario Hockey League (OHL) Guelph Platers. He was selected by the NHL Hartford Whalers in the ninth round, 164th overall in the 1983 NHL entry draft. He remained with the Platers until the end of 1985, getting a call up to the International Hockey League (IHL) Toledo Goaldiggers. Having broken his hand twice, his arm and his clavicle, Bill decided to discontinue his playing career, and moved onto other hockey opportunities.

Bill retired from hockey and made the jump to the Royal Canadian Mounted Police (RCMP) where he enjoyed a twenty-eight year career. During his tenure there, he served as the RCMP Assistant Commissioner overseeing all administrative and operational matters of policing in the Lower Mainland District (LMD) and five of their integrated units, which included – Integrated Homicide Investigative Team (IHIT), the LMD Emergency Response Team, LMD Integrated Forensic Identification Service and the Police Dog Service. The LMD has over 3,500 employees, thirteen detachments in twenty-eight communities and an approximate budget of $414 million. Bill held a variety of senior management positions during his policing career ranging from Chief Superintendent to Inspector of the Integrated Homicide Investigative Team.

He was invested as a Member of the Order of Merit of the Police Forces by the Governor General of Canada in 2014, and received the Queen Elizabeth II Diamond Jubilee Medal and the RCMP E Division Commanding Officers Commendation.

He serves as a member of both the International Association of Chiefs of Police and the Canadian Association of Chiefs of Police where he was the former director.

I caught up with Bill on September 28th, 2018. He had left the Vancouver area, and moved back to Ontario to take up the job of Deputy Chief of the Niagara Regional Police Services.

As a hockey player, Bill possessed all of the qualities that a coach wants; impeccable character, work ethic, accountability, teammanship, respect, leadership and a great sense of humor. He was a guy that I counted on when the game was on the line and was a key contributor to the two successful seasons that I had there as a coach.

I asked him for his thoughts on why so many retired junior, college and professional players take on career opportunities with either the police or the fire department.

"Those institutions depend on people working together to achieve a goal that's much bigger than the individual. It's the same environment as a hockey team and once a player has experienced that atmosphere, it's a nat-

ural transition. I joined the RCMP because I wanted to be in that team environment and be a part of something bigger than myself. I felt that it was where my values and talents could allow me to achieve success."

"What you're asking is interesting." He continued, *"I did a lecture yesterday for the Niagara Chamber of Commerce and the lecture was on leadership and lessons learned from my career. When I talk to junior police officers I identify four basic rules; 1 – always obey the rule of law, 2 – The team is bigger than any one individual, 3 – No one unit is bigger or better than any other unit and 4 – Don't ever forget who you work for. As a police officer, you work for the victims and you work for the community."*

"If we draw parallels to the hockey environment, we can agree that the first point where 'one has to obey the rules of law' or, the rules of the game would ring true. In the second point: 'the team is bigger than the individual', is also relevant. When we look at the third point: 'no one unit or no one line is bigger or better that any other' creates a strong team atmosphere which is again relevant. Looking at the fourth point; don't forget whom you work for can again be directly correlative to hockey."

"Those are my thoughts on policing. When I teach a course, I ask these four questions and of course bring up examples that I have experienced personally. However, when I talk about leadership, I say that the most important thing to me as a leader is trust. Am I trustworthy? Do the people that I lead trust me and do the people that I serve trust me. So, I ask them to ask themselves; 'are you trustworthy?'"

"The first question that I ask about trust is; do they honor the absence. By that I mean when I'm in a meeting – or in the hockey world the dressing room – and I get up and leave, do you disparage me? Do you malign me? Do you talk ill of me because if you do, that tells everyone else on the team that the second that they leave the room; you would do the same to them. This destroys trust and undermines team building."

"The second point that I bring up is; 'Do you put unspoken conflicts on the table?' If I have a problem with a guy, no matter how big or small that is, it erodes confidence and trust. Whatever that issue is needs to be confronted and dealt with. The last point, and it deals with social media and its prevalent influence on our lives; Do you blind copy (BCC) others on your

conversation? In the wrong context, this shows a complete disregard for the other person's privacy and again erodes trust."

Our discussion carried on into the more personal core values of players that leave the game and which, if any, core values would be the most helpful in a successful policing career.

"Hard work most definitely. When I first entered into policing I took pride in never booking off before the end of my shift. If a call came in a 5:45 and I was off at 6:00, I dealt with it. Some guys stop taking calls at 5:30 so that they can get out the door at 6:00. I never did that. There's lot of grey areas in policing. I always respected the rule of law and worked within the boundaries that have we have to work within to gather admissible evidence. I was always respectful of and, worked within the charter of rights and freedoms. This was very important to me and very important to me when I led units. We had to be very respectful of the law."

Take the game of hockey and I think that guys do the same thing. They need to respect the game and play within the boundaries of the game. Respect is respect whether we are talking about policing or talking about the game."

"Coming back to our earlier discussion, there are many parallels between the two. Players that work honorably within that environment find the same values in policing and that's why they tend to move in that direction."

Bill has a son that played junior hockey, but because of concussion issues, he had to back away from the game and is now in college. I thought that it was an interesting conversation, since the cycle was complete; Bill played hockey, got into policing and then his son played hockey.

"Were there values that you focused on with your son that translated back into hockey again?" I asked.

"Both of my kids are very hard-working, very committed, honest, compassionate and good to other people. I'm very proud of them for that. We always discussed honesty, respect, hard work and being a good person, but I always tried to model that behavior rather than just talk about it. I found that sometimes when I wanted to talk to my kids, it was best to jump into

the car and go for a drive. You have a captive audience and it's less threatening as opposed to sitting across the table from them and saying; 'Hey I want to talk to you."

I asked Bill whether he thought that hockey contributed to his success in the police department. What would have happened if he hadn't played, would the result have been the same?

"Hockey teaches you to compete, there are no short cuts, if you stop skating the other guy gets the puck; you stop working other people get ahead of you. It teaches the value of teamwork, the value of honesty and hard work, respect, getting along with teammates and dealing with conflict. Those are great values to bring to policing or to any occupation. The fact that one has to work on all of those values over their career makes the transition much easier I think."

Bill has always viewed himself as a guy who tries to make a difference and to make the world just a little bit better every day. Those were the qualities that drew me to him as a coach. His contributions to this book are greatly appreciated.

GARRY TOOR

FORMER PRO DEFENSEMAN, DENTAL SURGEON

Aside from Mike Valley, Garry, a former long-time hockey student, is also one of my longer hockey friendships. I met Garry one early five-o'clock morning at Burnaby Winter Club when he was fourteen-years-old (twenty-five years ago). He was a part of a small group of six hockey players that wanted to do skill development. Garry lived quite a distance from the Winter Club as did a couple of the other kids so it was early to bed, sleep in the car on the way to the rink, hit the ice hard, then back in the car to sleep, as he was driven to school. Never one to complain, always paying attention, always working hard, Garry was a teacher's consummate student.

That was the beginning of a long friendship.

Garry played his minor hockey in the Vancouver Thunderbird Minor Hockey Association, as a smooth-skating and highly skilled defenceman. Back in the early 90s, the Vancouver Super Series was one of the top showcases in Western Canada and he was always selected to play on the elite squad whether minor or major; PeeWee; or Minor or Major Bantam and he served as the captain or assistant captain on every team. There was no doubt that he would play junior hockey and he was selected to play for Langley Thunder of the British Columbia Hockey League (BCHL) when he was fifteen years old. This was quite the accomplishment at age fifteen, especially when you consider he was 5'9" and 155 pounds. What he lacked in size, he made up for in skill, hockey smarts and heart. Although he was recruited by the top NCAA schools at fifteen years of age, he elected to make the jump to the West Hockey League (WHL) Tri-City Americans when he was sixteen.

He was selected by Edmonton Ice of the WHL, in 1996, in the expansion draft and then was traded to the Prince George Cougars WHL franchise in 1997. These would be is his best junior years, when he became a two-time WHL All–Star as well as team MVP and top defenceman as a nineteen-year-old.

At twenty, Garry played defense in the Finnish Elite League (Liiga) for the Lahden Pelicans in Lahti, Finland. The following season he came back to North America to play for the Idaho Steelheads in the WCHL. From 2002- 2003, he played in the East Coast Hockey League (ECHL). Part way through the 2003 season, Garry joined the Muskegon Fury. It would be Garry's last year of pro-hockey, but a memorable one as Muskegon Fury went on to win the League championship by going undefeated in the playoffs (11-0).

Garry returned to begin training again that summer for the upcoming season in the hopes of working his way up to the AHL but with the NHL strike looming, he was concerned that opportunity would not be there.

Garry and I talked about his hockey future and he was a young man in turmoil. His uncle was a surgeon and they had sat down and discussed Garry's future after hockey on multiple occasions. His uncle recommended that he go into medicine or dentistry when he retired, because of his outgoing personality. Garry's uncle always supported him in his pursuit to be a professional hockey player, but as an ex-athlete himself, he knew there was a lot of life to live after sports and Garry would need another career, especially if hockey did not work out. Garry's family and extended family were first generation Canadians that believed that education was a long but predictable path to a better life. He was torn between the game he loved more than anything and the debt he owed his family for giving him the opportunity to play in the first place.

After much deliberation, Garry retired from hockey and started his academic career. After three years of little sleep and even less socializing in his undergraduate studies, Garry was offered a seat at the University of Toronto's Dental School. This was followed by a one-year internship at the University of Manitoba and a four-year surgical residency at the University of Toronto. After twelve years of school, Garry began to practice with his uncle, as an oral and maxillofacial surgeon. That brings us up to the summer of 2018, where we sat down at his residence and talked for a long time about the game and where it had taken us.

Garry's story, I'm sure, is like many others. A kid that was incredibly passionate about the game but being 5'10" and 180 lbs in a big man's league, he always had to prove himself as a defenceman. It's a classic tale of a player that arrived on the scene ten years too early. The Boston Bruins were watching him and were discussing whether he could play in their lineup. I knew the director of Amateur Scouting and Garry's name would come up often.

Garry was raised by a single mother and while there were hockey males in his life, myself being one of them, the grind of every day work and then supporting a son in hockey is a difficult one and one that did not go unnoticed.

"My mother would work hard every day and then do the seemingly impossible, fed me, take me to the rink whenever and wherever there was ice, would get me whatever equipment that I needed to be the best I could be. How could I not notice? Often kids don't notice the sacrifices that parents make, or even their siblings like my sister who got dragged around to every rink whether she liked it or not, they just take it for granted."

"While I'm sure that to my mother, it wasn't a sacrifice, to my sister, I can imagine that they're other things that she would have rather been doing. She never complained though and for that I'm grateful."

I asked Garry about where he got his work ethic from.

"I was very passionate about hockey and my whole life all I could think of was playing in the NHL. It was a childhood dream and I was willing to do whatever I could to get there. But that wasn't the only reason that I worked hard. Every day I watched my mother work to support me, and I didn't want to disappoint her, not in the playing in the NHL sense but because if she worked so hard for me, how could I not do the same for her to provide us a better life."

With the word sacrifice coming up in the discussion, I asked him if there were any regrets.

CORE VALUES

"I have no regrets about the game. The game defines you, shapes you and molds you one-way or the other. It helped me to understand that being part of a team, being a part of something bigger than yourself is important. You realize that people depend on you to succeed; coaches, line mates, the organization. So, as far as hockey is concerned it is the reason why I am where I am today."

"The only regret I have is that when I look back, I can see situations where I should have treated my body better. Being a smaller defenceman, I was always first to the puck. I would never take arriving second; it wasn't who I was. I had to prove myself every day and wanted no doubt as to my character and effort. As a result there were injuries and some injuries that were never allowed to heal due to the "warrior mentality" and today, during surgery or picking up my kids, there are times where my body feels every single one of them."

"Fighting through injuries was where I could have backed off, I think. The coach would always say, 'Can you just play power play?' and I would lie to the team doctor to get back in. Young and foolish, wanting to please; but, all players that do that and pay for it in the end. Old injuries all come back to haunt you."

"I always felt the pressure to play but I kind of enjoyed it in some strange way. I believed it's what you do for your teammates and to get the next the level. Your teammates know that you're not a hundred percent but the fans and scouts don't. You have a knee injury and you're not skating your best, but they don't know that. I think that looking back I should have taken the break and came back when I was the best I could be for the team and myself. Being mentally tough is part of the game but at times it can be detrimental."

When I asked Garry about how the game helped to shape his oral surgery practice, his first set of answers surprised me.

"Everywhere I was interviewed for residency positions, hockey was always a major topic of conversation. I think they appreciated that I would be a team player and work hard for them. In the end, I got my number-one ranked program and I am convinced that it was because of my past career."

Garry has always had a great sense of humor and was one of the guys that you loved having in the dressing room. His personality won them over and he was selected.

"My second opportunity came about when I applied for another residency in Toronto. The final question that they asked me was: 'Why should we chose you?" I replied. "Because I'm the guy you call in the middle of the night when it's my day off to help you with a case and then we grab a beer after. I must have had the lowest GPA ever allowed for such a position. However, the best grades didn't always translate to good hands or good teamwork."

"There is no doubt that I am where I am today because of hockey."

I've known Garry to ask the tough questions and his character was always something that his teammates and coaches could count on.

Garry added, *"Hockey will expose your character. Sooner or later you will have to look at look in the mirror and see who you truly are. There is nowhere to hide in hockey, sooner or later all will be revealed. Hockey is a great teacher for life. I take the lessons that I learned in the game into my practice."*

We shared some great hockey stories and one of my favorites occurred when he was in junior hockey. Garry always wanting to excel at everything that he did and would never waste an opportunity to get better. I was working at the rink on day and I got a call from him. "Coach, I'm having trouble with the accuracy on my shot. Would you mind if I came down and you looked at it for me."

"Of course" I answered then provided him with a convenient time for him to drop by.

Lacing them up and eager to get to the bottom of what was going on; he did a couple warm up laps while I put the net into place. I stood back by the boards and watched as he walked in from the point and let a couple fly. Over the net they went and off the glass with a resounding 'bang'. Next he skated across the blue line and took a couple more shots. The result was the same, over the net and off the glass.

Chuckling, I skated down, grabbed the net and pushed it up to rest on the blue line that he was skating on. I then moved the pucks to the far blue line, which at that time was exactly the same distance from the blue line to goal line. I asked him to shoot again. He gave me a funny look but humored me none the less, positioning a couple pucks where he wanted them and then proceeded to take several stationary shots. All the shots went top corner. He then skated in as before and the result was the same.

He turned and with that great sense of humor made some smart ass comment to which I replied, "Yes, that sound of the pucks ricocheting off the glass has a wonderful sound of power doesn't it." Worth a good laugh years later.

The final question that I posed to Garry was one about his child, a sixteen-month-old boy who is a terror in running shoes and one that won't slow down.

With a twinkle in his eyes he commented:

"This one I will have to keep out of trouble and he will be a handful." He grinned. *"By accident, he takes one to the nose and it bleeds. He doesn't cry, just gets mad that his nose is bleeding. He slides down the stairs face first because it's faster than crawling down. The kid doesn't slow down; he runs everywhere and is fearless."*

"What values from the game do you feel are important for you to share with your son?" I asked.

"Respect people, the game and hard work. It is important that he knows respect and becomes a good person. If by some chance, he does make it and he's an ass, then I have failed as a father. My mother put me into hockey to keep me out of trouble. She couldn't have cared if I made it to the NHL but she wanted me to learn to work with people and learn to be part of a team. To work hard for others, be respectful to the coaches."

"She just wanted me to be a good person and she felt that team sports were the best for me. She made sure that she found some great coaches to help achieve that. I have to add 'the right atmosphere' because as we have all heard, there some environments in this sport that 'aren't so great' I was

fortunate to have some great hockey people in my life that guided me along the right path. That is what I want for my son. Find the right people with the right character to guide him in growing up to be a good father, a good son, a good husband or a good neighbor. If I can't do that for him then I have failed not only him but my mother as well."

STEVE WICKLUM

FORMER PROFESSIONAL PLAYER, CEO SCOOLU

I have had the privilege of working with Steve for the past three years. Our first meeting centered on an online learning platform called "My Pro Hero". Today, Steve has taken that platform and merged it with a similar online platform called Scoolu of which he is a co-founder and the Chief Executive Officer. His platform is far more diverse now; involving many different professional sports such as basketball, soccer, football, baseball and hockey as well alternative professions such as the music industry and writing. The objective of this type of platform is to provide a student with direct access to the best coaches/trainers in the business, no matter what their passion is. Some of them include Spanky McCarty - Lady Gaga's drummer, Grammy winning producer Richard Furch, Paul Annacone – Federer's tennis coach, Brandon Paye and Idan Ravin – NBA Skills coaches and Todd Eldridge – Olympic figure skater and coach.

Coaching has been transformed by the World Wide Web and, with today's internet speeds and video technology; it is a natural evolution of the learning process. Steve's sports background centered around hockey with his junior career starting with the Smith Falls Bears of the Canadian Junior Hockey League (CJHL), and he moved from there to the SUNY (State University of New York) - Buffalo State roster from 2009-2012. From there Steve tried some minor pro leagues, playing in the Southern Professional Hockey League (SPHL) and the Federal Hockey League (FHL) from 2012-2014, before hanging them up to focus on his business interests.

Steve and I have engaged in many hockey conversations regarding developmental issues, not only in hockey, but also in other industries as well. His passion for linking the top instructors in the world with aspiring students has been a driving force behind his day-to-day operations. He travels extensively to meet with the best instructors available.

I think that Steve brings a unique perspective to the discussion on core values, more specifically from a teacher's perspective. Due to the fact that Steve engages in conversations with some of the best teachers in their respective fields, he gets valuable insights into what drives them and what they are looking for. While I teach, I can only engage in this conversation from my singular perspective. Steve gets to engage the best across a very wide teacher/student spectrum.

I pressed Steve on how he got into this type of business in the first place. He had a short minor pro career, retired and then moved quickly into his business venture. I asked him why this type of company.

"When I trained, there were a limited amount of high end hockey resources. Strength coaches were becoming a common off-season addition to hockey training, and there were some skating coaches available, but aside from hockey schools, there really wasn't anything out there that could really help propel me to the next level. I felt that I was missing out on elite training."

"Playing hockey at the different levels, one sees players that have more skill; better hands, better shots and better skating. I was a hard-working guy and was doing everything that I could do to get better. Being around more skilled guys at the different levels I played at, made me realize that there were differences in skill coaches. The objective then was to find those super elite coaches, the "gurus" of game, put them together on one platform so that players, whether amateur or professional, could realize their potential."

"There is so much money and time invested in sports today, especially hockey, why not have a platform that gives students access to the best teachers available? For me it was all about putting something together that would accomplish exactly that."

I thought that Steve's retirement from the game and the immediate rebound into his business seemed sort of urgent and I pressed him on this.

"I definitely think that it was because of the coaching that I received through playing. Not having really great coaches. Having coaches that didn't fully understand the skills transferrable to the game or even how to implement those skills. How to really teach a player. How to build up a player over several years, that makes that player attractive to the next level. I just didn't have the coaches that could do that. I knew that there had to be a better way. There had to be another source out there that I was missing and I began to think about the thousands or even tens of thousands of players that felt the same way as I did. That was the motivation behind it."

I've known Steve for several years and he is an intense guy. If there were ways to get better, he most certainly would have followed them. He is a consummate student; he doesn't like wasting time, he just wants results.

I can fully understand his thought process. I have experienced the same thing myself as a coach, where players have come to me and expressed the same views. The frustration is really two-fold; they wish they had started sooner or, they are upset that they have to now go back and unlearn many of their techniques and retrain themselves.

As previously mentioned, Steve has gained access to some of the most elite sport trainers available today, through his company Scoolu. I asked him what type of people they were and what they were looking for in their students.

"They are intense. What I mean by that is that they are intense about what they are doing. They believe in their information and they are going to hold that information in high regard and as a result, are very confident about what they bring to the table. They are very passionate about what they do and are definitely savants in their field. They have the ability to see things that others don't because they were seekers, looking for solutions. The have taken the time to get to the answers and then have developed a way to get those solutions across to their students."

"As for the type of student that they definitely appreciate, those are the ones that are students of the game. They want students that are passionate, that want to be a better athlete every day. They want the student that understands the difference between average and elite training, the student doesn't

want to waste time and is driven to get to the next level. You have to be a student that will buy in, that has an open mind and is willing to get out of their comfort zone. This seems to be the common theme talking to these elite trainers."

I asked Steve about his choice of platform, video interaction with one-on-one instruction; what did he see as the pros and cons of this kind of training?

"I think that there are a couple issues, the first one being the parent. This type of technology is rather new. Parents have become familiar with IPads and IPhones for taking video. I remember years ago, there was always one guy or someone assigned on the team to capture video. This has changed dramatically. The problem is that the developmental or teaching industry still depends on physical interaction, which parents want. They want to see their kids sweat and see them physically having fun however, they are not really up close and personal with the on ice trainer and as a result, don't know the quality or even relevance of skills being taught. Parents also have trouble bridging the video technology to the online one. Kids however are more accustomed to doing so and we see kids every day, going to NHL.com or YouTube to watch highlights. They are far more familiar with how a video pertains to them. Parents pay the bills and as such the industry still progressing rather slowly."

"Another negative for the parent/player is that unless they are fortunate with an elite trainer being available in their immediate area or are ready to travel, they do not have access to the best teachers available. As you know, some of our clients have flown you in to Toronto to work with them. You've also had clients fly in from Russia, China, and the US to work with you one-on-one. This is very expensive and while some can afford it, many cannot."

"Same goes for the instructor. They either desire the best students or look for better ways to manage their time. Walking downstairs to their office is much more efficient than driving one hour to meet a student and then another one hour back home. Due to the global nature of our business, they can attract students from all over the world increasing the likelihood that there is a great student on the other end of the video session. With the increased number of students available, there becomes increased pressure *on the student to have the right values that fit the learning environment. High-end teachers prefer high-end students. This doesn't mean only professional players but those individuals that exemplify the same character traits. Ultimately, it is all about supply and demand."*

"It only made sense that we create a platform that benefits both the students and the teachers economically and logistically."

I believe that this is the new way of teaching; video assessments and then online instruction. As Steve so clearly outlined, the sport's world is ever-evolving and there is a need to align the student with the best teachers available. I always tell parents that their child will run out of time before they run out of money. Just make sure that the dollars and time are well spent.

CAM STEWART

FORMER NHL PLAYER, DIRECTOR OF PLAYER DEVELOPMENT KO SPORTS

I have had the pleasure of knowing Cam for several years. I first met him at one of the development camps that I was running for KO (Kurt Overhardt) Sports, in Detroit, over the summer. We have had many discussions over the years about the changing landscape of youth development, the evolution of the game and the makeup of the NHL.

Cam has an extensive background in hockey. He was born in 1971, at a time when hockey was certainly more physical and the demands on the player were different back then. He was chosen 63rd overall by the Boston Bruins in the 1990 NHL entry draft. His career spanned many years, and he played for the University of Michigan in the CCHA conference, from 1990 to 1993. His did not return for his junior year, but decided instead to turn pro, joining joined the NHL Boston Bruins organization. He remained in the Boston system playing for the both teams until 1996. He then signed with the IHL Houston Aeros, in 1997. This is where he contributed to a Turner Cup Championship during the 1998-99 season.

As for his seven years in the NHL, he played for several organizations; first the Boston Bruins, before moving to the Florida Panthers in 1990-2000 and he ended his career with the Minnesota Wild in the 2000-2001 season. Known as a skilled gritty left-winger, Cam retired from professional hockey in 2001, after experiencing problems that stemmed from a concussion that he received while playing professional hockey. He moved to an assistant coach/front office advisor position with the Houston Aeros of the AHL, an affiliate of the Minnesota

Wild from 2002-2007. Unfortunately, Cam had to leave the game because of those concussion issues but he now offers his knowledge and experience to players trying to navigate the road to junior, college and professional hockey.

He is currently employed as the director of player development for KO Sports and represents the east coast; predominantly the Metro Toronto area. Known for his knowledge of the game, impeccable professionalism and his passion to help the players he represents, Cam's mentorship has helped many young players achieve success.

Cam is a very humble human being. He loves working with kids and helping them to improve. Having as much experience in a career as he has, playing and coaching, has given him a lot of wisdom about what it takes to become a consummate professional.

"What are some of the changes that you have noticed over the years?" I asked.

"The game is a lot different now than from when I played" Cam started, *"Every team has a skills coach, goalie coach, strength coach, specialty coach and even video coaches. This gives players so much more opportunity to improve their game if they have the desire to do so. There was none of that when I played. If you were lucky, you could take some skating in the summer or maybe attend a local hockey school but aside from that, we were left on our own. Even look at the training camps today. If players don't show up in shape they are sent home. When I played we used training camp to get into shape."*

"Another area that the player benefits from is medical and advisory. If a kid receives a hard hit or if there are issues with his game, it can always be discussed, sorted out and dealt with. I remember getting several concussions in a row and the word was always, "Get out there Stewart". They had no way of telling what the damage was and because we wanted to keep in the lineup, we geared up and played. It was a constant worry for all the players that if we were out of the lineup, the team would pass us by. While players often have to be in the right place at the right time to get an opportunity, sometimes it works in reverse. A kid gets an injury and they before they know it, they are on the outside looking in."

"This is what happened to me. I was centered between two great wingers when I was in Boston. I broke a finger and I was out of the lineup. The next thing I know, I'm running around as a third and fourth liner hitting everything in sight. I had 119 points in Michigan and was considered a goal scorer. The day I broke that finger, everything changed."

"That's the nature of the game. Crap happens and when it does, mental toughness has to take over and one has to be ready to do what it takes to get back into the lineup. Back when I was injured, there was no one to advise me, no one that was on the side of the player. It was a tough grind and coaches were expected to win. Players had to get out there and do their job and do it well if they wanted to keep it. I had to adapt after the injury and that is often hard for a young player."

I mentioned to Cam that during my tenure as a junior coach I saw a lot players come through the tryout camps that, while perhaps super stars on their team, had difficulty coming to terms with the fact that there were now thirty guys just like them out there. They knew how to play but did not know how to compete for their job.

"That is a common discussion I have with the guys that I work with." Cam added, *"The game will spit you out if you don't have a healthy understanding of your strengths and weaknesses and know how to compete. It is hard for players and parents to watch their son or daughter thrive at one level and then disappear into the mix at the next. They have to know how to separate themselves."*

"I always tell players to love what they do and love who they are. Don't try to be someone else. Play the game that they know how to play and then work on their weaknesses. Players often try to emulate some pro player that they respect instead of selling their own unique set of skills. Compete, take instruction from the coaches and be a part of the team game. One can still show who they are and be part of a team."

"It is important that they understand that each level is a little faster, a little more skilled and if they think at any time they are good enough, they will get exposed. It is important that they keep working to improve no matter what level they are at."

CORE VALUES

I mentioned to Cam that another area that can be overwhelming for players is the sheer number of players that show up to team's tryout camps. When I was coaching the Richmond Sockeyes in 2003-2004, we had ten teams of players trying out for maybe six positions. It was hard for players to understand how to compete against so many different kinds of players. Even though the coaching staff explained what we were looking for – make the guy next to you better, move the puck quickly, skate hard on the back check, compete in the corners – some couldn't grasp the team concept and would showcase their skill over carrying the puck. Some players worked hard but not smart, and some ran around hitting everything in sight.

"Every player has a role to play in a team system. It is important to know what you bring to the team and what the team expects of you." Cam went on *"Sometimes one has to adapt in their role like I did to get ice time, until an opportunity presents itself. One has to be prepared for an opportunity. Train hard, work on the little things that allow for success and gain confidence from the coaches. Demonstrate strong defensive play, compete hard, go to the net, win your face-offs, keep your feet moving and follow the team game plan, however that is laid out."*

I asked Cam what character traits he tried to reinforce in the young kids today, who demonstrate enough skill to get them to a professional career?

"I think that kids today need to constantly work on their game. That takes commitment, accountability, discipline and hard work. Everyone is trying to get the same opportunity and the minute that a player takes his eyes of his goal, someone steps into his place. That's the nature of the game. It also takes mental toughness. There will always be adversity which they will have to battle through."

MIKE VALLEY

FORMER PROFESSIONAL GOALTENDER, NHL GOALTENDER COACH

Mike was born in Richmond, British Columbia in 1976. His family moved to South Delta where he played his minor hockey as a goaltender for the South Delta Minor Hockey Association.

I had the pleasure of first meeting Mike when he was fifteen years old. We have become close friends since and still reach out and talk to each other frequently. Our working relationship started in 2005, when we co-founded a sport's research company called Next Testing. Here we worked closely together until 2010, pioneering the field of performance testing on ice. Until then, I knew very little about his minor hockey days. His mother worked in the Parks and Recreation office located inside the North Delta Recreation Center where I worked as an iceman and we would occasionally chat about Mike's hockey and his desire to be an elite goaltender.

She approached me one day and asked if Mike could drop by for some ice time. He managed to get a ride down to the rink late one Friday night with one of his best friends. Back then, late night ice on the weekend was often open and he was more than welcome to come and work on his goaltending while I was servicing the rest of the building. He was one of the most focused and intensely driven players I had ever seen in all my coaching experience. I was more than happy to allow him to use the ice, as I went about my midnight duties. Andrew was his shooter and every once in a while I would lace up and join them for some shooting competition. He was a very capable goaltender and we would sit and discuss eastern philosophy after some of the sessions, since Mike knew that I had been trained in martial arts. It was always something that intrigued him and over time, he adopted a lot of the concepts into his every day training.

Mike didn't started playing hockey until he was twelve years old. I asked how he managed to pick goaltending as his first choice? I mentioned that perhaps he took the position because he wasn't good at skating. I was kidding of course but in my experience, I had met some goaltenders that used that excuse as the main reason they started in net. Of course that was worth a laugh and Mike continued.

"For some reason I just loved the thought of being a goaltender. I loved the gear and the masks and when I was young I always had pictures of goaltenders in my bedroom and in my school locker. I had played some soccer and there I was a goalkeeper, I played field lacrosse and there I played goaltender and in baseball, I was the catcher. For some reason I was just drawn to the position, perhaps it was because of the pressure and always being in the game."

Mike played his minor hockey career in the South Delta Minor Hockey Association. When he was sixteen he tried out for several junior teams but could never stick. He had to make a choice; either stay and play midget rep hockey in South Delta or play somewhere else. Mike's parents are Swedish and through a family friend, Thomas Gradin, who played for the Vancouver Canucks, it was arranged for him to travel to Sweden and try out for the Vallentuna BK J20 (Second Tier Junior Hockey League in Sweden) junior hockey team, which is about twenty-five miles north of Stockholm.

He made the team and this was the beginning of his truly amazing hockey journey to get to play in the NHL.

Of course I asked Mike about what his parents thought of his quest to head to Sweden to play hockey.

"My parents have always been supportive, driving me to hockey practices and games. My father would keep stats for me when I played. They knew that I wanted to play at the highest level and if there was any chance for that to happen, I knew that I couldn't go back to midget hockey in South Delta. I had to go where I could play at a higher level and get as much ice

as I could. The great thing about Sweden is that ice is free, supported by the community and if the ice is open one can use it as often as they like. With the decision made to go, my parents put me on the plane and told me that it was up to me to find financial support when I got there. I was sixteen years old."

"Thomas had arranged a tryout for me. I am fluent in Swedish so it was a natural choice for me to try out there, but in Sweden there are no billet families, I knew that if I made the team I would have to find both a place to live and a job to support myself. "

"I was selected to play for the team and was lucky, finding a very small hut to rent behind a German couple's house. It was big enough for a small stove to cook my meals, a bed and a tiny fridge, which I purchased. I was allowed to use their washing machine but not their dryer. I managed to find work at a stable several miles away to make money to pay for my rent and food. Every morning early, I had to get up, climb on my bike and ride through the snow to the clean the stables and then head to hockey practice."

"I took every opportunity to skate that I could. In Sweden they flood the soccer fields and every chance I could; I put on skates and went to work. It was very difficult time and it taught me a lot about myself. I stayed there for a year-and-a-half. With all the ice time that I managed to log, I probably accumulated 4 extra years of training. I realized early that the only way that I could catch up and get recognized was through hard work. It was the one thing that I could control."

"When I got back home in my eighteenth year, I was ready to give it my all for any junior team that would allow me to be a part their training camp. It was kind of weird actually." Mike added, "When I left to Sweden I couldn't get an opportunity. When I came back, I discovered that everyone had heard about this kid that went to Sweden to play junior hockey and were eager to have me at their camp."

"All of the hard work and training paid off and I signed with the British Columbia Junior Hockey League Chilliwack Chiefs. Harvey Smyl was the head coach and gave me a great opportunity."

"What was the difference this time around?" I asked.

CORE VALUES

"Living in Sweden made me realize that I had the ability to do what was necessary to achieve whatever I wanted. It was a tough but very rewarding year and a half. I had to work hard every day and I was committed to make the most of the situation. I came back with the attitude that 'No one would ever outwork me'. It was an attitude that I carried with me through, junior, college and pro. I realized that it was something that I could control; my career was completely in my hands."

From the Chilliwack Chiefs, Jeff Sauers, the head coach of the NCAA Wisconsin Badgers, recruited Mike during the 1996-97 season.

"Sadly, Jeff passed away in February of 2017 at the age of seventy-three. He was a coach that really cared about his players and they played for him. He had a great coaching history in Wisconsin. He had turned the Badger program into a success winning two national championships. He retired as the winningest coach in Badger history".

"He had come to watch me play at Chilliwack and I can't say that I had the greatest game. We had talked and I had told him that I would be the hardest working guy on his team. As, I mentioned before, hard work was something that I could control and I felt that as long as I keep focused on getting better every day, I could make a difference. Coach Sauer was old school and really valued hard work and a commitment to excellence and he brought me on board to play with the Badgers."

After his second year with the team, Mike was given a contract by the Vancouver Canucks and he played his 1989-99 season with their affiliate team the Manitoba Moose of the AHL. He played four years in the AHL, six years in the ECHL (East Coast Hockey League) and then two years with the Swedish Elite League. He managed to get bench and practice time with the Canucks but never cracked a game. Mike retired from professional hockey in 2004.

"Mike Kennan was the coach and I knew that he expected hard work and that was something that I could give."

When I asked Mike about his past and what he felt was the reason he couldn't crack the NHL lineup.

"I think that a couple things came into play. First of all I wasn't quite good enough." He admitted, *"But I also had a problem with holding onto loses or mistakes too long and I think that stopped me from progressing the way I could have. Having been an NHL Goaltending coach for the NHL Dallas Stars, from 2010 to 2015, and operating my Elite Goaltending schools, one gets to see that the best let things go. I remember when I was young, we would be playing street hockey out in the street and when I got scored on it was just a goal and I moved on. I would go to a hockey game and win or lose when I was young; somehow I realized it was just a game. Somewhere, it got too serious and I would relent over a mistake that I had made or a goal that had gone in. The trick is to let it go and move on."*

Mike retired from the Dallas Stars organization after experiencing some serious health problems. He was bitten by a tick and was infected with Lyme disease. Complications arose over several years and while dealing with that condition he found out that he had developed a heart issue. It was a rare disorder called Wolff Parkinson White Syndrome (WPW), where an extra pathway between your heart's upper and lower chambers causes a rapid heartbeat. Most of the time, episodes of fast heartbeats usually aren't life-threatening, but some serious heart problems can occur. Of course with athletes, this can pose a problem when participating in highly intense activity so extra care must be taken. With Mike, this was discovered by chance, when a doctor recommended a heart exam. As a result, he had to undergo an emergency heart operation to correct the problem.

These two experiences changed his life. We discussed how his health issues changed how he views his life now.

"When playing sports and competing, one often loses track of really what is going on. Hockey is a game and the game is exactly that, a game. I used to get so emotionally connected to my mistakes that I couldn't let go. When one experiences an illness or serious health issue, it often put's one life in perspective. That's what it did for me. Just after my operation, I took a solo hike in the Grand Canyon to kind of find myself again. Nature has that amazing way of making one stop and appreciate the simple things in life. I remember the long hike down to the base of the canyon. I was alone with my thoughts and appreciating the view. I set up camp, just enjoyed the quiet time, the fresh air and my surroundings. After a refreshing sleep, I awoke

early before sunrise to start my hike again. I was climbing upwards and stopping to take a look around when I realized that the sun was just coming up over the top of the canyon. It was spectacular. I had reached a narrow part in the trail and the canyon floor was a hundred or more feet below me. Heights don't agree with me but I decided to put that in the back of my mind, sat down and hanging my feet over the ledge and just enjoyed the amazing view. It really put my life into perspective when I realized how many such views in my life I had simply passed over."

"Every day I get up now, I try to live it like it's my last and I don't sweat the details. I wish that I had of figured that out years ago."

I asked Mike that if there was any advice that he could share with aspiring young goaltenders?

"Achieving one's goals takes an incredible amount of work and one has to buy into that philosophy. To play in the best hockey league in the world is no easy task and it's one that takes effort, dedication and discipline. In the end one has to remember that we play it for fun and that day that it stops being that, is a day that the passion starts to fade. It is important to let go and learn from the mistakes and not hang on to them. One works hard so that they can enjoy the game even more; it's the battle that matters and how one performs in those battles. Enjoy the fight, realize your mistakes and let go."

Mike had a great closing comment and always one to give credit where credit is due, he brought up a great quote from Stu Barnes, a nineteen-year NHL vet who ended his career with the NHL Dallas Stars: *"The NHL has a way of exposing you!"*

Mike added: *"No matter how good you are, there's someone pushing you, you may get three goals one day and then go without for a month, you may think your fast and then you get exposed. Every day one has to go to work. Get complacent and you get exposed and before you know it, you are on the sidelines."*

PETER HARROLD

FORMER NHL PLAYER

I met Peter in 2017 through a very close friend of mine, Hal Katernick. Hal is a cognitive trainer that lives in Bellevue just outside of Seattle Washington. Peter, who has an autistic son, was introduced to Hal and his training program, which helps autistic children. Hal has achieved some significant improvements and, afterwards, impressed by the results, Peter explored the possibility of training/teaching in that area of development. Having a hockey background, and with the fact that I had experience in Hal's area of expertise, it was a natural introduction.

I really can't recall how many hockey conversations that I have had with Peter. He is one of the most humble people that I know and has a firm grasp on his strengths and weaknesses in all areas of his life. He is very articulate and I'm not sure that I can do him justice when transcribing his stories about how he became an NHL player and his commentary on his core values; but I will attempt to do so.

Peter, as he put it, comes from a very competitive family. His older brother by seven years, Josh, had a good hockey career, playing junior hockey for the Cleveland Barons of the North American Hockey League (NAHL) and he received a scholarship to Miami University (Ohio) where he played for four years. He then moved up to play two years in the East Coast Hockey League (ECHL) before jumping to the Worcester Ice Cats of the AHL. He played minor pro for six years, bouncing back and forth between the AHL and the ECHL but not quite making the final step to the NHL.

Everyone in his family was active in sports and very competitive. As Peter puts it, *"They all hated losing and when one grows up in that environment, it's contagious and becomes a part of one's psychological makeup. The one thing that I learned early: being one of the youngest in the family, I realized that everyone seemed to know more than I did. As a result, I spent most of my time keeping my mouth shut; observing and learning from others."*

Peter followed in his brother's hockey footsteps, playing midget hockey for the Cleveland Barons U18 and then moved up to play for the same NAHL team that Josh had played for in 1999, where he played through the 2002 season after which he received a scholarship to Boston College. He played four years at Boston College and was named captain in his senior year, when his performance on defense and natural leadership helped them get to the championship game of the Frozen Four (college hockey's version of the Final Four). Ironically, Peter's team lost to the Wisconsin Badgers, 2-1, who were captained by Adam Burish, who has also contributed to this book.

I opened my conversation with Peter by posing a direct question about the core values of the professional player. Was there anything that stuck out in his mind?

"In my experience, I don't think that any one thing lent itself to determining that. It is a collection of values that, when combined together allowed me to play at that level. What was obvious at every level was that the great players put the work in."

"I was happy with my career to that point. Until my senior year of college, I hadn't seriously entertained the idea of playing in the NHL. Of course I wanted to, but I didn't really think it was a legitimate possibility. I had a good start to my senior year and the team was playing really well, and my confidence began to build. It wasn't until later in the season that I really began to entertain the idea that I could actually play in the NHL. I had been selected to the First Team All-American in my senior year, and I really began to believe that if I kept working I could get to the NHL. All I wanted was just a legitimate shot and I would go in and try to make the best of the opportunity."

"After my college season was over, I had a couple of offers from different teams, and my agent and I decided that signing with the Los Angeles Kings would give me the best opportunity to develop into an NHL player. At the time, Los Angeles had struggled, and their roster was loaded with players who were nearing the end of their careers. It would be a good chance to learn from them, and possibly step in if given the chance. I went to camp with no expectations, just kept under the radar, worked hard, kept my mouth shut and my head down and tried to do what the coaches asked."

"I always hated the negative guys, the ones that complain when something goes wrong. I never liked being around those guys and didn't want to be one of them. I worked hard and knew my strengths and weaknesses and stayed within them."

His first year he played twelve games with the NHL Los Angeles Kings playing the remainder of the season with their AHL affiliate the Manchester Monarchs.

"The following season, I moved up to play the last few months of the season with the Kings. The following year I made the team out of training camp. I had a realistic grasp on where I fit into the organization. There were guys that skated better than I did, guys that stickhandled better than I did, and guys that shot better than I did, but I thought of myself as a cerebral player. I could read the play and make good decisions."

Peter had won the Hockey East Best Defensive Defenseman award during his 2005-06 season.

"How did you become a forward?" I asked

He started laughing. *"I never played one single game as a forward before I got to the NHL. They said I had been playing well, but we had some defensemen come back from injury and they were working younger guys into the lineup. They wanted to find a way to keep me in the lineup so they asked me to play forward. The organization was exploring options to see how to improve or change things up and they were willing to give people opportunities. I had a choice to make: I could accept what the situation was and do the best I could, or I could argue and complain and end up in the press box. The answer was obvious to me. It's always better to play than not. I have watched many players over the years slip through the cracks and it was in most part because they weren't given an opportunity, or because they didn't do what was asked of them. This is professional hockey. If you don't perform or do what's asked of you, you get replaced. That wasn't lost on me and I understood my role very well."*

He explained further, *"At the end of the day, I was getting paid to play hockey and if that meant that I got paid to work out, paid to practice, and paid to sit on the bench, there are a lot worse things I could be doing. I knew my job was to do what the coaches asked of me and it was that simple. I was asked to fill in as a forward in the lineup and accepted it as a challenge. I have felt the pain of being passed over, or cut, or being told you're not good enough. It hurts. What we do with that pain is a choice. We can use it as fuel to get better, or let it eat at us, which makes the situation worse."*

"The most games I played in an NHL season were sixty-nine with the Kings during the 2008-09 season. One season I only played nineteen games. I can't say I never complained, but if I did, I made sure it was away from the rink or with someone who truly understood the situation. I tried my best not to be negative in the locker or at the rink. At the end of the day it's a team game, and the guys that aren't playing have three jobs: get better, stay ready, and support your teammates. I think that is why I lasted longer in the league than my talent would have predicted. I did what was asked of me and tried to focus on only what I knew I could control."

"I think that I could have done better or played longer. I did what I knew and looking back now; I know that I could have trained differently, worked on different skills. I don't harbor any regrets about my career in hockey. Only that I wish I'd known some things back then that I know now. I think that's pretty common among retired players and that's what draws many of them back into hockey. They want to make it better for the next guy."

All in all, Peter played ten years in professional hockey, retiring in 2016 after his final year with the AHL Chicago Wolves. He played a total of 274 games in the NHL. His career also included being selected to play for Team USA in the IIHF World Championships in 2009. Peter was also given the captaincy several times in his life including his senior year with Boston College. I asked him what traits he had that allowed him to be successful in that role.

"I think that there are many kinds of leaders. Some lead by example and some speak up when it's necessary. I was a pretty even-keel player. I never got too high or too low and I tried to keep the game in perspective. In general, I tried not to be too critical about guys in the dressing room. That may have been a shortcoming of mine, not recognizing or having the courage to rip a guy that needed it. The only thing I believed should be condemned immediately is lack of effort. I didn't encounter a lot of that once I got past juniors. In college and the pros pure laziness really wasn't much of an issue since everyone there was fighting to get to the next level."

"Coming back to the leadership thing. I don't know if I can precisely define a good leader. Because there are lots of traits a good leader has, it can manifest in many different ways. Some guys talk too much and that can be detrimental, others talk when they think it's necessary but sometimes need to talk more. It's a tough thing §to define. They have to walk the walk. Good leaders don't tell people what to do; they set the tone by doing things the right way, all the time."

I also wanted to ask Peter about opportunity, chance, and luck. I said, "I realize that in your mind, making it to the NHL, at least how I understand it, had a lot to do with luck. An opportunity presented itself and then you made the most of it. It still means that you had some skill and you still had to perform. Many try and don't succeed though, so when did that realization that you could play or wanted to play come from?"

"As the season went on, the team was having a great year and so was I. It was only then that I started to entertain the possibility that perhaps I could play at the NHL level. Fortunately for me, I had coaches that understood what it took to play in the NHL, and they were preparing us to play at the next level. They would subtly start a sentence, "When you play at the next level…", when speaking to my teammates and me. 'When', not 'if'. They would say it more overtly from time to time, but those little things added up and slowly built up confidence in me that maybe I could play at the next level. I ended up being named an All-American that season and we went to the NCAA finals. Although we lost, I think that we over achieved. We were

young, but we had a phenomenal goalie in Cory Schneider, great coaching, and talented guys that wanted to win."

"I was more surprised at the attention I was getting. I think that humility is an important value as well. I remembered the old adage that "rookies should be seen and not heard" and it was instilled in me at a young age. That served me well through my pro career. The game is changing and younger players are having to play a bigger role in the team's success, so observing, listening, and quickly absorbing as much as possible is crucial for individual and team success in the NHL."

"Were you just a quiet guy?" I pressed.

"I guess. I wasn't the kind of kid that wanted to stand out. Fitting in was just fine with me. I also wasn't a confident kid away from the rink yet. When I was playing I knew that I had some skill and was good at hockey so I could open up around the rink a little more, but the jump from college to the pros was very intimidating."

"I remember my first year with the Kings. I had Rob Blake and Mattias Nordstrom in the dressing room. They were both much bigger and more talented than I was. It was hard for me to feel confident around those guys. I just kept my mouth shut because I sure as shit didn't have anything useful for them to hear. At training camp I always talked to guys my age and kept my mouth shut around everyone else. I had always been an observer and was comfortable just blending in. In hindsight I likely missed out on a lot potential learning experiences, because I understood pretty quickly that almost all of the older guys, especially Blake and Nordstrom, were incredibly great guys. They went out of their way to give advice and engage with everyone. Just being quiet wasn't the ideal way to be, but it was just how I was at the time."

"I knew what my physical limitations were. I knew that I was fast but not the fastest, I knew that I had OK hands but I wasn't going to dangle anyone out there. I had a healthy perspective on who I was and the skills that I had. I knew that I had a good sense of the game, I could move the puck and saw opportunities and I knew that it was up to the coaches to put me into situations that played to my strengths. I never tried to over extend my abilities and became a player that they could rely on and use in a variety of

situations. I was definitely a role player. I knew my place and was ok with that. That didn't mean I didn't work at getting better but I always knew where I fit in."

"One season I played nineteen games and I sat out the rest. I thought to myself, there can be worse things that I could be doing in my life. I was getting paid to work out, practice, and bag skate. It could be frustrating at times, but perspective matters. Being part of a team is being a part of something bigger than you. There's an old adage that gets used a lot, 'Take care of the team and the team with take care of you'. It's kind of corny but it has been true in my experience. In hockey everyone has a job to do and they have to do it well. There are only so many super stars and everyone else has to fit in and do their job to make the team successful. Sitting, and being the kind of guy that observes, helped put that in perspective."

"I believe that this is actually a great analogy for life. Everyone has to do their part for a team, a family, a company, or society to be successful."

"Being a quiet observer allowed me to learn what not to do. I learned from those around me and didn't want to duplicate their mistakes. This approach served me well in pro. When a player does something wrong and the coach yells at the player for the mistake, then someone who wasn't paying attention makes the exact same mistake, coaches generally lose their mind. He just spent time trying to educate the team, and another player couldn't even be bothered to listen. The second guy to make that mistake always gets ripped worse than the first guy."

"When you look back on your life, are there any lessons that you learned or people in your life that started the 'push'?" I questioned.

He chuckled and answered, *"I've been helped by lots of people along the way. When I was eleven years old I was a 'pudgy' kid and I remember my uncle, who taught at the same school that I went to, looking at me and he said 'You know Peter, we are going to have to do something about that'. I don't know if he actually said that or that's what I imagine he thought. Either way, I'm glad he decided to help. We started doing more athletic things together and he was the one that got me into better shape. We would hit baseballs, shoot pucks, play golf, and do strength and conditioning work. I* have to give him credit for pushing me in the right direction. That kind of push was one that I needed then."

"I can remember every single year when I was young, my father asking me if I still wanted to play hockey. He wanted to make sure that I was happy and still enjoyed playing; he never pushed me to play hockey. One of my favorite memories is of the time my dad asked me, before my senior year at BC, if I still wanted to play hockey. I was fortunate enough to receive a full scholarship so I was attending a very expensive school for free. I laughed and said to him, 'Yeah, I think I'll play this one out'. The more time that passes between the present and that moment, the more I truly appreciate him asking me that. My parents provided me with opportunities to learn from good coaches and teachers with the single requirement that if I chose to play, I had to give my best effort all the time. That requirement has served me well my whole life. My mom and dad spent a lot of time and money putting me into positions to enjoy playing hockey and succeed. I'm very grateful for everything they did for me."

"I think my brother was the biggest influence on me, especially with regard to hockey. Growing up, my older brother would push me, and I would push myself to be like him. As I mentioned earlier, we grew up in an intensely competitive family so I always wanted to try the things he did, and try to be as good as he was at them. I learned from his successes and his mistakes. Having a brother like him was crucial to my development."

"I was fortunate to have lots of people help me in my journey. I guess you could say it took a village to raise me."

"I would advise young players to always remember two things. The first thing is allow mistakes to be a guide for improvement, not something to be feared or used to make you feel bad. The second thing is to work hard. Learning is a lifelong endeavor and it's a part of everything we do. The results of one day or one season, win or lose, are secondary to the feeling you get when you know you gave your best effort in the pursuit of better."

ADAM BURISH

FORMER NHL PLAYER, STANLEY CUP CHAMPION

I have had the pleasure of knowing Adam since 2010. He reached out to me to work with him on a shooting camp in Madison Wisconsin, when he was playing for the Dallas Stars. Always, the organizer and not wanting to leave his friends out, he included players Tom Gilbert, Joe Pavelski, Blake Geoffrion, Brad Winchester as well as several other pros.

He started his junior hockey career with the Green Bay Gamblers of the USHL in the 2001-02 season. The next year Adam was drafted in the ninth round of the 2002 NHL entry draft, 282nd overall by the Chicago Blackhawks.

During his career with Green Bay, he was recruited to the Wisconsin Badgers of the WCHA NCAA division in 2002, and played there till his senior 2005-06 season, when the team was crowned national champions after defeating Boston College 2-1 in the title game. Adam served as the captain that season and assisted on both goals in the championship game. He graduated with a degree in economics. He left the university, in 2006, to join Chicago's AHL affiliate, the Norfork Admirals, for their 2006-07 season.

Adam recorded his first career goal with the Chicago Blackhawks on January 22nd, 2008. As a member of the team during the 2008-9 season, he became a Stanley Cup winner.

He signed a two-year deal with the Dallas Stars for $1.15 million per year as a free agent after his 2010 season. When his contract expired with the Stars, he reunited with University of Wisconsin teammate Joe Pavelski to sign a four-year contract for $1.8 million per year.

It was during his 2013-14 season with San Jose that he had surgery to repair a lower back injury and was placed on injury reserve. During the following season, Adam was placed on waivers by the Sharks and was sent down to play with their AHL affiliate team, the Worcester Sharks. Adam was loaned out to the Chicago Wolves late in the 2014-15 season and upon completing this season with the Wolves, his contract was bought out by the Sharks releasing him to free agency.

Unable to gain another NHL deal, Adam signed his first contract abroad, playing in the Swedish Hockey League (SHL) as a free agent in 2015. He left the team in 2016 to focus on other interests.

In summary, Adam played nine years in the NHL for Chicago and Dallas and finished his pro career with the San Jose Sharks. Along the way, he was rewarded for his efforts by winning a much-coveted Stanley Cup with Chicago.

Adam co-owns a high-end steak house in downtown Madison, Wisconsin called RARE with his father, Mark: It consistently receives rave reviews from its clients on atmosphere, service and a quality meal. It won a diner's choice award in 2015.

When I reached out to Adam to help with this book he was gracious as always and glad to help. All pro players have a story and Adam's story was centered around the comments that he would never play junior, and after he conquered that, he would never play NCAA hockey let alone win a championship. Well he conquered that in style and when told he would never make the NHL let alone win a Stanley Cup, he put all his naysayers to rest.

One of Adam's greatest contributions to the game, aside from his work ethic, is his interaction with his teammates. Having coached hockey for many years, there is one guy that is the glue, one guy that helps bring the team together. Teams that don't have that kind of chemistry, rarely win championships. Adam is such a teammate and this is his story.

I caught up with Adam at the end of summer. School was back in and the NHL season was starting exhibition games. Having retired from the game, Adam was busy running his steak house and enjoying the rest and relaxation after an NHL career.

I asked Adam a little about his childhood and where his values came from.

"My mother and father were always very professional. It was always about how one treated others, how they acted. I was raised this way my whole life. As a result, I hated the bully in school, the guy that was too full of himself. I learned early on that you treat people how you wanted to be treated."

His hockey journey was something that I consider extraordinary.

"I was always a very skilled player. I mean I was a top Wisconsin amateur player, not a top NCAA or NHL player." He corrected, *"I could play the game and I didn't really have to work hard to have success at that level. At the age of sixteen that all changed. I was in a very bad car accident. I was in the back seat of a BMW that my sister was driving. She went off the road and the car flipped end-over-end three times tossing me out the back window and sixty feet through the air. If I was to try and fit through that back window under normal circumstances with the rear window out, I doubt I could."*

"This resulted in massive injuries and a lot of rehab. I finished my high school year in a wheelchair. All I could remember was asking the doctor; 'When can I get back on skates?' His answer was; 'Let's just get you walking first'. There was no doubt in my mind that I was going to skate again. I wanted to play junior hockey and then move on to be the captain of the Wisconsin Badgers and there was no way that I was going to be denied. I can't remember there being even a doubt in my mind. I think that coming back from that accident changes you and when one sets one's mind to a task or challenge, it's just going to get done."

"I worked hard and made the jump from Madison Edgewood Prep school team to the USHL Green Bay Gamblers in 2001-02. My goal was to move up from there to play for the Badgers which I did the following 2002-03 season. As I mentioned before, I had my goal set on becoming the captain of

the team and that happened in my third year with the team. In my senior year we won that NCAA Championship."

"I was drafted in the 2002 NHL Draft by the Chicago Blackhawks in the ninth round 282nd overall. However, I wasn't concerned about playing in the NHL at that time. My mind was completely focused on the Badgers and I wanted to win a championship with them. Once the season was over, I set my goal on the NHL."

"Again, there was no doubt in my mind. I knew that I had to work for it and that was something that I was familiar with. I just knew that I was going to play. My work ethic and attitude was all positive and I was completely focused on my objective."

"I signed a contract with the Blackhawks and while I played nine games for the team, I spent most of the year in the minors with Chicago's affiliate team, the Norfolk Admirals of the AHL. The following year I played for the Blackhawks winning the Stanley cup in 2010."

That spawned the next conversation. Very few people win championships and having won a couple myself as a coach, it is a road that is seldom traveled.

"Coaches often miss the point that a great team wins championships. I don't mean that skill doesn't matter but if the guys don't get along, the team goes nowhere. I've played on teams that had cliques, vets that picked on rookies, guys that were loners. I hated that. We never seemed to go far. Something about dressing room chemistry is what's important. The Badgers, the year we won the championship, we were the closest group of guys. We hung around together and were inseparable. We still keep in touch today. During the summers we get together and hang out."

I remember having a conversation with one of Adam's close friends, Tom Gilbert, who played with Adam on the Badger's team. "Burs is always the guy that gets us all together, barbeques, golfing, whatever. He kind of keeps everyone in touch."

Joe Pavelski, when I asked him about Adam joining the Sharks. *"I put a word in for him. Adam is a great team guy, great in the dressing room. The one everyone loves having around."*

When I asked Adam about winning the Stanley Cup he replied, "*That team played together and partied together more than any team I've ever been a part of. They hung around together and played hard for each other. I don't think that it mattered who coached that team, they were going to win that year. They were a great example of a great team in every sense of the word.*"

Looking back over his hockey career, I asked him if there was anyone that stood out in his mind and helping him get better at the game.

"*I have to say Mike Eaves. He really taught me a lot about the game, how to be better defensively and offensively. He helped me to become more professional. Mike helped a lot of guys that way. He demanded hard work and expected a lot out of us. He had a great impact on my game for sure.*"

I have known Mike for quite a few years, meeting him around the rink when I was in Madison training some of the pro guys. We would get ice at the LaBahn Arena and often Mike was at the rink. He was always approachable and had a real passion for the game. It was just after they expanded the rink with a new practice center and dressing rooms where he showed me around the facility. Mike and I have had some great hockey talks and he always had great things to say about Adam, his effort, teammanship and leadership.

When I asked Adam what the game has helped him bring to his business life he responded:

"*I think that seeing the teamwork in hockey and how it resulted in winning championships really helped to create a great working environment in our business. Every work environment is in essence a team much like hockey. At our restaurant, we tell the employees that we are working for them. We want them to get whatever they need and we are there to help them anyway we can. If they are happy at their job then they bring their best every day, which in turn benefits our customers. We pride ourselves in great service as well as a great atmosphere. It all comes from being a great team and working together.*"

CORE VALUES

Adam closed with a great comment, *"I have a very close friend in the music business who is one of the top people in the industry and he gave me a saying that stuck with me. I have it as a plaque on my desk in my office as a reminder. It says: 'Do Simple Better!' It is so true and when I think of my hockey career, that was what I tried to do each practice and each game. It is what we tell our employees to focus on each day at work."*

SHAWN HORCOFF

FORMER NHL PLAYER, SKILLS COACH DETROIT REDWINGS

I had the pleasure of meeting Shawn in 2016, when I was in Anaheim working with some of the Duck players. He was being put through some hard skating drills and upon completion, we had a chance to sit down and chat about skill development. As with all of the NHL players that I have had the privilege of working with, he was always looking to improve his performance. He was always ready to ask hard questions and it was clear that he was committed to hard work and being the best that he could be.

Shawn is a Canadian-born former professional hockey player, from Trail, B.C. He was selected by the NHL Edmonton Oilers ninety-ninth overall in the fourth round in the 1998 NHL entry draft. He played for Edmonton for eleven seasons serving as their captain for three.

His junior career started in the British Columbia Hockey League (BCHL) in 1995, playing for the Chilliwack Chiefs. From there he was selected to Michigan State University in the Central Collegiate Hockey Association (CCHA) in 1996. He was considered a contender for the CCAH All-Rookie Team after a successful first season, but his second season had better numbers even though he played fewer games. This led to his draft selection by the Edmonton Oilers. His senior year was his best, where he posted his best totals in goals, assists and total points leading him to be selected as CCHA Player of the year and he was a finalist for the Hobey Baker Award (the top player in college hockey). Shawn graduated with degrees in Finance and Mathematics.

CORE VALUES

His first year out of college hockey resulted in his missing the Oiler's line-up out of training camp, so instead he signed with their affiliate team, the Hamilton Bulldogs in the American hockey league (AHL). Here Shawn not only led the team in scoring, but he was ranked sixth overall in scoring in the AHL. This led to his being recalled by the Oilers on December 4th, and he scored his first NHL goal on December 13, 2000. As a result of being called up to Edmonton, he missed appearing in the 2000-01 AHL All-Star Game. He remained with Edmonton for the rest of the season getting five games playoff experience against the Dallas Stars.

Shawn has had an impressive career, appearing in the NHL Young Stars Game in 2003, and he led leading the Oilers in goals during the 2003 Stanley Cup Playoffs. In 2003-04 he was named the Oilers Outstanding Defensive Forward after setting career highs in all point categories. During the NHL lockout in 2004-05, he signed with Mora IK of the Swedish Elite League, finishing fourth in overall scoring. He took over the number one center position during the 2005-06 season, and posted career highs in goals and assists. During this season he also tied Wayne Gretzky's team record for most points in a period, assisting on four goals in the third period in a game against the Detroit Redwings. During the 2006 Stanley Cup Playoffs, Shawn was part of the Oilers team that lost in the Finals to the Carolina Hurricanes.

Shawn has represented Canada internationally three times, winning gold in 2003, 2004 and silver in 2005 at the World Championships. He was selected to the 56th NHL All Star game where he won the Fastest Skater in the Skill Competition. Due to a shoulder injury and surgery in early 2008, he missed the last half of the season but on July 16, 2008, The Oilers announced that he had been signed to a six-year $33-million contract extension. In 2010, he was named the thirteenth captain in the Edmonton Oiler's history.

On July 4, 2013, upon completion of the shortened Lockout season, Shawn was traded to the Dallas Stars where, after two seasons, he signed a one-year contract as a free agent with the Anaheim Ducks, in 2015. That was early in 2016, and it was when I had the pleasure of meeting him. Shawn was named director of player development for the Detroit Redwings in September of 2016. Since that time we have shared many conversations on development, and he is always an enthusiastic learner and passionate about helping newcomers to the professional ranks: The Wings have made a great investment, bringing him on board.

An area that I was interested in discussing with Shawn, because of his long exposure to the NHL game, was the changes in player makeup over the past ten to fifteen years.

"One of the biggest things I notice in players today is most of them aren't very good at dealing with adversity. When they get to me in Detroit, most of them are highly skilled and the best player at their previous level. Then they get a pro game or two and things haven't gone so well. Because they have no, or little, past experiences in failure, their mental makeup has no tools to deal with the problems. It's the kid that realizes he has deficiencies, who is open to coaching and new ideas, who can then absorb and implement them, that is the player that will go on to have success at the pro level."

With all of the training both off ice and on, players seem to be much better athletes today than they were years ago. I asked Shawn if he has noticed a major difference in players' athleticism, today.

"Are they better athletes? I'm not so sure? But, I do know they are better hockey players. They're much more well-rounded and complete physically. It's very different now from when I was young. I played three or four different sports all year round, up until about fifteen years old. That's all changed now, elite kids play or train for hockey all year round, and don't have time for other sports. Having said that, I come across very few well-rounded players at a young age. Maybe they are elite skaters and have never had to learn how to protect the puck down low or in tight spaces. They always just beat people with their speed and were rarely in those positions. Maybe they had great hands and didn't have the ability to drive wide or beat guys off the wall with quickness so they didn't work on their skating as much. And almost all of them have no idea where the defensive zone is, because most kids are drafted on their offensive ability and skill. They don't realize that for ninety-five percent of them it's their ability to defend that's going to keep them in the league. If they want to have a long career it's going to be their ability to earn trust in the coach, to put them out and not get scored on in important situations."

CORE VALUES

This brought up the issue of work ethic and a player's commitment to get better. I asked Shawn what his primary concerns were as a pro skills' coach?

"Another issue that I see is a lack of focus and a capacity to think under extreme stress. A player can go out there and work hard but that doesn't translate into success during the game. Players today have to maintain a very high level of conditioning and their brain has to work well under fatigue. What I see with kids today is that, while their conditioning is very high, their ability to make smart decisions when they are tired just isn't there. Their brain shuts down and they start to make mental errors. All the top guys play a lot of minutes. It comes down to their ability to make great decisions later in the game or when in a tough series like the playoffs, even longer."

I posed the question that if he had any advice to give youth today, regarding their intangibles, what would that be?

"*For me it comes down to two things; work ethic and competition. Most kids that get drafted already have a certain amount of physical gifts. It then comes down to who wants it more? Who's willing to pay the higher price? Who is willing to make the most sacrifices? Then the second point on competition comes into play. I've played with and seen players that have a great work ethic off the ice and in practice, but when it comes to a game that gets tough and physical, they shy away. There's so much skating in today's game that you have to be good in tight spaces; you have to be able to win one-on-one battles. Most coaches say, at the end of the night, whoever wins the most one-on-one battles will win the game...and more often than not they're right. A high work ethic will hone a player's individual abilities, but a high competitive level will win players games, and winning games wins championships."*

I brought up the differences that I have seen over the past twenty years. While the game used to be a lot more physical, with far more hitting, the new rules have allowed the game to transition more towards speed and skill. I asked Shawn if he agreed and what major differences that he has noticed in the make-up of the players today as a result?

"I agree. I feel that the game has gotten a little softer. The rules have changed and the game has gotten faster and players demonstrate more skill. However, it is not my job to debate the changes. They are what they are and we have to coach around them. My job is to develop the players to fit the game today. While I agree it is softer game, a problem that arises with some players when the playoffs come along is less gets called, it gets a little grittier out there and now players have to adapt and compete. It becomes a challenge for some guys. Again, it comes back to their ability to face adversity and compete."

Having my own analytics' company for the past ten years, I have noticed certain trends. The space out there is getting smaller and smaller. I asked Shawn what changes he has witnessed and where does he think the game is going?

"Players are much better athletes today. They all have skill; they all skate well and are stronger. It all means that there is less space in which to play. Guys like Sidney Crosby can thrive in today's game; he is so good down low at protecting the puck and creating space for guys. I think that today's game suits him more and more. It is the guys that can create more space, who can work well in those small areas that have success. There are guys like Connor McDavid that skate at a high level of speed. There are a lot of guys in the league that can do that, but he is one of the only players that can make plays at high speed with the puck. Elite players can control pucks at high speed and still make plays."

Everyone seems talk about teamwork. There was a great YouTube video on the Las Vegas story, and how they picked their team around guys of great character, guys that were good in the dressing room. How much importance do teams place on that character trait? Were Vegas an anomaly?

"I think it's very important and I was taught that, when I first came into the league in Edmonton. That's one part of the game that will never change. You always want great teammates, guys that are there to pick you up when you're down, push you on the ice to get better, challenge you to reach places you didn't think you could. I think you saw that last year with Vegas. You read all year long how no one believed in them but the players didn't care because they did. And they proved that it doesn't matter what *the truth is, when you believe in something strongly enough it will eventually become reality."*

Obviously there is a lot that goes into player selections for the draft. Teams look at overall points, there are a lot of scouting networks out there and I'm sure that teams interview coaches or team personnel. Do they do deeper dives into the character of a player?

"Yes, we do all that and more especially on the drafting side. Once we draft them, the first thing I try to do is build a relationship with them. That is my biggest priority during my first year. Most of them are years away from becoming pros and have a lot of learning to do. How can I expect them to do things I ask and push their bodies and minds to the limit if they don't trust who and where it's coming from. I need to learn what makes them tick? What motivates them? What are their weaknesses and strengths? Those questions are also answered a lot of times from the people around them. They know how the players carry themselves. Their parents, coaches, trainers, teachers, and teammates are all good sources of information. Social media nowadays makes it hard for these guys to live a private life."

I mentioned to Shawn one issue I had as a developer, and that was dealing with the negative/positive feedback loop. Players, as is their nature, tend to lean the way of the least conflict and those coaches that run drills and not skills seem to attract a lot of clients. The negative side of running drills sessions it that there is usually a high volume of players participating so critique is more often related to effort. The positive side of just running drills is that if the kid is working hard, rarely does he hear a disparaging word. In skill development, which requires a much keener eye and more one-on-one interaction, some players take it personally and even think that I don't like them. Did he run into the same issues?

"I totally agree. I've had a few players that tell their coaches or agents they think I don't like them because I'm hard on them. That couldn't be farther from the truth. I'm the hardest on the guys I think are the closest or have the greatest chance of becoming NHL players. I want to see how they react to being pushed to change. Not all players are open to it and it's the ones that aren't, that think they're good enough already and know everything, that rarely succeed. Those are the ones that find very little success at the

pro level. Mentalities like that, I have very little time for. The guys I love are the ones that are constantly looking to get better. Guys that are willing to go outside their comfort level and try new things. Another thing at the development level that you have to realize is these players are kids. Their minds and bodies are still developing so you have to stick with them. What you have at eighteen will not be what you have at twenty-one."

ETHAN WOLTHERS

WORLD CHAMPION
BMX RIDER & USHL JUNIOR PLAYER

Ethan Wolthers is not only an amazing athlete but a very humble one as well. After speaking with his parents it's easy to see that the apple doesn't fall far from the tree.

I got to know him in the summer of 2018, when he flew into Vancouver to train with me. His advisor had reached out a couple of months, previously, to see if I was available to train him both on and off the ice in my studio in North Delta. He was a top goal scorer that season in the Anaheim Junior Ducks, a highly successful Midget AAA program but wanted to take his game to another level. His father Marcel and I connected and organized his visit.

I was very impressed with him on our first introduction in my small training studio. He was very courteous and respectful, offering a firm handshake and a "Nice to meet you coach". It was obvious that he was eager to get to work and after a brief orientation we got down to business. It was instantly obvious that he was a special athlete. Eager to learn, and possessed of an incredible work ethic and a professional attitude, one could tell that he would not only go far in hockey but in life as well. I had no idea that he had begun to play hockey when he was twelve years old.

He was accompanied by his father (Marcel), a gracious and supportive parent, who stated that he was only there to assist Ethan, or as Marcel said, "be his taxi driver" and not push him in his career.

Over the next few days he opened up about his previous sporting experiences. He informed me that he had retired from his first career, BMX bike racing at the age of nine years old, after winning six world and three national championships. He had decided to try football and lacrosse, both of which he had excelled at, but he fell in love with ice hockey when a friend invited him to birthday party at the Ice Station in Valencia. While they were there, his father signed him up for a Hockey 101-camp where he trained for two weeks, and then was put on an in-house team. The rest, it appears, is history. His passion for playing hockey and his incredible work ethic and desire to learn accelerated him quickly and he ended up playing for a Los Angeles Jr. Kings Pee Wee AA team that fall after only skating for six months.

I asked him to be a part of this book. His story is inspiring and goes to show that given the right attitude, one can go far in life, no matter the direction.

Ethan's childhood as far as two-year-olds go, was not normal. His older brother Nicolas, who is three-and-a-half years older, has been an inspiration and driving force behind a lot of Ethan's accomplishments, and moreover, in his entire life. His brother learned to ride a bike and as far as Ethan was concerned, at eighteen months, he was going to ride one as well. At the age of two, the training wheels came off and he was on his own. When I talked to his mother, Monica, about this we had a good chuckle. *"It was competition from the start. Ethan admired his older brother and whatever Nic could do, Ethan wanted to do and do it better. His brother was a real motivation to Ethan."*

From an early age Ethan was driven to be the best he could be but, it started with a love of riding, which he learned from his older brother. I asked him what drew him to BMX racing, *"It was the speed, I like the jumps and the track but I liked going fast and it was something that I was good at"*.

A phrase that we hear a lot from players is that they need to have fun, to enjoy the sport and the moments. However, like everything in life there are great days where we love what we do and there are days where we don't. Racing was no exception.

CORE VALUES

What drove Ethan through the hard times? When I asked his father, Marcel stated, *"Old fashioned values of respect, hard work and discipline is what our family is based on. Ethan loved riding and then there were days, albeit very few, when he didn't want to go. I would tell him that he had committed to riding and we were going to the bike park together. I would tell him that he would ride and train the three hours that he had committed to. Once on his bike, his passion would kick in again and he was off. It was just getting there sometimes was all that mattered. He had learned to work hard at the skills, so pushing him, other than getting him there, wasn't necessary."*

He also added, *"It is also important that kids get the same message within the family. My wife reinforced the same values and we demanded that from all our children. That is really important in creating consistency."*

Ethan's mother was an Olympic hopeful in gymnastics and knew the value of hard work as well as coachability; *"All of our children played sports. We taught them to be polite, respectful and to work hard, of course, but we wanted our kids to be coachable. I remember my gymnastics coach getting frustrated because some of his students wanted to do things their own way and in some cases would even argue with him. I would always wonder why they were there, if not to learn."*

When I asked Ethan his thoughts he responded, *"Mom and Dad were great, they were always supportive. There were days that I didn't feel like practicing and Dad would insist on me doing my training and would take me to the park. Once there I didn't need motivation since I loved riding. Winning championships is very hard work and both Dad and my mother taught me early to be consistent and to keep finding new gears to elevate my training. The hardest thing to do is to train really hard when you really don't feel like it. They helped me to developed good work habits and then I came to expect that of myself".*

Winning one world championship is an accomplishment for any person, but to win six was incredible. What was his secret I challenged?

"When I was very young I discovered that I was good at riding. I guess that it came from wanting to copy my older brother, but I found that it was something that I was passionate about, so working hard at something you

love to do isn't really difficult. When I won my first championship that was amazing. The feeling of accomplishment was incredible. When you win once and you get that feeling you want it again. The difficulty was to keep finding new gears to win. To be rewarded for all my hard work made working even harder that much more satisfying of course, but people challenge you even more because you have won. You have to keep pushing your boundaries. Every win is harder and I had to make a choice to keep working harder and harder, which made wining that much more satisfying. After a while, working hard becomes a habit and I would just do it."

When I asked Marcel what the underlying secret of Ethan's success was he added, *"Ethan always wanted it, maybe he learned to compete as a result of trying to do what his older brother did. All we did was guide that passion, reinforcing work ethic, discipline and coachability. Parents or even coaches, for that matter, have to push the values of hard work when kids are young and if they push often enough, they become a habit. Ethan loved riding and winning."*

He associated hard work with winning but as the competition challenged him, he had to keep finding new gears of hard work to prepare for each race. As a result, Ethan had already won the race in his mind before the race even began.

Monica added. *"He was very strong mentally, even at a young age he would say to us; 'I got this'.*

Marcel said, *"This he did on his own. He had learned the value of hard work and knew that if he just outworked people, he would have success. Monica and I just enjoyed watching him compete. We would just take him to competitions and he would do all the work. We would just support him."*

Ethan decided to get into team sports after his sixth world championship and picked two familiar sports: football and lacrosse. Due to his coachability and work ethic, he excelled at both. It was only when he put skates on, at that fateful birthday party when he was twelve, that he realized that he had found something new that inspired him.

We talked about the thrill of skating.

"I love speed" Ethan said, *"The feeling of wiping around on the ice reminded me of BMX racing. There was speed in skating and with all the riding I did, my balance for skating wasn't that bad. Another thing that helped was the leg strength from my knees. Riding hard is tough on the legs and this really helped me get low on my skates"*.

His mother remembers the first times at open skate where Ethan found his speed and would weave through the crowds of teenagers. *"He was so fast and he loved it! He had the biggest smile on his face because of the joy of speed on those skates"*.

"No matter the sport" She added, *"He always had the biggest smile on his face while riding, carrying the football or, now, when he's skating."*

"I also loved scoring" He added; *"It's a tough game with a lot of talented players and scoring provided the reward for my hard work."*

Working hard and getting better is just a part of Ethan's make-up now. *"I loved hockey but realized that I would have to work really hard to become good at it. After practice, when everyone would leave, I would stay out for a couple hours more and work on my skills."*

When I asked him about his goals:

"I want to play at the highest level I can. I know that it will take a lot of very hard work but I don't mind that. We will see where I end up, but right now, signing with Cedar Rapids Rough Riders of the USHL is awesome and I want to do very well there. The coaches are great and have given me a great opportunity. It is all up to me!"

Ethan also committed to UMass Amherst. His career looks very promising and there is no doubt that with Ethan's attitude, he will achieve whatever he desires.

BEN ISRAEL

NCAA COLORADO COLLEGE

Ben had just signed as a defenceman with the Coquitlam Express in the BC Junior Hockey League, after being traded from the Chilliwack Chiefs at the trading deadline in 2013, when I first met him.

He had reached out to me to take some shooting sessions on his days off or when practice permitted. People that are familiar with Ben know that he is bald. He has a condition called alopecia, and lost all his hair when he was seven years old. I would normally have used the phrase; "suffered from" but this would be far from the truth. It is as much a part of his character as his great sense of humor. He told me that his doctor mentioned that if he quit eating gluten and dairy, there would be a good chance that it would grow back. I asked him if he had ever considered it. His answer, with a devilish smile, was; *"Hell no, I love bread, ice cream and all that good stuff."* I loved his spirit. It was easy to see that he was a player with conviction, who had a great outlook on life and, from the intense fire in his eyes, his passion for the game burned bright.

I got to know his story over the many informal sessions we had that season. He was a wonderful, attentive student and always had a smile on his face. Early in the pre-season tryouts I got to know his story of perseverance. He explained to me that while he couldn't perform the off ice running test because of a major injury to his Achilles tendon, he could still play due to the support of the skate boot. He also informed me that this was his second injury.

"My first injury occurred when I was seventeen years old." Ben explained, *"I was getting ready to play juniors on the East coast for my senior year of high school. It was late in July, and a several of my friend and I were relaxing around our family pool. Never one to miss a challenge, I thought that I could make the jump from the second floor balcony into the pool. I miscalculated the distance and landed on edge of the pool deck shattering the heel bone of my left foot. "*

"I was rushed to the hospital, where the doctor told me that my heel bone or "calcaneus" had imploded. The surgery resulted in eleven screws and a metal plate being added to rebuild my heel. I was told that it would be four to six months before I could attempt skating. Recovery was a very tough but I was allowed to return to game play exactly four months post-surgery. The stiff boot of my skate really helped to stabilize my foot allowing me to skate long before I could run."

He played that year, from December on, with Detroit HoneyBaked Hockey Club and had a very successful season in spite of the heel injury. Upon completing his season with HoneyBaked, he decided to attend an early spring tryout camp in the CCHL (Central Canada Hockey League) with the Smith Falls Bears, to get some games in and get ready for the BCHL/USHL camps, which were held at the end of August.

"It was at this camp where my Achilles tendon was severed, approximately 75% during a freakish accident." Ben added, *"A player pushed off during an escape move along the wall but didn't realize that his blade was positioned above the protective heel cover on the back of my boot. The blade on the push-off, sliced through my sock and cut through the tendon. This accident occurred only ten months after the heel surgery on exactly the same foot."*

I have had my Patellar tendon ripped in half, when a dog tripped me going down a flight of stairs, and then had the same tendon torn in half again nine weeks later after a very successful first surgery. Coming back from such a major injury is difficult at best, having experience in that department, but to have two such dramatic injuries in the prime of one's development was a testimonial to his desire and passion to make the most out of a couple of dramatic circumstances. I asked Ben how hard it was to go through rehabilitation for his foot again.

"My mom and dad always taught me about hard work but my role model was really my father. Every time there was a negative he would say: 'Ben, you can take this as a negative or you and turn this negative into a positive'. I looked at this as an opportunity. It was obvious that I couldn't skate but I could still work other areas of my body, I could work on my cardio by doing rowing, I could watch video, or I could eat healthier and I could do core work or whatever. I had more time on my hands so I was determined to put that to good use. I mean it wasn't easy but I put a positive spin on it and that really helped. I was a young healthy guy and that allowed me to heal quickly."

"The second injury was really hard, mentally. I had to do exactly the same rehab that I did the first time; the same ankle exercises and everything. I had worked my butt off to keep in shape and get healthy and almost exactly the same thing happened again. It was tough on me. I worked hard and it was still tough to get through it the second time. I was all excited about playing and then I was held back again."

"The rehab went well and I was able to play three months later with the help again of the stabilizing skate boot. While I was unable to run or do most of the demanding physical testing, I managed to make the Chilliwack Chiefs of the BCHL in August of 2012. I was then traded at the deadline in 2013, to the Coquitlam Express where Barry Wolfe was the head coach."

Ben was one of the hardest working guys that I had met and he always had a smile on his face. It was easy to see that he was passionate about the game, had an incredible work ethic and was a perfectionist. He hated that fact that he was average at something. I asked him where he developed that attitude.

"I really owe it all to my father. He instilled that in me since I was seven and eight years old. He owned his own paving company in Michigan and had worked really hard to build up the business. He always stressed that hard work was important. He used to take me down to the warehouse on weekends when I was seven and eight and make me sweep the whole floor. One of my favorite stories was when I was nine years old. I went into the

warehouse one day and he handed me a thirty-pound backpack power blower and told me to go and blow the leaves off the parking lot, while the wind was blowing the leaves back onto the parking lot. I was there for four hours, and I couldn't figure out what to do. I worked my first eight-hour day when I was nine years old. I had to work around the shop."

That was worth a chuckle on both our parts. I have met his father and can easily see him passing on those work lessons. I asked him if he could remember any others.

"There is another." He laughed, *"I was twelve years old and my father decided that it was time for me to have a job. Up to that point I was doing basic crap around the warehouse, sweeping floors and picking up stuff. I have a cousin who is the same age as me, well two months younger actually, so he took both of us down to where the paving crew was working. Up to that point, I was an errand boy once in a while, but this time he pulled the foreman aside and told him to put us to work and if we were slacking he would be in trouble. He then turned to me and said; 'I'm going to start you at $5 an hour'. I was thinking that was awesome, I was making money. Then he turned to my cousin and told him that he would get paid $6 an hour. I couldn't believe it. He turned and told me that the owner's kid would get no special treatment and walked away. I couldn't believe it!"*

We both broke into laughter at this point. I told Ben a couple stories about my father and they brought on the same result.

I asked Ben where his passion to play came from.

"I started playing hockey when I was six, I did learn to skate before that. My cousin had played Division 1 College and had mentioned to my dad that I was a pretty aggressive kid; had a lot of energy, liked to wrestle when I was a kid and that sort of thing. My dad threw me into hockey after that and I loved it. I was the kind of kid when I was younger that when it was baseball season I loved baseball, when it was hockey season I loved hockey. I loved sports and loved competing. Once I got to thirteen or fourteen, I went full time into hockey. I was really good at baseball but it was to slow for me. I needed more action and while I liked the game, I loved the action and intensity of hockey. There are a lot of things going on when you're playing.

That's when I really developed a passion for hockey and I was very lucky that my father supported me."

I asked Ben what his future held for him. He is in his senior year at Colorado College and is motivated to play at the highest level he can.

"I'm at an interesting crossroads in my life; I'm in my senior year of college. My whole life I was driven to be the best of the best, get to the NHL, win a Stanley Cup. I was driven by goals before, but I realize now that I'm not on pace to be the next Eric Karlsson. At this time of my life I'm more focused on the day in and day out philosophy. I think that a realistic goal for me at the end of the season after graduating from here is to sign an AHL tryout and give myself a shot that way to get to the NHL. I think that is a very realistic goal."

"Some people find shopping fun. Some people find traveling fun. For me, I loved working towards a goal. I loved the progression. I worked on skating and loved getting better. I watched game tapes and got better. I practiced skills and got better."

I shared a story with Ben from when I was fifteen years old. I was a pretty good badminton player. The secondary school was a block away from our home and during the spring and summer months, they would have a badminton night mid-week. I decided to join and I think that in one of my first games against an adult, I got beat 21-0. It was the most humbling experience in my life. I hated losing but to lose like that was like someone had kicked me hard. I was determined to beat him so every lunch hour at school, I would challenge a couple of the kids to play me two on one so that I could train harder. It took me the whole summer to beat him, but it was the most satisfying win I can remember. It was that picking away one point at a time; 21-1, then 21-2, then 21-3. I'm not sure to this day whether he let me win that final game but I know how much I enjoyed the battle and the quest.

I asked Ben where his competitive nature came from.

"I think that comes back from my childhood and working so hard. Another reason is my dad. Dads play games with their kids; they play soccer or something else. My dad played games with me but he never let me win. He would say that I gave you some points but you never beat me. It would

drive me crazy. I think that it formed from there. My father coached a youth soccer team, where I played. I think we had a 900 winning percentage or something like that. We hated losing and I hated losing. To this day, I can't stand losing at table tennis, cards or anything. I love the challenge and I love the fact that with hard work one can get better every day."

Ben's mental fortitude and perseverance have always been an inspiration to me and I have used his story many times when kids have become disheartened because of a life setback or an injury.

CHRIS CONNER

PROFESSIONAL HOCKEY PLAYER AHL, NHL

At 5'7" and 180 lbs, Chris had to work hard his whole life to prove himself. He started his career in juniors, playing for the Chicago Freeze in the North American Hockey League, or NAHL, during the 2000-01 season. He then moved to the Compuware Ambassadors for 2001-02 and then back to Chicago Freeze in the second half of the season. He was selected to play NCAA hockey for Michigan Tech in the WCHA division from 2002-2006 and moved to the AHL Iowa Stars, an NHL Dallas Stars affiliate team in 2005. He got his NHL experience during his 2006-07 season, playing eleven games for the big club. He remained in the Dallas system from 2005-2009, after which he made a move to the NHL Pittsburgh Penguins system. He played there from 2009-2011, moving up and down between their farm team and the main club.

In 2011, he signed with the NHL Detroit Redwings, playing mostly with their affiliate club, the Grand Valley Griffins, and he played only eight games that year with the main club. From there, he signed with the NHL Phoenix Coyotes and played sixty games with their farm team in the AHL, the Portland Pirates, moving up to play twelve games with the Coyotes that season. After that season, he went back to the Penguins' organization from 2013-2014, and then made the jump to the Washington Capitals AHL affiliate, the Hershey Bears, where he played two games for the main club the following 2014-15 season. He moved, in 2015, to play for the Leheigh Valley Phantoms in the AHL, where he is currently playing.

Since his initiation into the AHL, in 2005, he has scored 181 goals and 297 assist

I first met Chris Connor at a KO Sports camp that I was running s for a total of 478 points in 606 games played. His NHL experience garnered him 180 games where he accumulated 22 goals, 28 assists for a total of 50 points as a gritty, hard-nosed, aggressive role player. His see-sawing, thirteen-year career in professional hockey (so far) has been challenging and one that he has faced with conviction and enthusiasm.

This is his story.

in Farmington Hills Michigan, in 2013. He was a fiery hard-working player that easily caught my eye. At that time he was playing in the Pittsburgh Penguin's organization, moving back and forth between the Wilkes-Barre/Scranton Penguins of the American Hockey League (AHL). What I respected most about Chris was his accountability and his desire to get better every time his was on the ice. Not one to make excuses, he always challenged himself and when he was unsure of a skill or tactic, would always come up with a well-thought out and direct question as to its purpose and application.

"I've always been that way." Chris stated when I spoke to him recently about his hockey career. *"There is so little time to get better and there's always an urgency to do so. I don't want to waste any time in going down the wrong path and then have to turn around and start all over. I always wanted to know why I'm doing something and where I can apply it."*

We had a good laugh about Ryan Kesler, a very close friend, from when they were very young. *"We went to kindergarten together. Ryan's mother had a book she showed us and it was all about what we wanted to be when we grew up."* He chuckled. *"I always wanted to be a hockey player and Ryan wanted to be an engineer. I go to college for engineering and Ryan goes to the NHL."*

Chris admits that being a smaller player never bothered him. *"Some kids have that small-man syndrome, always having to prove themselves and then worrying about being small. I was never worried. I knew that I was smaller and knew every day that I had to prove myself but was my height* was never an issue. I felt that I had skill and could compete, it was just that everyone else seemed to have an issue with small players."

"My father always believed in hard work and, while he had never played hockey, he knew when I was or wasn't working hard in a game. He would bring it up saying that hard work is always noticed and when you get people's attention through your hard work, they start to appreciate other things that you do. That always stuck in my mind and helped me throughout my career."

Chris learned early, that one always has to get out of one's comfort zone. It is the only way to know that you are on the path to getting better. My father always had a saying that I shared with Chris. *"Make uncomfortable comfortable."* To which he whole-heartedly agreed.

"One of the reasons that players get stuck at a certain level is that they don't like to be uncomfortable." He added, *"I learned early on, that I had to get better every day and because I loved the game, working towards being a more skilled player was never a problem."*

We discussed his career to date and the challenges that he has faced as he worked his way up through the different levels to the NHL.

Chris, always humble commented, *"I realized that I wasn't quite good enough to stick in the NHL, I can admit that now and I have never blamed anyone for my inability to stay there. I looked back on my career and there were times where I thought, yeah I don't need to really work on that, that's not my game and that's not a skill or tactic that I use often. Over the years, one realizes that every skill is used at some point in a game and no matter how seemingly insignificant that skill or technique was, sooner or later one would have to use it. As I matured as a player I realized that even the smallest details matter. Over the years I have learned to focus on those things a lot more and they have helped to build the game I play today."*

Chris played 180 games in the NHL and we discussed the reasons why he managed to move up and down between the AHL and NHL so often.

"I prided myself on being a diverse or flexible player. I had good speed and competed hard so could contribute on the third and fourth lines. I took pride in my play-making ability, saw the ice well and could score at the AHL level, so that provided a lot of confidence to the coaches and general

managers that I could get the job done and contribute no matter where I was placed in the lineup. I wasn't a liability defensively, so when a player on the top team got injured, I could slide into any position and contribute both offensively and defensively."

"Again…" he added, "I always worked hard to get that opportunity. Too many players get complacent at the level they were at, or thought that they would never get called up. As a result, they did just enough to keep their jobs at the AHL level and didn't do the extra to make the next step. Accountability is a big issue. I always took responsibility for where I was and realized that I had to earn everything that I got. There were no political agendas, just old-fashioned hard work and a desire to get better every day. This is an attitude that I still have today, even though I have already played professional hockey for thirteen years."

Connor has three children: a girl, Brynnlee, aged seven and two sons, one a barely a year old, Easton, and an older son, Caden, who is nine years old, and who is loving the game. *"I tell him all the time that he has to work hard and that he needs to have confidence in himself. He has to have fun out there and fun is getting better every day and then using those skills when he plays."*

We discussed "Confidence" and how a young player can learn to become confident.

"First of all, hard work will allow you to get better every day and also allow you to out-compete other players, which in turn creates its own advantages. If a player is not afraid to be out of their comfort zone and not afraid to learn, then they always know that ultimately they will be better. As parents and coaches we must always encourage learning and when they acquire a new skill, we must be positive and praise them for doing so. This builds that learning without fear environment that ultimately helps to build confidence."

It is an attitude that has helped Chris overcome many challenges over the years and has turned him into the player/person that he is today. I asked Chris if anything stood out in his mind that he could have done a little better.

"I think that I could have taken some advice early in my career. At times in our hockey life we tend to get a little too confident and while that helps overcome some of our short comings, we can always learn from others. I think that at times, I could have listened to others. Work a little more on this, work a little more on that...."

"Also, I was a confident player but sometimes I faltered. I was told that I was good enough to play at the highest level and I think that getting called up for games demonstrates that, but at times, I myself lacked confidence. People believed in me but one gets distracted away from who they are, when they start watching elite players and realize that there is still a lot of work ahead. Each level is different and while I was very confident at the AHL level, sometimes I struggled at the NHL level. It wasn't so much that I couldn't make plays or skate at that level, I wasn't sure completely if I could all the time."

"What separates the great players from everyone else is they put in the work and learn every day. At times, I forgot that those qualities were my value system, so given the right direction; there was never any reason to think otherwise. I think over time, one comes to realize that they could play at a particular level given enough game time, but at the NHL level, there is a pressure to perform every night, especially as a call up or as a rookie. One needs to just believe that they can play and never doubt themselves."

It goes without saying Chris has had a long and productive career at a very high and intense level and is still producing. I asked him about how he manages to keep up the pace, year after year.

"Fortunately, the one piece of advice that I did take from experienced vets was that one has to take care of their body. I was always fit, always worked on my conditioning and flexibility. Playing two or three games back to back are tough on the body so I would use ice baths, roll out after games, do whatever I could to keep my body healthy. In this game, one will always suffer injuries but it is important to take of the little ones before they grow into bigger problems. I always did that figuring that prevention and better maintenance would help me have a longer career."

KALEIGH FRATKIN

PROFESSIONAL PLAYER

Kaleigh is arguably one of my most familiar hockey students. I first met her when she was ten years old. At the time, I was working with both of her brothers, Casey and Jesse, and she would come along and engage in the training. (Both brothers went on to play BCHL junior as well as collegiate NCAA hockey.) As a result, Kayleigh was pushed to compete with them her whole life. This family competition, coupled with her passion, drive and accountability, helped accelerate her development. As a result Kaleigh has competed in a variety of hockey environments.

In 2008-09, Kaleigh played defense for the US Little Caesars 19U woman's team, in the Tier 1 Elite Hockey League – Woman's Division (EHL). During that season she was recruited to play for Canada at the U18 World Junior Women's Championship.

Coming back to British Columbia the following 2009-10 season, she played defense for the Vancouver North West Giants in the Major Midget League (BCMML). That season, she was also affiliated by the Aldergrove Kodiaks of the Pacific International Junior Hockey League (PIJHL) where she was called up to play five games that season, and was the first woman to play junior hockey in British Columbia.

From there, she was recruited by NCAA Boston University, where she played from 2010-2014, acting as assistant captain of the team in her senior year. Upon graduation, she made the jump to the professional Canadian Woman's Hockey League (CWHL) for the 2014-15 season. The following 2015-16 season, she moved to the professional National

Woman's Hockey League (NWHL) in the United States. She played for the Connecticut Whale in 2015-16, New York Riveters in 2016-17 and then signed with the Boston Pride in 2017 to the current 2018-19 season.

She has had quite the hockey journey and has faced many challenges along the way. We got together at the start of the 2018 season and I thought it would be great to discuss the values that led her to be the player that she is today.

She has had a lot to live up to. Her father served as a British Columbia provincial court judge, her mother was, and still is, a self-made successful sports apparel entrepreneur and her brothers have successful junior and NCAA careers. I asked her how this has impacted her core values, and about the differences between the men and women's game and her career.

"Both my mother and father were very hard-working people. While we were taught to put in an effort to anything that we did, whether sports or school, our parents led by example. My mother started her own apparel company and the amount of work that she put into her business every day left no questions about the work required to be successful. My father's being a provincial court judge, meant he had responsibilities and had to work hard in a different way. My brothers were highly competitive and being around that type of environment certainly shapes one's core values."

"In the sport environment, I've always played with boys and I never really looked at myself as a girl playing sport. I always viewed myself as an athlete with something to prove every day. I'm not saying that as a girl or woman, I didn't want to prove the critics wrong, but that wasn't really the view I had when I was on the ice or in the dressing room."

As one of Kaleigh's skill coaches over the years, I have seen her perform more than adequately against elite level junior, college and professional players. I totally agree with her comment. This is the reason that I affiliated her with the Aldergrove Kodiaks in the PJHL. At that time she was playing defense for the BC Major Midget team, the Northwest Giants. I discussed her coming to our practices, with the owner Rick

Harkins, to see how she fit in with the team. He agreed that we should affiliate her after seeing her perform and talking to the veterans players.

Due to a couple defensive injuries, we offered her the opportunity to play in a league game versus the Ridge Meadow Flames. People in the hockey world, who know me, will admit that I am not one to shy away from controversy and, her being the first woman ever to play junior hockey in our league, did not go unnoticed by the opposition coaches and general manager. They both approached me and asked why I would do such a thing.

I would like to be clear that they weren't being disrespectful in their communication but rather they were concerned about her safety because of the intensity level of the league. I have had the privilege of meeting many character hockey guys over the years and the staff of the Flames were no exception. I explained quite clearly that I had worked with her for years and that she was more than capable. I explained that the reason that chose an away-game was so that the naysayers couldn't say that I hid her in our home line up to protect her and knowing them well, they could appreciate my thought process.

That game, Kaleigh won 3rd star and more than earned the opposition staff's respect. They came up afterwards and told me that I was correct in my assumption that she could indeed play, and they had enjoyed watching her compete.

As a result, Kaleigh has had the unique opportunity to play within both the elite men and women's programs. I asked her about the differences in core values between the two.

"I don't really think that there is much difference in core values between the elite women and men. We can obviously agree that there is a difference in strength and size, but as far as character, I can't say that there is much disparity. I think the biggest difference comes from the players just below the elite category. I think that one of the reasons for this is due to the depth of the talent pool. There are not near as many females playing ice hockey, as there are males."

"Another factor, of course, would be motivation. A male hockey player can see a clearly-defined road, from an amateur program up through junior,

college, semi-professional and into the NHL. For a young girl, passionate about hockey, the focus is different; play for an elite girls' bantam or midget team, look to make the Women's National team and then hopefully get a college opportunity. It has only be the last ten years that the Canadian Woman's Hockey League (CWHL) has been around and the US version (NWHL) has only been around for the past five. While these leagues are becoming more recognized, the branding and media support is very poor, meaning that the drive to play for the teams for self-gratification doesn't really exist."

"What I mean by self-gratification is that a boy can easily recognize many NHL players, they are in the media spotlight and want that 'goal'. This is far easier to identify with, not to mention the salaries that they are paid, than woman's professional hockey, which is more obscure."

"The problem with the Canadian National program is that it draws players from all over the country and if one lives in British Columbia, there are not that many spots available. Female players, as a result, kind of get lost in the shuffle, and if they are lucky enough to get recruited to an NCAA program, their dreams are more or less fulfilled. The pro league is now getting some notoriety. Having played in the league for the past five years (she signed a contract to play during this 2018-19 season, with Boston Pride of the NWHL), I see more NCAA as well as National Team players making the jump over; more as a way to continue playing a game that they love, as opposed to making a career doing so. The money that players are paid is barely enough to get by; many having to take up secondary jobs such as coaching. After a couple of years they decide that they have to move on. Most girls that graduate from college are twenty-one or twenty-two-years-old and like me really haven't figured out what career move they want to do make. They join, play for a while and then have to exit the league due to financial situations."

"Another influencer is the quality of coach that engages with female programs. While I don't want to be disrespectful to the coaches that I have had, I just want to be clear that the career trajectory of the coaches that engage in elite female programs, don't receive the financial remuneration that their counterparts do, who moved up through college, into the professional ranks. As a result, the coaches that are driven to higher careers on the male side of the game are under more scrutiny, have to win more, and have to develop

players to a higher level. In the end, I don't think that the overall quality of coaching at the female level is as good as on the male side."

I pushed her further, "So, taking all these variable into consideration, then, what would be the most noticeable character differences between the two as a whole"

"I think work ethic and accountability are probably the two most noticeable. Having participated in both types of practices; overall, girls don't work as hard as the guy's do. Many of them are quite satisfied where they are in their skill execution. Also, coaches tend to read off that and they don't push as hard as they could. As we discussed before, I think that this is because they can get away with it due to the depth of the talent pool."

I affirmed her comments, adding that during the many years that I have coached junior and senior women hockey players I always ask if they want to be treated like hockey athletes or women athletes. The point is that hockey is hockey and there is a code of conduct and a work ethic that goes with the sport, which should be adhered to, not separated because of the female or male gender.

"So all that being said" I then asked, "Many pro players make the move into coaching or environments that simulate that team setting such as the police or fire department. What are you plans moving forward?"

"I worked this summer in an office job and found that it just didn't suit me. Programs that provide the same ideology as a hockey team for women are a little different and hard to find. Hockey players like to be a part of something bigger, to compete, and fight for a cause they believe in whether male or female. However, for myself personally, working in an office job just doesn't seem to fit that profile. I think that I would like to get into coaching or only recently, I have been considering going back to school to get a degree in fashion design. My mother loves the work that she does, it is her company, and she is her own boss, loves working with people. I can see myself doing the same thing."

MATHEW BARZAL

NEW YORK ISLANDERS, NHL

I met Matt several years ago when he and I connected over some shooting sessions in my studio in North Delta. He was playing for the Seattle Thunderbirds at that time and while being already recognized as an elite playmaker, he wanted to focus more on his shooting skills, so he could add another dimension to his game and increase his offensive output. He was one of the hardest-working and most focused players that I have met and it was clear to me that Matt was a highly competitive and focused athlete. This, coupled with his sarcasm and quick wit, always made our sessions a fun and engaging affair. I had the privilege of working with Matt again last summer, when he partnered up with Nick Petan of the Winnipeg Jets for a couple of refresher sessions. Watching the intensity level of the two of them competing with each other was something to behold. I still chuckle at the back and forth commentary that occurred between the two of them. They were trying to kick each other's butts in a spontaneous shot velocity and accuracy competition.

Matt was drafted sixteenth overall in the 2015 NHL entry draft, by the NHL New York Islanders. Matt has enjoyed a very successful junior hockey career, being selected first overall by the Seattle Thunderbirds in the WHL, where he scored fourteen goals and forty assists for fifty-four points in his rookie year. This performance had him ranked seventh overall in the NHL midterm draft rankings. He made his NHL debut, on October 15, 2016 but returned to the Thunderbirds to lead them to a WHL championship where he was named the WHL Playoff MVP. Matt returned to the New York Islanders, full-time, for the 2017-18 season playing 82 games, registering 22 goals and 63 assists for 85 points. His outstanding performance led to him to win the Calder Memorial Trophy as the NHL's best rookie, becoming the fifth Islander's player to win the title.

Matt's outstanding skills and his drive to be the best he can be, have led to numerous accomplishments, that started when he was very young and which show no sign of slowing down:

- Brick Super Novice Tournament Top Scorer 2007
- BC Hockey Player of the Year, Coquitlam Express 2013
- BCMML (BC Major Midget League) Most Points 2013
- BCMML All-Star Team 2013
- WHL West First All-Star Team 2016, 2017
- WHL Playoff MVP 2017
- Rookie of the Month, January New York Islander 2018
- Calder Memorial Trophy 2018
- The Hockey News, Teemu Selanne Award (Best Rookie) 2018

I caught up with Matt the day after he had just completed his second game of the 2018-19 season, against the Nashville Predators. He had just finished practice and was gracious enough to talk about his humble hockey beginnings.

"When I first met you in my shooting studio, it was easy to see that you were very passionate about hockey. Was there a time that you can look back to and identify when it all started or was it something more gradual?" I asked.

"As far back as I can remember I was always passionate about hockey". He started, *"I used to always play mini sticks or street hockey whenever I could. It was something that I loved to do. When I was young, I would spend hours with my dad stickhandling, shooting and tipping pucks; whatever I could do to get better. I would be out there before practice, after practice, three or four hours a day. That probably helped because it was challenging and fun, but when I look back over my hockey career, it was just something inside me, I think, that I was very passionate about."*

"You had an amazing start to your first season. Was that a goal of yours that you set out to do or was it more of a momentum thing?" I continued

"Doing as well I did that season wasn't really my goal. Coming into camp, I was on a two-way contract and was more focused on just finding my way, making the team by competing hard and securing a spot on the roster. After that, it just kind of took off. I had a great start and some great line mates, the coaching staff gave me an opportunity and it just kind of took care of itself after that."

As I had mentioned to Matt, there are very few players that I have met who have his level of competitiveness. I asked him where it came from.

"I don't know where it came from actually. I think that from a young age my father pushed me hard, but in a good way. It was never about the points it was always about my work ethic. That was instilled in me when I was young and still to this day, I'll call my dad thinking I had a good game; got a couple points and he will say that at times, my effort level was off. He was a plumber by trade and every day he got up at 6:00 a.m. and headed off to work. I got to see how hard he worked and he never complained. He would sit me down and say; 'You don't want to be carrying a lunch pail to work every day Son'. I mean there's no disrespect in that kind of work but he knew how much I loved the game and that if I put in the work, I'd have a better opportunity to make it. "

"For as long as I can remember, I have always been competitive, always wanted to win. It wasn't just hockey, it may have been gym class, team work outs or even at home playing cards, I hated losing. As a kid, I almost had a fear of losing. I just hated losing, no matter what I did: playing golf, soccer or even playing outside. It's hard to understand really. My father had played junior hockey and had played with some great guys like Brett Hull and a couple others that ended up playing pro. He knew how to recognize talent and how hard one had to work at it. He felt that if I put in the effort I could make a pretty good life for myself in hockey. The biggest thing for me was appreciating the effort he put in every day.'

"It wasn't just hockey. I can remember jumping rope so that I could keep active. I also played lacrosse and would be in our garage for thirty minutes

to an hour every day, throwing the ball against the wall. I was always trying to get better, no matter what sport I played. As I said earlier, I hated losing and I knew that the more I practiced the better I competed."

"I also heard somewhere that Joe Sakic and Sidney Crosby used to shoot pucks all the time when they were young so I felt that I should do that as well."

Matt is an exceptional athlete and I'm sure that with his drive and athleticism, he could have had success in any sport that he chose to play. He was also good at lacrosse, a sport that a lot of hockey players transition over to, after their regular season ends. Was it his hard work that allowed him to succeed at hockey, or was it more his passion?

"From my observations, any good NHL player has a real passion for the game and if you have serious passion and that competitiveness, things will fall into place I think. I was always working on my game, stick in my hands all the time, roller-blading in my cul-de-sac, stickhandling or shooting pucks. For some reason, I wanted to play professional hockey. Guys like Sidney Crosby, Pavel Datsyuk and Patrick Kane, watching them when I was young, were real role models for me. I watched them as I grew up and they were real idols to me, I wanted to be just like them. It all depends I think, on who you look up to, and they helped motivate me to be better every day."

There is an old saying that it takes a community to raise a child. I had people in my life, apart from my father, who inspired me to be a better person and a better hockey player. I asked Matt if there were people in his life that had helped guide his hockey career and if so were there any stories that he could share?

"As I mentioned before, my father was hard-working and a real inspiration. He worked hard every day and I never came from a whole lot. I never had the best gear when I was younger and that kind of humility, respecting the process and never having everything given to me, helped shape me as a player. He used to say to me that if I couldn't go out and work on what you love for an hour or two then there's a problem. There are never any shortcuts and while I had a real love of the game, he taught me that no matter what ones passion in life, it still takes effort to be good at it."

"Being on a winning team with good coaching that set high expectations and great teammates, helped as well. I played for the Burnaby Winter Club and I always played on a team that demanded winning more than others. We always wanted to go 20-0-0 every year and that culture of wanting to win, pushing oneself to make that happen, helped reinforce hard work and competition. Anything but a win was unacceptable and losing hurt."

Teamwork is a huge part of Matt's game. He has a reputation for being a great playmaker and that takes not only great vision, hockey sense and patience but an unselfish attitude as well.

"I just love going to the rink, going to practices. I find myself more excited for practice sometimes than I am for games. I don't know why but I just love competing against my teammates. I think sometimes they push you harder. They know your moves and you always have to adapt. It they beat you in a drill, you also have to face them in the dressing room. "

"The team game is what hockey is all about and setting up a teammate is a great feeling. It's a way to give to each other. Scoring is a great feeling and I love sharing that with my line mates."

I asked Matt what he felt his strongest character attribute was. He is fiercely competitive, has a great work ethic, is accountable and a great teammate.

"I think my work ethic, but my passion to learn, my passion to get better is way up there. It doesn't really matter what I do. When I play video games, I don't play them that often, when my buddies are killing me and it's something new, I want to get better right away. Doesn't matter what I do; I want to learn how to be good at it. Being open-minded is very important, taking in everything you can get. I just love working on new things every day and getting better. I guess I would have to say that wanting to learn all the time and being competitive would be my best attributes."

Matt has both experienced and accomplished a lot in the time that he has been around hockey. As a result he has spent time with a lot of players; those that are successful and those that have fallen short. What character traits did he notice that separated the two most often?

"Yeah" Matt exclaimed. *"It all comes down to one's 'want', it's just their 'want'. Everyone has to put work into this game and the ones that don't make it often say that they put in so much time and effort. I ask; 'Did you really put in as much time as you could have? Did you really work as hard as you could every single time you were doing it? I hear all the time that guys like Sidney Crosby, Connor McDavid and even myself were naturally gifted. Yeah maybe somewhat, but at some time those guys; Crosby and McDavid were working harder and putting in more hours and it just paid off more in the long run. Hockey is a sport unlike football and basketball, where ones' natural athleticism takes over. Because of skating, stickhandling and shooting, it is all about repetition and even at an early age you have to put in the work. If you don't have that drive early on, it's tough for it to pan out I think."*

"One more thing, as well." Matt added. *"Everyone used to talk about pro players and say how hard they worked. As I got older, my friends, and even people that I didn't know, would say the same thing about me. But, one doesn't know how much effort they are really putting in until they are around someone else that is working hard. Growing up, I surrounded myself with players that had the same passion for hockey and Dante Fabbro, a real cool friend of mine, was one of those guys. We would spend countless hours together working on shooting and saucer passing. We would push each other hard. He was as competitive as I was and hated losing as much as I did."*

Carrying on, Matt stressed, *"It's all about the extra hours one puts in. You hear guys talking about players; criticizing who they were in Novice and Atom and then asking one day, how they got so good. Maybe they just worked a little harder every day. It's those extra minutes over a couple years that turn into hours that start to add up. Some people think that working hard for three days here and there is good enough. Getting good at this game is a long process. You don't see the results in a week, it takes years of consistency; it is truly a marathon and not a sprint."*

"It is a commitment to the process. I was always the last guy off the ice and when one considers all those minutes of handling a puck, those hundreds of extra shots over the course of a season, they start to add up and make a difference. I would go home after a game and watch NHL highlights; my mind was always on hockey. Seeing highlights, doing the extra, pays off in

the long run. I see guys post on Instagram about some skills they are performing. They think they have put in the work, but it's the work that one puts in, when no one is watching, that matters. My parents are the only ones that have seen that drive and truly know how much time and effort I put into training."

"Most guys get home after a practice or a game and what do they do? Play a video game, watch a show on TV? I would go and work on my game. If we lost, it really bugged me and I hated that feeling. I would do what I could to make sure that it didn't happen again. I would put in the extra work."

"In the end it all pays off, I was never the best kid in Novice and Atom. During the summer, kids would go away on holidays, we wouldn't. My father would have to drag me out of the back yard where I was shooting pucks. When I was in PeeWee and Bantam, my skill started to show, but the gap between others and myself wasn't that much. As the gap increases, the best players don't take the time off, they still push themselves more to get better. I have seen McDavid and heard things about him. Yeah, he works harder and there is a reason why guys like him are better. It doesn't happen overnight and you're not just born a good hockey player, you have to work at it. I remember running on the track when I was twelve and working so hard I couldn't breathe. I try to bring that effort to everything that I do."

"Another thing that is important is that one needs hard competition to get better. It shows us what our weaknesses truly are, if we are accountable to ourselves. It is also important whom we associate with. Dante Fabbro and I spent countless hours together and he pushed me and I pushed him. That makes one competitive. When I played in tournaments and saw a player that was good, I wanted to be better than him. Taking on a challenge and then settling for nothing but the best, has to be part of your makeup. To see a challenge and then going after it without excuses, that is, in my opinion, what defines a pro."

ANDREW COPP

WINNIPEG JETS, NHL

Andrew was born, in 1994, to Anne and Andrew Copp in Ann Arbor, Michigan. He grew up playing a wide variety of sports: soccer, tennis, football, basketball and, of course, ice hockey. His father was his hockey coach during his youth and early teen years and while having never had played hockey when he was younger, he picked it up when he was in college and fell in love with the game. His mother, Anne, was a figure skating coach and understood the values of hard work and respect.

Playing so many sports helped develop the natural athleticism that he demonstrates today and allowed him to excel at these sports as he matured. This was demonstrated during the 2011-12 season, where, while splitting his duties with the US National Team Development Program, he set a state passing record of 557 yards on Sept. 24, 2011, in the Skyline High School Football program.

I first met Andrew Copp in 2012, at a KO Sports camp that was held in Farmington Hills where I was instructing. At that time he was playing for the US National Development program. Andrew was a regular attendee at the camps and with the exception of 2016, where I had major leg surgery and this past 2018 season; I have had a great opportunity to get to know him.

The first time I met him, I immediately recognized him as a fierce competitor and avid student, completely focused on getting better every time he was on the ice. He put his heart and soul into every drill. I found him to be very humble, always assisting with the younger guys and leading by example.

As a result, I was not surprised to learn that he was named captain of the University of Michigan Wolverines in his sophomore 2012-13 season. He was drafted 104th overall in 2013, to the Winnipeg Jets. In March 26, 2015, Andrew signed a three-year entry level contract with the Winnipeg Jets in the NHL, opting out of his senior year of college with the Wolverines, and picking up his first career point in his first professional hockey game on April 11, 2016.

His elite amateur career started with the Compuware Bantam Minor AAA team in 2007, where he moved up through their system playing on the Compuware U18 team during the 2010-11 season. He was selected for the US National Team Development Junior Program, which played in the USHL, in both the 2010-11 and 2011-12 seasons. In 2011-12, Andrew was given a scholarship to the NCAA Division 1 University of Michigan Wolverine team where he played for three years and where he gave up his senior year to play with the NHL Winnipeg Jets. He won a goal medal at the 2012 Under-18 World championships, held in Piestany, Slovakia. In 2013-14 Andrew was selected assistant captain of the U20 team that competed in the World Junior Championships.

Andrew was gracious enough to chat with me prior to heading out the next day for a series of exhibition games. There is always a lot of work for NHL players to do in the way of preparation and to give up an hour to discuss his hockey life was greatly appreciated. I started with a question that I was always curious about .He had always played a wide variety of sports which is very uncommon with today's youth hockey players.

"Becoming an elite athlete that could compete very well at ice hockey and football, as well as other sports had to come from somewhere?" I questioned

"I always played a lot of different sports." He started, *"My parents thought that it was good to keep me busy and it was a great environment to be in. With my dad coaching me in hockey and my mother being a skating coach,*

they always demanded that I worked hard and pay attention to the coaches. Being in a sports environment that always expects you to work hard and pay attention really helped me build good habits of always pushing myself. What also helped was going to a private school when I was young. My parents found that I wasn't pushing myself in public school and really wanted me to challenge myself. The teachers there were great in that they always expected me to work hard, listen and learn and challenge myself to always be better."

"I think that when one is pushed when they are young, especially developing good work habits, it rubs off. I found that when I studied, I was smarter at school. Being smarter at school helped me get better grades. You get better grades and then you study harder. The same happened with all the other sports. I worked hard at skills, my game improved. My game improved and I had better results. The better results I got the harder I trained. This cyclic process really helped me understand the value of hard work."

During our conversation he mentioned that his father had coached him through most of his youth hockey career.

"Was it hard having your father coach you?" I continued.

"No, he treated me just like everyone else but I knew that I didn't want to disappoint him. However, there was one time I kind of took him for granted." He chuckled: *"My dad was making a coaching point and I rolled my eyes. Well, he snapped and told me that if I ever did that again he'd kick me off the ice. Needless to say that I never let that happen again. He always stressed respect for the coaches. They put their time in and deserve that respect."*

When I asked him if there were any other hockey lessons that he remembered his dad throwing his way he again laughed and added:

"My father had dropped me off one day at the rink for a skating lesson. The strict rule of the instructor was that if you were later than two minutes getting on the ice you were sent off and couldn't participate. I guess I lost track of time and I was a couple seconds late. She turned and sent me off the ice. I now had to call my father to come and pick me up. Was he pissed, and then I started thinking, this will be a fun ride home. On the way back my dad stopped by a track outside a school, told me to get out and to start

running laps. I can't remember how many laps I ran before he instructed me to sprint the sides and jog the ends. That then led to me doing leapfrogs down the sides and jogging the ends. This took place for an hour or so and after he thought I learned my lesson, we got back in the car and headed home. I was NEVER late for anything again after that."

"Another funny story about my father" He added, "My brother is a goalie and they were playing in this pretty important tournament. Both my brother and other goalie were goofing around and were late getting on the ice. My father informed them that they were going to sit on the bench for one period and the team would play six on five. I think the score was 7-1 or something like that but he didn't care. It was more important that he taught the lesson than worrying about winning."

"He has preached the same consistent story all my life." Andrew continued, "He didn't care how many goals I scored, it just mattered how hard I worked. Even today he will get kind of disappointed if I screw up a play but really give it to me if he feels that I wasn't' work hard."

"Were there any other people in your life that really helped to define your work ethic?" I asked. I grew up in a hardworking community and had watched my father work tirelessly with home projects such as pouring a new concrete driveway himself or helping friends with home renovations and that really helped shape my perspective.

"I was never the best in sports I played when I was young. I remember watching the best players and they would always be doing something extra. It was the same in all the sports. I wasn't the best baseball player but I played with some really talented guys, the same with tennis and soccer. They all worked hard and having them to look up to kept me focused; knowing that I had to do what they did or even more if I wanted to be better. When I went to Michigan, I was given a walk-on opportunity and I knew that in order for me to make the team I had to work hard for my opportunity. All of these early lessons in my life really helped me become the athlete that I am today."

"I keep coming back to the word cyclic." He commented, "I kept realizing that the harder I worked in school or in sport, the smarter or better I became. This led to more success and then the cycle just repeated itself over and over again. After a while, ones work ethic becomes a part of who they are."

"When you made the Winnipeg Jets, there was a tough time at the end of your second year when you were sent down to the affiliate AHL Manitoba Moose. The following season you were back up again with the Jets. How did you deal with the adversity?" I asked

"I think that it is always about choice. One can look at the experience in a negative way and blame others. I took it upon myself to try and make a difference. I was the first person on the ice and the last person off. I did whatever I could to be a great teammate. As I mentioned before, in all the sports I played I was never the best. That in itself is a humbling experience. No matter how good you are, there is always someone better. The only way that I could overcome that deficiency was to work harder than everyone else and this is what I did. I put in the effort and trained hard that summer to make sure that I was ready for camp the following season."

One always wonders when an athlete has worked hard to achieve his goal and then finally achieves it, do they every get a little 'cocky' when playing in the best hockey league in the world. Andrew seemed to me to always be somehow grounded. When he competed in the World Juniors, or captained the Michigan Wolverines, I could never tell, so I asked him, "Do you ever get a little too overconfident or 'cocky' now that you've played a couple years in the NHL?"

Andrew had a good chuckle over that question, *"Listen, I have a very close friend and he was always way better in baseball than I was and while I'm a better hockey player, it's kind of a moot point to brag about something when someone else can rub your nose in it. Whenever I would get a little cocky, he would take me down a peg. I was very fortunate to have friends around that had great values and we would always point out any character flaws in each other; which in turn kept us all grounded. He is in the world of finance right now and it's the same thing, we talk several times a month and he always keeps me grounded. He puts a lot of work into his business so the work ethic that he had in sports certainly carried over into other areas of his life. I came to realize that my work ethic and attitude would be the same no matter what I do. It's a habit now, and once one sees the result in one area, it carries over to everything else. It's always about* who we are in our attitude, our accountability and how hard we work. My parents were always demanding of us in how we acted: respect, work ethic, accountability, and our actions always spoke louder than words."

What I found interesting about Andrew's athletic career is that he really had an opportunity to play a secondary sport at a high level. That was football. He tried out for the US Junior U17 Development and was one of the last cuts. At the start of the season, one of the players was injured and he was called back to participate.

"I was playing quarter back for the Skyline High School Football program. I had just started at the position and felt that I couldn't let the team down so I turned down the opportunity. Later in the season, another player got injured and they said that I could participate with the hockey program and still keep playing football. I ended up injuring my shoulder at the end of the season and didn't get a chance to go through the playoffs with the guys. It was a pivotal time in my sports career, I think. I didn't get the taste of a football playoff run or a championship and while I was good at the quarterback position, I liked hockey. The opportunity to play for the US Development program kind of won over and looking back, maybe the injury was the turning point in my hockey career."

Another topic we got into was the "chip on his shoulder" attitude that I had noticed in the one-on-one battles at the skills camp. I mentioned that I had a brother who was ten years older than I was and who thoroughly enjoyed getting me going. Thankfully, he moved away to live with my older sister when he was in grade twelve. All I could remember was that he constantly kept poking me until I would snap and then I would come out swinging. He would put his hand on the top of my head and hold me off laughing at how upset I was. This happened for three years of my life and I still think it had something to do with my anger management issues that resurface every once in a while. I asked him where his edgy attitude came from.

"Not like that." He chuckled, *"I think that it came from the fact that I wasn't one of the top athletes on any team I played for. I guess that I wanted to kind of prove to everybody that I had what it takes. I think that chip helps my NHL game by keeping me going when there's a tough road trip.*

CORE VALUES

Sometimes it slips when I play three games in a row, but if I make a mistake or get scored on, that 'chippiness' comes back quickly."

We had some good laughs sharing stories of some of our game experiences. In closing I asked him what advice he would offer younger players, trying to work their way up to the professional level.

"I think that they need to be aware of how hard work makes one better, whether or not it has to do with school or sports. Sometimes the improvements are very small but they are there. When one works harder, the improvements come even faster and this kind of reinforces the cycle of work and reward, work harder and receive more rewards. Being very good at something is not luck and requires a lot of dedication and being willing to change. Also, surround yourself with good friends with good values. They will help in your journey when perhaps you go off path or get to full of yourself. Good friends keep you grounded."

Andrew is one of the players that truly impressed me with his attitude and commitment to excellence. One could call him the perfect student. It will be fun to follow his career over the next ten years.

DYLAN LARKIN

DETROIT REDWINGS, NHL

I had the pleasure of working with Dylan at a KO Sports Skills Camp in Michigan in the summer of 2014. At that time he was playing for the US National U17 team. He is one of those guys that are easy to remember in that he always hits the ice with a smile on his face. There was no question in my mind that hockey was a sport that he was very passionate about. It always reminded me of the eagerness and enthusiasm that those six and seven-year-olds have when they can't wait to get out on the ice and play. He was always eager to learn and get down to work.

Dylan has played elite level hockey since his bantam years when he was rostered with the Belle Tire Bantam Minor AAA, a traveling all-star team located in Detroit Michigan. He played in that organization from 2009-12, after which he joined the US National Team Developmental Program (USNTDP) in 2012-203, and competed in the U17 World Hockey Challenge. He stayed with the program competing in the World Junior Championship U18 during his 2013-14 season.

Drafted by the Detroit Redwings 15th overall in the 2014 NHL entry draft, he was recruited by the University of Michigan and played there during 2014-15. He made the jump late in the season to the Grand Rapid Griffins in the American Hockey League AHL, an affiliate team of the Detroit Redwings. He started his NHL career in 2015 and has never looked back. His international experience includes a Team North America appearance in 2017 at the World Cup Championship and a stint as assistant captain at the World Championships in 2017 and 2018.

CORE VALUES

His talent, work ethic, strong team and leadership skills, has management convinced that he can help lead the Redwings to a future Stanley Cup, and they have selected him for an alternate captain role that includes a new five-year deal worth $30.5 million for the 2018-19 season.

Dylan brings a lot to the table in the way of skill, attitude and leadership and I was fortunate enough to catch up with him at the start of the 2018-19 season.

To get the professional level and accomplish what Dylan has requires a certain passion and affinity for hard work. I asked him where that work ethic came from.

"I think that it comes from way back. The basis comes from my father, and the lessons he told me. He has never had anything given to him, he's a self-employed, self-made businessman who started his own beauty supply business, made calls and was on the road as a sales man. Seeing how hard he worked really stuck with me."

"Another thing that really helped was my competitiveness. I was a younger sibling to my brother who was two years older than me. Obviously he was bigger, stronger and faster when he was seven, eight, nine and ten years old. He used to drive me crazy. Pond hockey season would come around and I would always be after him to come and play one-on-one, pass the puck around or just shoot pucks. It would have snowed the night before and he would say; 'nah, there's too much snow and I don't feel like it shoveling it'. I would say screw it and I'd head down and shovel it off. I would have the whole thing done except for maybe a strip or two and he'd show up to help. I'd be dead tired, but we would compete hard against each other. I'd be so choked when he beat me, even when I was exhausted and that really drove my competitive side and made me want to work even harder."

"With all of the competition between us, over time, it just instilled that competitive spirit in me and I hated losing. I was never the best player in Michigan when I was growing up, so I had to work for it. When I made the US National Team Development Program (USNTDP), I was a fourth line center. I would hear all the stories about Ryan Kesler and Rocko Grimaldi. These guys were successful and high draft picks and I would hear

how hard they worked and how many pucks they shot after practice in the shooting room. I would try to do my best to take it to another level. "

"*The shooting room at the USNDTP would be kind of full after practice so I would work out, shoot a couple pucks when I could fit in and then go down and shower. I would stick around afterwards in my street clothes, would wait for everyone to leave and then take my stick, gloves and all my stuff and head back up to the shooting room. All the trainers and coaches would have left the building and I would stay till seven or eight o'clock at night just working on my shot. I was always working on the little things and I think that being so competitive really helped.*"

I was telling Dylan that I had a brother that was ten years older than I was and between three and six years old, he and his friends would tease me so much that I would snap. Of course, there was no way that I could do anything but I would come out swinging which would make them happier. Did his brother ever get him riled up?

"*Oh yeah. My brother would egg me on and would slap me or something. I would cross the line and throw a mini stick at him or smack him with my stick. There was no way that I could beat him one-on-one so I would do something to really piss him off and then I would have to run and he would catch me. I would always have to get the last blow in.*"

I brought up a story that I had heard that he had done something to the ceiling of his room when he was billeting.

"*I was seventeen at the time; it was my second year at USNTDP. I took a roll of black hockey tape and made the words 'NHL' on the ceiling of my room. When I got up in the morning or when I went to bed at night, or was just laying there I could see the letters. It helped me visualize my goal and when I left, my billets removed the tape and of course they had to repaint the ceiling. I wasn't thinking of course but my billets, not complaining, told the coaches about the letters and then it was passed on after that I guess.*"

"Having been in the NHL now for several years," I asked, "What are the values that the young players coming in either have or don't have?"

"*I don't think that it's skill. Everyone can skate, stickhandle and shoot. The first thing I notice is their game sense. The difference that I noticed between* the AHL and the NHL is not really the skills or how strong they are, it is how they think the game. If they can pay attention to what the coaches are saying and understand the system, they still need to find ways to play the game. The biggest thing for me is seeing a young guy that can come in and play the game."

"As for myself, I don't want to be a robot. It's learning when to go, when to hold onto the puck, when to get open, when to drive or hold up or just chip the puck in and learn to fight another day. I think the best players in the NHL, at the end of their shift, when they are exhausted and they see an opportunity to make a play, they will do after it nine out of ten times. It may go sideways three or four times but they're going to take that chance. I think that you have to take those chances once in a while."

I think that it takes a lot of courage to play that way. I asked Dylan if he had to earn what I call "wiggle-room" before he could become more adventurous.

"Yeah, I think so. You get a first round draft pick coming in will get more of an opportunity than a guy coming up from the AHL or free agent signing. I don't know why it's like that."

"My dad had a great saying:' If you put the puck into the net it solves everything.' And it is true. I mean, it's not as easy as it sounds but if a guy can find a way to contribute to and chip in some offense the better. The sooner that a guy can be more creative within the system; find ways to fore-check, get the puck back and make a play, the faster that one can earn the coaches trust."

"I remember my second year when we had the end of the year meeting. Ken Holland, the Wings' general manger, told me that if I wasn't a fifty-five or sixty point player then I had better win fifty-five percent or higher of my face-offs if I was going to get any ice time. This is what you have to do if you want to be a center-man in the NHL."

I asked Dylan if he approached the game any differently, now that he has more games under his belt.

"Yes I do and we have talked about this many times. What is takes to be a great offensive player. How to slow the puck down and protect it, how to make plays with puck. Zetterberg is probably one of the slower guys out there but he always finds ways to make plays. He is so good at protecting the puck and slowing the game down."

"In the first year I was so concerned about speed and then the defense learned how to play me. The next year I had to adapt and change how I entered the zone; maybe hold up and look for a late man, slow down coming late into the zone to be a different option. Great offensive players value the puck. They understand the second and third pucks like off the cycle, how to get into lanes. Take guys like Ryan Getzlaf or Zetterberg for example, they know how to change the pace of the game. The more one watches great offensive players, the more they see how they maintain control, get to the right areas and slow the game down. It is something that I'm constantly watching and learning through experience."

If there was anything that you could say to the young kids coming up, what would it be?

"Passion for the game is very important and wanting to learn. You have to be a sponge. As a young player in the NHL you have a great chance to be all eyes and ears. Watch and take things home with you. Passion is the love of the game and wanting to learn makes you better but you still have to work hard. It is a tough road. After the season, there are guys that want to be on the golf course all summer, but if you want to be good at this game you have to work at it whenever you can. A game here and there doesn't hurt but you have to get back at it."

BRENDEN DILLON

SAN JOSE SHARKS, NHL

I met Brenden several years ago at a goaltender camp in Richmond. He was taking every opportunity to improve his skills and shots from the point were the order of the day. Over the past couple of years, we have had some great hockey conversations about drive, desire, attitude and never giving up when people say you're not quite good enough.

He was born in Surrey British Columbia in 1990, and that is where he played his minor hockey. Over the years, he has had some setbacks yet his never-say-die attitude has kept him achieving the goals that he is so passionate about.

At the age of fifteen, he was passed over in the Western Hockey League (WHL) Bantam Draft yet managed to catch the attention of the Seattle Thunderbirds after one year of Junior B Hockey. At the age of sixteen he played in a league where I was coaching, the Pacific Junior Hockey League (at the time was called the PIJHL – Pacific International Junior Hockey League) for the Hope Icebreakers. Anyone that knows where Hope is, knows that the drive from Surrey is not an easy task and demonstrates his commitment to doing whatever it takes to get experience, and get better. I remember him as a hardworking, gritty defenceman and to play that way in a league of nineteen, twenty-years-olds at sixteen years of age is not an easy thing to do.

His work ethic and attitude earned him the attention and respect of the Seattle Thunderbirds, who signed him to a player's contract in 2007 and this is where he remained until 2011. He was passed over in the NHL draft but, as before, dug even deeper and was determined to achieve his ultimate goal. His hard work, physical play and strong defensive game garnered him the attention of the Dallas Stars of the NHL. They signed him to a three-year-entry-level contract at the end of his senior year in the WHL.

He started off as many WHL player do, playing two years in the AHL for the Texas Stars, Dallas's affiliate team before moving up to play with the Stars for good in his third 2012-13 Season. He was also selected to play for Canada in the 2013 International Ice Hockey Federation (IIHF) tournament. Again, his work ethic and commitment to development allowed him to succeed where so many others had failed. He was traded to the San Jose Sharks, in 2014, for Jason Demers, a third-round draft pick. He has been with the Sharks ever since, and his contract has recently been extended to the 2020 season.

His journey has not been easy and the only thing that kept him forging ahead was an unbridled passion to play in the NHL.

We did some training together in the summer of 2016-17 and it is where I got to know him more personally. It was easy to see that his desire to improve was a well-developed habit. When I pushed him on that point, he offered some great insights:

"Hockey has always been a passion of mine. I remember playing with mini sticks in my basement when I was young and listening to the local hockey radio talk show discussing the Canucks game that was played earlier that day. I remember thinking to myself that I could actually make a living playing the game that I loved."

"My father was always a great motivator for me" He added, *"When I played basketball he would make me go outside and shoot hoops saying that if you want to get better you have to practice. The same thing was with hockey, you want to get better to you have to put in the time and do extra practice. His message was always the same, no matter what you do; you have to put in the extra to get better."*

"When I wasn't selected in the WHL Bantam Draft, it was an eye opener and clear statement that I needed to get better. I worked hard and going to the Hope Ice Breakers as a sixteen-year-old rookie was the best thing that happened to me. They had great coaching that believed in me and gave

me the chance to play. Competing against the senior vets at sixteen was a great learning experience and let me know that I had to get a lot stronger and faster."

Each step of the way, Brenden had to earn his keep however, the support that his mother and father have given him over the years has allowed him to grow as a player. *"Dad would drive me to the rink or whenever I needed to be to get better. Never a complaint, he just got me there."*

When I asked him whether or father pushed him at all he replied, *"Not really, he always said that if you want to get better you have to put the work in. When I was young he made it clear what I had to do to get better, but my drive to play at the highest level was my own motivation. I was not going to be denied and I would do whatever it took to get there."*

His next setback was missing the NHL Draft. *"I looked forward to that draft and when it didn't happen, I was disappointed. I had worked hard, but realized as before, that I would have to do more and work even harder to get an opportunity."*

When I asked him about sacrifice, he was clear, stating, *"I don't think that I had to make any sacrifices. I wanted to play in the NHL so bad that missing a weekend or an activity with my friends was not really sacrificing. I knew where I wanted to get to and knew only hard work and a commitment to improve would get me there. Looking back I wouldn't change anything."*

What core value did he feel helped him the most in his quest?

"I would probably say mental toughness and hard work. Every time that I was passed over, I set a goal to prove people wrong and worked harder. Life is full of disappointments and I feel that they are just obstacles to overcome. With the right mind set anyone can accomplish their goals."

I have watched Brenden play for the Sharks ever since he joined the team. He looks on his journey as a marathon, not a sprint. I see him improving just a little each year.

When I asked him about this he answered, *"I'm always asking the vets why they use the curve they do, why they train a certain way, what advice can they give me. If I get better every year, even just a little, I feel that I'm helping my teammates and the organization. They have treated me very well and it's my way of giving back. I know that I have to work hard, there are many talented players in this league and I know that one has to keep moving forward."*

As for his future in the NHL?

"It is always up to me. I have to improve every year and I have never backed away from a challenge. I set goals every year and work hard at achieving them. My life has always been that way. Not selected for a WHL team, work hard and make a team. Don't get drafted, prove them wrong, work hard and sign a contract. Get put down into the minors, climb back up stay with the main club. Success in life is a fight and not one that I will ever back away from."

JOE PAVELSKI

CAPTAIN SAN JOSE SHARKS, NHL

I first met Joe in the summer of 2010 in Madison Wisconsin. It was teaching at a shooting camp that was organized by Adam Burish, who was playing for the NHL Dallas Stars at the time. Joe was an intense practice player and I like to remind him of an incident that we still chuckle about. We had just completed a series of shooting drills and all the pucks were in the net. I remember a couple of the guys went to retrieve them and were passing them back to a designated area one by one. Impatient, Joe intervened pulling all the pucks out of the net and then bending over from the waist with his stick flat on the ice, he pushed them over where everyone was standing, all at once. He felt that there were a lot of skills to cover and didn't want to waste time.

He is a consummate professional. He goes to work every day, is not afraid to engage in the tough questions about how to get better. He is a consistent performer who hates to let his teammates down. He is also a student of the game, looking for every possible advantage skill-wise and tactically.

Joe Pavelski was born in Plover Wisconsin in 1984. He has had a very successful minor career, winning a Wisconsin State Hockey championship with his high school team the Panthers in 2002. From there he moved up to play for the Waterloo Black Hawks of the USHL, and won the Clark Cup Championship that season, with Joe winning the USHL Dave Tyler Junior Player of the Year Award.

He was selected to play NCAA hockey for the Wisconsin Badgers in the WCHA and during his first season was named to the All_WCHA

Rookie Team of 2005. During his second 2006 season, Joe helped the Badgers win the NCAA Division 1 Men's Ice Hockey Championship, and led the team in overall points.

Joe was drafted by the San Jose Sharks in the seventh round, 205th overall. He joined the sharks during the 2006-07 season, scoring a goal in his first game, which made him only the eleventh player in the Sharks' history to do so.

Joe earned the accolades of team management as one of the most consistent players during the next 2007-08 season where he played in all eighty-two regular and thirteen post-season playoff games. He was a revered shootout performer netting seven goals in eleven attempts that season. As a result of his hard work and consistent play he moved up the lineup and at the start of the 2014-15 season he was named as one of the four alternate captains on the team. This was changed to team captain on October 5, 2015, making Joe the ninth acting captain in Sharks history. He has made appearances in two NHL All Star games: 2016 and 2017.

Joe has garnered some great international experience and was selected for the USA Olympic men's team in 2010 and 2014. He earned the nickname "Captain America" in 2016 when he was selected as the team captain of Team USA.

Aside from his busy NHL commitments, Joe finds time to do charity work in the summer, hosting a golf event that raises money to purchase hockey equipment for families that cannot afford it in the Stevens Point area.

I have had the privilege of knowing Joe for the past eight years. This is his story.

I mentioned an on-ice incident at the start of Joe's introduction and when I talked to him, I brought it up again. It brought up a couple chuckles.

"Wasting time has always been an issue with me. I remember practicing shooting pucks when I was young and I always felt that I got more out of high quality reps. I had maybe half a bucket of pucks and when practicing,

it seemed like a waste of time to shoot fifty pucks, retrieve them and start over. Every time I went into a rink during my high school days, I would circle around and scoop what I could find. By the time I graduated, 'I'd gathered up three full buckets. This was a lot better and I felt that I could really concentrate on my technique and get it right and not have to worry about running out of pucks. After I was tired, I would then use the break to rest up, collect them and start over. That day on the ice with you, I felt that there was only a short amount of time to cover a lot of skills and wanted to get the most out of the session."

I certainly appreciated that approach. I asked him where else he applied the same philosophy.

"Every practice or pre-game skate, I try to cover one or two skills that I want to sharpen up and try to do high quality repetitions. There are some slot drills where I practice quick turns and releases both forehand and backhand that tend to occur during games."

"This time wasting philosophy – was there something that triggered you to ingrain this into your training?" I asked.

"Actually, I remember a story that Jay Woodcroff shared with me. He played with the Redwings when they won the cup and was telling me about Nicklas Lidstrom. Lidstrom's eye hand was incredible and I remember playing against him and we would try to chip a puck by him and he would always be able to knock it out of the air. He said that Lidstrom used to bounce a ball off the wall in his mother's kitchen, just kind of volley it back and forth. I decided to try the technique myself. I found that if I could bounce a ball against the wall and keep it in the air, I could get in three hundred or more touches in a couple minutes. There was no way that I could get three hundred pucks shot from the point."

"That occurred while you were pro." I continued, "You still had a philosophy of work rate relative to time. Where did that come from?"

"Actually, there was one. My younger brother had lost a championship game in high school to a team that they should have beat and after the game when he climbed into the car, he was all upset and depressed. My father was always direct and hated pouting. 'We're going home and we will grab the dogs and go rabbit hunting. Do you think that the beagles

care that you won or lost. You had your chance to prepare all year, you had a chance to work hard and you fell short. When you have the opportunity to train, don't waste it. You should be able to look back and not have any regrets. Don't let it happen again but now it's over, move on.' It was so true. We have to use the time that we have been given and not waste it. That always stuck with me."

"Were there any core values that really stick out in your mind that contributed to your success?"

"Core values are really a blend; I can't say that it was really one thing or another. Respect for me was big; respect for your teammates and respect for yourself. When you go from your minor team to junior, from junior to college or from college to pro. You have to respect that you can do it. You have to respect yourself and your underlying habits that allowed you to get better. Everyone works hard but quality of work, focused work and not just running around for a forty-five second shift. Hard work is what earns you respect from your teammates and coaches."

"I remember a quote from a book "The Secret of the Pros", the answer really is that there is no secret. Everything has already been done before. The trick is to get off the couch and get into action. My interpretation is who can get into action or get into the hard work part of their training the fastest. There is a lot of wasted time. Players skate around shooting a couple pucks and it's the guy that gets into action the quickest and then add that up over a long period of time, it is who accomplishes more."

"Champions in all sports, whether golf, football, soccer or hockey work on their fundamentals. They don't take shortcuts, just get into their training faster and get the work done."

I brought up a favorite saying of my father, "Make your uncomfortable, comfortable!" If you're not out of your comfort zone, you're not learning and you're not getting better. We discussed the fact that to young players, everything is uncomfortable and of course as one learns an action becomes more comfortable. The question then becomes, once the movement become comfortable, is the technique correct?

"I find that becomes one of my greatest concerns." Joe replied, *"I go to work on something and then it starts to become comfortable and then I have to*

ask myself, am I doing it perfectly or have I just become comfortable. I always have to be aware of where I want my game to go and then be aware of my technique when I'm doing high rep training. Nothing worse than working hard at something and then finding out you're doing it wrong and you have to start all over again."

"Did your father push you in your hockey?"

"Never. My father was always supportive but he never pushed me at any time during my career. We were always raised to work hard and be respectful. He told me early that my coaches would know more about hockey than he did so respect and pay attention to them and work hard."

"With you having a seven-year-old son now, that plays hockey; what core values do you try and instill?"

"Being a father is tough, no question. I really enjoy watching him when he's in the moment working hard and competing and not really thinking about anything else. It is important always to reinforce hard work and respect. That shows through when he's playing. But, I think that it comes from a love of the game and having fun competing and getting results. That tells me that he is working hard in the game for the right reasons and not just because he has to but he wants to if that makes any sense."

We discussed leadership.

"Leadership is an interesting conversation. There are many kinds of leaders. I try to look at it from several different angles. If our line is going good and another line is struggling, for example, we can't afford to worry about them, it just takes away from our game. We have to keep our game going strong. We have to look at ourselves first and know where our mind set is at and then encourage them to keep at it. A leader has to set a standard and then keep it. Show that he wants to be there, wants to improve and wants to compete, it is contagious. A leader, I think, looks in the mirror and makes sure that they are doing what they expect in others."

"Another character trait that I feel is important is discipline. When I was in junior I received a handout about discipline that really stuck with me. It basically stated that any player could have a great offensive day or a bad one but every day you're able to play defense. It is all about your character *and discipline. It really hit home with me. One obviously has to work hard at offense but it is also reward driven. Working hard at defense has little if any recognizable reward. It is all about commitment to the process and working for your teammate. There are a lot of values that define one's life but discipline is often overlooked."*

"It was a great handout and I always remember it."

We talked about the philosophy of defense and a person's attitude towards it. As a young player; because I played the role of a defenceman, I realized it was a quick way to get the coach's respect and a way to earn more ice time. The other approach to playing strong defense was based on puck possession relative to offensive output. Put quite simply, we agreed that strong defense put pressure on the opposition resulting in more turnovers; more turnovers resulted in more puck possession which in turn, leads to more opportunities to generate points.

"That type of defensive philosophy really took off when Todd McLellan came to San Jose for the seven years he was there he really preached a philosophy of 'win more face-offs, get a lot more starts'. The idea was that when you win the draw you start off with the puck, resulting more puck possession opportunities. The discipline there is sticking with it. There are a lot of skills to work on but if getting better at draws helps the team, then one has to commit to it."

"This also falls under accountability. If it is a weak area of your game, get to work on it."

Joe is a guy that holds himself accountable and I asked him where that came from.

"I always knew that hockey was something that I wanted to do. My parents established a hard work ethic but they just supported me, never pushed me. My dad always said; 'Listen to your coaches, they watch a lot more games, have a lot more experience and they know a lot more than I do, so respect what they have to say'. So, whatever plan they put together was the plan that I would try to execute. The accountability was playing within the system; do what they asked. For me it was doing what I could to help the team and doing it well would lead to more ice time. I never had any complaints

with coaches, I understood that they had a plan for the team and they were trying to find the best way to compete so that we could win."

"You know as a player when you're taking shortcuts, it doesn't feel good going half way."

"As a player, I know my strengths and weaknesses. It all comes back to my value foundation. I know as a player that skating is not my strong suit but I know that I can manage a thirty- to forty-second shift. When it gets longer than that, everything gets exposed. I go into a game knowing to keep my shifts shorts, don't cheat by extending shifts, and understand my faceoff roles. I know my skating routes and systems, so I can go into each game already prepared and just let it rip."

RYAN KESLER

ASSISTANT CAPTAIN, ANAHEIM DUCKS, NHL

Ryan Kesler is just such a player. He's the guy that people love to have on their team but they hate playing against. Ryan Kesler was born in Livonia, Michigan to Mike and Linda Kesler. His father, Mike, has been around the game for many years, coaching minor and junior hockey and also ran hockey schools in Livonia which Ryan attended every year till he was seventeen. His minor hockey experience in Detroit saw him play for Compuware, HoneyBaked and Little Caesars – all considered elite traveling teams.

As Mike tells the story, Ryan was playing AAA hockey and then at the age of thirteen Ryan was cut from every AAA team that he tried out for. What is not common knowledge is that at that age he had been diagnosed with Osgood-Schlatter Disease, an affliction of the knees, after experiencing a growth spurt. As Ryan explained, he could hardly skate and certainly couldn't run, let barely walk. He ended up playing for his dad's '83 birth year team, all a year older than Ryan, in the Livonia Minor Hockey Association.

He had to ice his knees after every game and practice skate just to get by. He was in so much pain that by the age of fifteen, he had to decide whether he wanted to play hockey or not. It was here that he had to make a choice – prove everybody wrong or quit. And it was here that he had to shape his attitude towards pain and mental toughness. As he grew, the pain subsided and with new motivation, he excelled. In June 2000, he was drafted in the fifth round by the Brampton Battalion of the Ontario Hockey League (OHL).

The OHL is a premier eastern junior developmental program and is part of the Canadian Hockey League (CHL). Ryan decided instead to play for the US National Development Program, due in part to the fact that it was close to Livonia. This allowed him to focus on his education without leaving high school. During the 2000-01 season, he entered the US National Development Program where he spent two seasons recording ninety-nine points in 131 games.

Ryan accepted a scholarship to play college hockey at Ohio State University for the Buckeyes, a member of the CCHA. During his tenure there, he was awarded the Ohio State's George Burke Most Valuable Freshman award. In 2003 Ryan entered the NHL entry draft where he was ranked sixteenth overall among North American players. He was chosen twenty-third overall by the Vancouver Canucks.

His first season with the Canucks was split between the NHL team and the AHL affiliate team, the Manitoba Moose. With the 2004-05 being the NHL lockout season, Ryan spent the entire year with the Manitoba Moose finally making the jump to the Canucks in the 2005-06 season, where he completed all eighty-two games.

His life has been complicated with injuries and controversy but he has risen through the ranks of the elite to be considered one the best two-way players in the NHL. He earned the Selke award in 2011 and was nominated again in 2016-17. He is well known for his work ethic, tenacity and prowess in the face-off circle. He competed at the World U18 Championships in 2002, the World Junior Championships in 2004, the Winter Olympics in 2010 in Vancouver and in the World Cup for the USA in 2016.

I first started working with Ryan when he was with the Vancouver Canucks, a couple years before he was traded to the Anaheim Ducks. His agent had reached out to me to see if I would mind working with him to get his shooting back on track, after shoulder surgery in 2012. He showed up at my training center in North Delta and we started his rebuilding process. It was immediately apparent that he only believed in hard work, making no excuses, and doing whatever it took to get better.

It was several weeks later that I received another call from his agent to see if I would work with him at a private, in-house ice rink owned by Chad Kroeger from Nickelback. That was where I really came to appreciate both his sense of humor and his incredible work ethic.

I was let into the parking area through security and led down to where the rink was located in the basement. There was a back entrance and Ryan was in there waiting to see me. The conversation was direct and simple: he wanted me to put him through some skating and puck drills. For over an hour we worked on various skills, discussed mechanics and I challenged him on some new techniques. Afterwards, as we sat in dressing area discussing some of the exercises he had performed he asked me a very pointed question, *"Well, what do you think?"* I paused, grinned and replied; "How honest do you want me to be?"

I then gave a quick and negative breakdown on what I thought of his release, his need for being more explosive, his lack of deception in his turns, etc. etc. I paused and waited for his reply. All I got was a wide grin and a thank you for the honesty.

With that we shook hands and I left. I remember chuckling to myself as I drove away. "Yeah, he must think I'm crazy". A couple of minutes later, my cell phone buzzed. It was Ryan's agent and the first thought through my mind was. "Ah great, must have tweaked something by being so negative and now I'm going to get my butt kicked".

As it turned out, Ryan was a guy that wanted criticism. He just wanted to be the best player he could be and all he needed were the facts and someone that would give it to him straight. The rest is history and I have worked with Ryan ever since. I am incredibly grateful for his friendship and for sharing his story with me for this book.

Ryan had a passion for hockey but his work ethic was driven by his father; who, as he explained to me, was s man *"who worked hard all his life to put food on the table and clothes on their back. He never made excuses and never accepted any."* Ryan went on to say that his father couldn't care less how many goals he scored, just how hard he worked. It was all about the effort.

CORE VALUES

Ryan brought up the infamous Basement Drill that his father designed. *"I'd come home from a game and Dad would look at me with that you didn't give your best effort look and down to the basement we would go. I'd put on my gear minus my skates and he would have me run the stairs, do pushups and burpees until I was going to puke. There is no question that my father believed that work ethic defined an athlete. He always demanded a 200-foot game and never relented. He taught me how to be a professional."*

Ryan commented further, *"I was never the most talented player and even today, there are many players better than me. I learned that hard work always beats talent that doesn't work. I knew that no matter what, I always had to work harder than everyone else and that I could make no excuses. My father was instrumental in teaching me those lessons. It wasn't just the Basement Drill (he chuckled here) but I got to see him work hard every day. He didn't make excuses so how could I?"*

"I came to realize that we in essence are an extension of our parents. I, through my hard work, could represent my father's values and show people that he was a very hardworking man and that I was an extension of him."

"I look at my own son, Ryker" He added, *"I expect him to work hard and while I want him to have fun, I expect him to work hard and not quit. I think that it's important for parents to demand more of their kids."*

"We work hard as parents, trying to pass on the best values that our parents gave to us. One of our proudest moments happened just a while ago. One of our best friends took our daughter, Makayla, and Ryker for a hike with them. They always chirp each other at home and drive us crazy. We received pictures back from them of Makayla and Ryker holding hands and helping each other out. You realize as a parent that you're doing a good job when other people are commenting good things about them when they are away from you".

We discussed many issues and some hit home. Sacrifice was a big one.

"I wish I knew back then what I know now" he stated, *"I knew that I had to give everything I had to prove to people that I deserved what I got. In doing that I pushed my body to the limits. I think that there is a time and place to do that and when I look back now I see I only knew one way. With*

all the injuries that I have had, it gives one an opportunity to see the mistakes in one's effort and mistakes in one's training. Sacrificing one's body for the cause has been tough and looking forward I have to learn how to adapt, While playing hard has always been who I am, I also have to learn to play smarter."

I asked him what he thought were the weakest attributes of the young players trying to get into the pro game.

"I think that the four areas that I see most of them fail at are; work ethic, mental toughness, discipline and respect. Kids today don't really face many challenges. At the first sign of adversity they disappear. They depend too much on their talent and at the pro level, everyone is talented, it's just how much they want it, how much they dedicate to their training, how they fight through those challenges. Much of the time, the best kids never really have to earn their ice time; they start to feel that they're entitled. At younger ages, that may work but not at the professional level where consistency in effort has to be given every night, especially as a rookie trying to earn their way."

"I also think parents and especially coaches today are too soft. They worry too much about winning and let the top kids with talent get away with too much. Players like me have always had to work hard and when we thought we gave enough, we had to give more. It's only after a long battle with one's mental toughness does your talent start to arrive. Too often, I see talented players lacking the mental toughness side of the game. Most of the kids today are too soft!"

He was telling me what it was like to play in the NHL as a rookie. "Coaches pushed players all the time and if you weren't mentally tough you quit. There are a lot of expectations on winning and effort. As a vet, you've earned your way, but as a rookie we had our butts kicked and while I hate some of my former coaches I can see how their actions pushed me to be better".

Having a son that loves hockey; are there any words of wisdom that he could share.

"The problem with today's game is that it becomes a business way too early. Weight training and the push to be the best starts too young and the most *important thing is to have fun at a young age. To Ryker, it's a game still. I tell him to have fun but always work hard. Enjoy the game and learn to love it without all the extra pressure we put on them."*

"I think that parenting is so very important" he added, "Work ethic has to be taught so that even when one is playing or practicing they understand that working hard is the most important thing. That way, if they learn to work hard everywhere in their life, when they play, the effort that they need to put into the game to get better while having fun, is already there as a foundation".

"As it has been said, the apple doesn't fall far from the tree. Our kids represent our values and who we are as people when they are away from us, so it is important that we get it right".

PATRICK MARLEAU

ASSISTANT CAPTAIN, TORONTO MAPLE LEAFS, NHL

I had the pleasure of meeting Patrick in 2015, when he still under contract to the NHL San Jose Sharks. I was on my way to Anaheim to teach and he asked if I could stop by his residence where he had a small shooting training area and talk about shooting. Two qualities that stood out immediately were his passion to always get better and the fact that he is an incredibly humble athlete.

He is a Canadian hockey player, born in Aneroid, Saskatchewan, and drafted in the first round, second pick overall by the San Jose Sharks of the NHL. He started playing there as an eighteen-year-old in 1997, serving as captain from 2004-09. He then ended his tenure in 2017, and signed with the NHL Toronto Maple Leafs.

His accomplishments are many; He is the Sharks' all-time leader in goals, even strength goals, power play goals, points, shot and games played. He scored his one hundredth career point on December 12, 2017 in a loss to the Philadelphia Flyers, and became only the sixtieth player in NHL history to do so. His 500th career goal came against the Vancouver Canucks on February 2, 2017 making him the forty-fifth player in NHL history to accomplish that feat. He played his 1,500th game on October 18, 2017 making him number eighteen on the all-time list, passing such greats as Steve Yzerman, Brendan Shanahan, Niklas Lidstrom and Johnny Bucyk to mention but a few.

He has won gold medals with Team Canada at the 2010 and 2014 Winter Olympics.

Patrick is considered one of the fastest players in the NHL, and his high skill level and gentlemanly conduct have earned him two nominations for the Lady Byng Memorial Trophy, as well as high praise from both fans and other league professionals.

His junior career started with the Seattle Thunderbirds of the Western Hockey League (WHL) where he played from 1995 to 1997, and where he earned the role of captain in his 1996-97 season. As a rookie sixteen-year-old, he exploded onto the WHL scene scoring thirty-two goals and adding another forty-two assists for seventy-four points, leading his team to a playoff loss against the former Memorial Cup champions, the Kamloops Blazers. Although they lost the series 4-1, they took the three losses to overtime.

His well-deserved accolades and accomplishments, of which there are many, could easily fill up many pages of this book. However it is who Patrick is as a friend, father, husband and teammate and the values that he brings to his everyday life and professional career that have inspired me. I hope that the lessons that he has learned in his life journey help you in yours.

"I was raised on a farm in Saskatchewan" He started. *"On a farm everyone has to pitch in. There are always chores to be done and everyone has a responsibility, whether feeding the pigs or cows, bringing them in from pasture, or harvesting a crop. We always had to take care of chores before we could do anything. In this atmosphere, one learns how important responsibility and hard work are. Also, one sees that the whole family is doing their part and that really builds a sense of teamwork and the need to be responsible. My brother would get up and feed the cows or the pigs in the morning and it was my job to take care of them in the afternoon. When either harvesting or moving the herd from one pasture to another it was all hands on deck."*

I shared with Patrick that I had to work during the summer on my uncle's farm in the Peace River Country, just outside Fairview Alberta. When I was ten-years-old, I was handed a double-headed axe, shown the wood pile and told that by the time I left to go back home, at the end of the summer, I had to have the wood shed filled.

"In the summer, I remember asking my dad, 'Can we go swimming?' and his reply would be; 'When you're finished your chores, maybe you can go after supper'. It was always, chores first and then fun after. I realized early in my life that teamwork contributed to success of the whole group. When a family depends on crops and livestock to put clothes on our back and food on the table, the only way it works is through teamwork."

"Where did your passion for hockey come from?"

"It's hard to say, I remember falling in love with the game the first time I played it. I always loved the game and then when I found out that I could actually get paid for playing, I was all in. I was relentless with my dad about hockey and was always after him to take me somewhere to play. Funny enough, my kids are the same way now and are always after me to take them somewhere to skate."

"I was also fortunate that my father had experience in the game. He had tried out for the Weyburn Redwings Junior team but was a little young. They wanted him to go and play for their affiliate team, however, his father said that there was too much work to be done on the farm and he couldn't go. As a result, he never played at a high level but he was my coach for most of my early life up through to PeeWee."

"I played my PeeWee hockey in Swift Current. My father and mother would drive me to practices and games twice a week and once on weekends. It was a lot of trouble so when I was fourteen, because they were only allowed to take several out of town players, I decided to move away from home to stay with my grandmother who lived there. Of course my mother was upset but I told her that hockey was what I wanted to do."

"While my father coached me up to PeeWee, the coaching never stopped there." He added, "Even into bantam he would give me advice. We would be on the bus out on a road trip and the parents would always sit at the front and the players at the back. I would always go up and sit with my father and talk hockey: How did I play? What could I have done better? What areas do I need to improve on? Sometimes I didn't like what he had to say but I still asked him anyway. He was always giving me feedback, I was willing to take the advice and that helped me improve faster I think."

Patrick played junior hockey as a sixteen-year-old and after a two-year stint in the Western Hockey League (WHL), he made the jump to pro hockey, showing up at training camp at seventeen-years-old (and turning eighteen during the season) with the NHL San Jose Sharks and he never looked back.

"You climbed the ladder from amateur hockey, through junior to the NHL fairly quickly." I commented: "Were there things that you did differently than other players?"

"Not that I can think of." He responded: *"I never questioned my ability to play at a high level. I think that I had confidence in my ability to play; I worked hard, worked on my skills and tried to make the most of my opportunities. I knew that commitment to improving every day would ultimately get me there. I don't remember going to camp thinking that I wasn't going to make it. I knew my role, knew what I had to do and just went out and did it. When I look back, maybe I was naïve in thinking that I would just make the team but that's how I viewed the challenge back then."*

I have had the privilege of knowing Patrick for several years. We discuss different training philosophies, stick issues, game issues, etc. He is always driven to get better and I asked him where that drive comes from. I run into pros that get stuck in their ways and seem very reluctant to accept change. Having played for over twenty years in the NHL, and at a time in his career when he could just be playing for the game, why is it that he still strives to be better every day?

"I've always looked at getting better. I read a lot of self-help, and sport psychology books. The game can and will continually humble you if you don't constantly look for ways to get better. I have to stay on top of my game since it is every changing."

"People are looking for changes and new ideas. They are constantly looking to expose other teams' weaknesses or countering opposition strengths. With video today, there are so many tools at a team's disposal. If you have a weakness now it will be exposed, there is nowhere to hide. If you don't improve the game will throw you out."

"How has hockey changed over the years? You have been in the league twenty years plus now. You came in when you were an eighteen-year-old rookie and now you would be considered a wily vet. What are some of the changes that you have seen in values over the years?"

"I would say consistent work ethic and maybe a sense of entitlement. Going back over the years, rookies were given little respect and had to earn their way. Today, young players come in and tend to expect more. I watch a lot of hockey, both with my sons and professionally and work ethic seems to be lacking at times. If a kid has talent and just puts in the work, I feel that they have a very good opportunity to play now."

"The other thing that I noticed is in how team personnel attitude towards players has changed. For example, last year in Toronto, Lou Lamoriello, our general manager was great for the guys; he was more concerned about the person than the hockey player. I know that meant a lot to me personally. He was always asking: 'How's the family? Are you doing all right? It was obvious that he cared about his players. He wanted to have good people that were good hockey players on his team. That has translated into winning teams where he was the general manager."

"Kyle Dubas, who just took over, is the same way. I think that there is more emphasis on the players now as individuals and how they are handling the 'hockey life' so to speak than before. I think that with all the social media and media coverage today, there are different kinds of pressures on the younger players today."

"As a hockey parent," I asked, "What are issues that you see today and is there any advice that you could pass on?"

"I think that parents tend to get too involved in giving the wrong message to their kids. I hear things like; 'my kid is better than that kid, my kid should be on the first line, my kid shouldn't be playing with that kid.' What this does is create a false sense of entitlement. They need to focus on their own son or daughter's issues and not be constantly comparing them to others. They need to focus on the mistakes that their own kids make. These are great teaching moments and in most cases, great life lessons."

"As a parent, I hate excuses. Take my oldest son, Landon, for example. I don't care how many goals he scores, it is all about how much of an effort that he puts into his games and practices. It's a team game and everyone has they're part to play. We always reinforce work ethic and teamwork.

CORE VALUES

When he comes home and complains that someone didn't pass him the puck, I ask him what he could have done better, how could he have helped his teammate to pass the puck; could he have gotten more open, or could he have called for the puck louder? It is important that he understands that no matter the circumstance, he can always be better and that he needs to take some ownership in the situation."

"With things being so different today, do you find that the values that you were taught and experienced on the farm are more difficult to pass on to your kids?" I asked.

"It is more difficult for sure. Back on the farm, we all had very important responsibilities and in today's society, it's not that easy to identify and I'm not sure if the kids today actually have that in them. I think that all hockey, or even all team sports for that matter; have the opportunity to pass on the same message that I experienced growing up on the farm."

"I also think, from my observations, that too many young players tend to blame others for their own failures or lack of success. In professional hockey, accountability is so important. With the speed of the game today, everyone has a part to play and must do so to the best of their ability. There is no time for finger pointing, everyone has to be accountable."

"I think that families need to have discussions with their kids and to ask what exactly their son or daughter wants out of the game. Then they need to explain how to be a good teammate, what it means to respect coaches and other players, what does it mean to accountable, how do they define work and effort, try to be a leader on the ice and away from the rink. They also need to ask tough questions on the core values of the family; what is expected, how they need to act away from the rink, how to be a good person, how to be a good friend. Good values start at home. These are discussions that we've had with our children."

RANDALL JOHANSEN

FATHER, PRO PLAYERS RYAN (NASHVILLE PREDATORS NHL) & LUCAS JOHANSEN (HERSHEY BEARS AHL)

One such positive coach and mentor is a friend named Randall Johansen. I have had the privilege of knowing him for many years, and of coaching both of his sons: Ryan who plays as a forward for the NHL Nashville Predators and Lucas, a defenceman drafted by the NHL Washington Capitals. It is not often that a father has one son rise to the level of prominence that Ryan and Lucas have, let alone two. He attributes their success, in part, to his being a very positive and supporting father.

We recently had a great discussion about core values and one that he kept coming back to, as his most important, was 'Confidence'.

"With Ryan, when he was three years old, we used to go to a local rink that had a combination of public skating and a mini hockey program. They used these plastic sticks and pucks and we would skate back and forth down the length of the rink passing the puck. We did it every time we went and with all the traffic skating around out there, it was difficult. Some people couldn't stop and neither could he. They would bump, he would fall down, get back up and keep going. I was never negative, just kept encouraging him. When there was a NHL game on I would point out guys that could carry a puck with their head up and how they passed to each other. This gave him motivation and after a while he would he could zip around people, pick up my pass and give it back."

CORE VALUES

Not all kids are as lucky to have a father who understood the game, or who offered the same level of support.

"If there was open ice somewhere, Ryan wanted to go, so we would pack up the car with our hockey gear and off we would go. He loved the game and every moment he could spend on the ice no matter what time, he was always eager to practice."

When I spoke to him about Ryan's early days, when he was five and six years old and coming up through the minor hockey programs, I asked what was the most important attribute that he had as an aspiring young player.

"I have to say it was confidence. The passing and puck carrying drill we did when he was very young instilled in him the confidence to do so when he was older. I always coached in a positive way, always encouraged him when he fell or couldn't carry the puck. I was always looking for small improvements and then pointing them out to him. All the positives kept him engaged in learning and he never lost the love of the game, learning new skills and then trying them out."

I had the pleasure of working with Ryan when he was fifteen and sixteen. He had come in with his father and a close friend to work on his shooting. He always had an eagerness about him and while focusing on learning new skill sets, would always turn the session into a fun competition.

Ryan's confidence and skill level garnered him the attention of the WHL scouts and he was drafted 150th overall by the Portland Winters in the 2007 Bantam Draft. He opted to make the jump to junior hockey with the Penticton Vees of the British Columbia Hockey League (BCHL) in 2008-09, to protect his eligibility to play NCAA hockey, after having been offered an athletic scholarship to play with Northeastern University.

His rookie season wasn't stellar with five goals and twelve assists in forty-two games played.

I asked Randall how Ryan had dealt with his rookie season, emotionally, since having coached Junior A and Junior B myself, younger players can struggle with the age, size and strength differences, with coaching philosophies and even with being away from home for the first time.

"It was tough on him". Randall explained: *"Penticton is a great organization but they have a plan for their rookies and vets. Ryan was frustrated and called saying that he was only getting six, seven, or eight shifts a game and wanted to come home. I told him that he had committed to the team and that he needed to honor that however, I would see what I could do and maybe talk to the coach or general manager about what he needed to work on to move up the lineup. I'm not an interfering parent and looked at other ways where I could help him. He was always motivated by positives so I started to take different stats for him during the season; completed passes, shots on net, strong defensive plays, hits, etc. and then would multiply them by three, the number of shifts that a vet would get."*

"This helped turn his attitude around" he added: *"I could point out that if he was a vet then he would be outperforming some of the older guys. We just focused on making each shift count and then looked at the positives."*

The following year, convinced of his abilities, Ryan decided to forego his Northeastern opportunity and joined the Winterhawks for their 2009-10 WHL season. He finished that year with twenty-five goals, sixty-nine points in seventy-one games, second among the league rookies and helping the team make the playoffs – one year after finishing last in the WHL. Ryan had a stellar playoff adding eighteen points in thirteen games and finished ninth in the league in scoring and first amongst rookies, having only participated in two of the four possible playoff rounds.

As a result of his offensive prowess, he was selected fourth overall by the Columbus Bluejackets of the NHL. The rest, we can say, is history.

"Ryan responds best in a positive environment" Randall stated: *"As all kids do I believe. I've coached young players most of my life and when they have positives around them, the love of the game grows and it sustains them through the tough times. Too often I see parents pacing in the stands yelling at their kids to skate harder. I can't imagine what the ride home with dad or mom must be like after a game like that. Parents put so much pressure on their kids to make something of themselves in hockey. Our family phi-*

losophy is that if we can raise our kids to be positive and be good brothers, friends, neighbors and contributors then we have done our job."

When I asked him about Lucas, his younger son, who was drafted by Washington, he admitted that Lucas was very different to Ryan.

"Lucas loved the rink because it was where his buddies were. Hockey is what Canadians do and he felt obligated to join his friends and participate. My wife often said to me over the years, I wouldn't be surprised if he told us one day that he would quit. However, he just hung in there. He is a good natural athlete and over time, some of the skills and teachings rubbed off and I started to see him challenge himself more and more. We were always positive and never pushed him."

Lucas was taken 119th overall in the 2012 WHL Bantam draft and played two years for the BC Hockey Major Midget League before joining the Kelowna Rockets for the 2014-15 season.

"Lucas was always a cerebral kid; always asking me questions. His interest in the game and passion for it grew with confidence. It didn't hurt that his brother played professional hockey and during the summer, when they were around each other, chirping was a standard part of the family dialogue. Ryan always encouraged him and Lucas started to ask Ryan a lot of questions about the pro game."

I have worked with Lucas many times and his attitude always impressed me. He always directed the conversation with questions as opposed to the teacher pushing the class. I always thoroughly enjoy his company and from my perspective he is a teacher's dream student.

Randall chuckled when I told him about how Lucas had recently walked up to me

and nailed me with some questions he had about shooting and skating. He trains at the rink where I have my shooting studio.

"Yes that sounds like Lucas. He is the thinking kid. He would come home from hockey and sit and watch every YouTube video on Karlsson, Doughty, Keith or whoever else was on his mind that day and study every move. He is driven to get better every day and loves the learning process."

Randall is one of those hockey parents that scouts and coaches love. Watches his kids play, always encourages and has a great attitude about life and the game.

His advice on confidence goes a long way and he shared many stories with me about his years of coaching and the theme was always the same. Being positive encourages growth and helps maintain the passion of the game. Learning a new skill is tough enough, let alone getting beat up mentally during the process.

Wise-words from a man that loves watching kids improve and is still very passionate about the game.

"I'm never negative around my kids when it comes to discussing hockey. I'm always telling them that if they need help they can always ask me. I'm there as a resource. If you don't want me to talk hockey you can always say: 'Dad I don't want to hear it'. I don't want to be that nagging parent that is always in my kid's face. However, when there is a good teaching moment, I try to explain to them either how the coach may be looking at them or the situation. I always explain that in hockey, they have to earn they're way; nothing should be taken for granted."

JEREMY RUPKE

HOW TO HOCKEY, YOUTH SKILLS INSTRUCTOR

I met Jeremy, by phone, in 2016. I had reached out to him to discuss coaching philosophies and was eager to learn how he had started his business. While I have not had the pleasure of meeting him in person, I have come to recognize that he has a great passion for the both the game and teaching. His domain is more specific to the recreational player, which I can completely respect and as such, he comes at hockey development from a different perspective than is portrayed in this book.

I reached out to him for his thoughts on the recreational player and to see what insights into their core values he could share. I asked him a little about his hockey history.

"I was a kid that grew up on a farm until I was seven. I loved hockey, not sure where that came from exactly because my mother or father never pushed me, but we had a pond that I would shovel off in the winter time and skate as much as I could. It was a way to escape I guess. One could go to the rink and no matter what I was going through; I could leave it on the ice. Working with a team was sharing a common goal. You're with your friends. It was fun times for me as I grew up."

Talking to Jeremy, one senses a humble beginning and a guy that works hard on what he believes in. Where did that work ethic and attitude come from I questioned?

"My father and mother got divorced when I was seven. We moved away from the farm, I have two siblings, and we lived with my mother. I wasn't easy for her. She worked three jobs, never complained. We didn't have a

car or TV but through it all, because I was young, I never realized that we didn't have much. We lived in a trailer then finally moved to an apartment. Years later, in my twenties I asked myself one day: 'Why do I work so hard and where did that come from?' Seeing her work so hard when I was growing up, instilled the same qualities in me I guess. I came to appreciate her effort, what she gave to us and how humble she was, never complained and while she never pushed her values on me, I guess I learned them from observation and association."

How did the hockey site start?

"I've always been inquisitive by nature. When I was living with my mother, we couldn't afford hockey and I didn't want to burden her with it because of the expense. It wasn't until I was thirteen that I was able to pay for my equipment and registration to play, although I played registered hockey as a kid. My mom and dad both played hockey, so I learned the love of hockey from my parents, but they didn't really push me to excel. Through the divorce period I took one year off, and then for a few years I was only able to play on weekends when I was with my dad. I didn't see much development as I only played games and wasn't able to attend practices. Through all that my parents paid my registration but around thirteen I was responsible to earn money and pay, or help pay."

"As a result, my opportunity to play at any elite level had passed of course but I loved the sport and wanted to be as good at it as possible."

"I searched online for whatever tips that I could find and would try to work on those as much as possible. I was also working on websites at the time and I thought there must be some good online site that taught skills or coaching. There were some good resources but they weren't complete, a little bit of information here and there but the navigation was poor and the content was confusing at times. I checked videos on YouTube as well, but some of them were a little questionable at the time. I remember seeing one where a guy described taking a slap shot was like swinging a baseball bat. I saw that the video had over 20,000 views or something."

"I felt that I could make a better website and I just wanted to create a resource that anyone, anywhere, could come to and learn. I realized that I couldn't just use articles so I started doing videos. I figured that if I had, *say ten videos to start that covered some skating, stickhandling and shooting tips that would be a good start. It kind of built up from there. I was good at web site development, so it was a natural progression to take it to the next level. Every once in a while, I would run into a good coach and he would show me something simple that would really click with me. It instantly made me feel better. I thought that if I could provide the same tips to the player that was searching like I was, I could help them improve faster. It was a way to eliminate some of the learning curve."*

"When I started, I never meant to make any money at it. I was making decent money on my other sites and it was more of a hobby. After a while, it built up some momentum and then advertisers started approaching me. I rejected them because they weren't hockey-based. Later on, **Hockey Shots [HockeyShot]** *approached me to do advertising on my site and that's kind of when I decided to put more effort into it and focused on the site and coaching full-time. They were hockey based and were in the business to help players get better as well. I thought that I was a good fit. As a result, their support gave me more time to focus on the content, become a better coach by finding more innovative ways to teach kids, which in turn allowed me to give back more to players."*

Jeremy holds no illusions about the fact he was a recreational player. He is a guy that loves helping players get better and in doing so, has kind of found a calling that services a certain clientele. That doesn't mean that some elite players; aspiring to junior, college or pro, don't find some benefit in what he offers. In dealing with the recreational players in my experience, I found that there are, what one would call: 'elite recreational players'. They are the guys that either played other sports most of their lives or had parents that couldn't afford it. Either way, they have that burning desire to be good at something they love doing and that was hockey. I questioned him on what differences he has noticed in attitude between the average and the elite recreational player?

"In most cases, the life core values are there; respect, being polite, etc. but the biggest difference that I found is really in the area of focus. Recreational hockey players are mostly just that, recreational. They have other hobbies and play other sports. Some play hockey just because their friends do, while others play because their parents want them to, and some truly enjoy the

sport, they just don't want to make a career out of it. As a coach, when I see them for the first time, of course I don't know what their real motivation is for being there. I'll see kids that listen and pay attention and I'll see kids that fool around and trip their friends."

"To find a kid that works his tail off is very rare. Maybe not rare, just more common at the levels above house league, because I coach at a lot of camps most of the time there is a mix of players from house league to AAA. Even at the house league level you will find kids who love hockey and work hard, maybe they started late, couldn't afford extra ice time and development, or take longer to pick up skills. I've just noticed most kids who aren't focused or don't care as much end up at that level. If I do see them, I think of them as just passing through. A lot of the time, the hardest working players will move up to rep or elite levels of hockey in a couple of years. They will improve faster than the other kids. You will still find super respectful kids that will work hard at games and practices but you won't see them put in the extra off the ice."

After coaching for the past forty-five years, I had to admit that when I was a younger coach, having players fooling around and being a distraction drove me crazy after a while. I asked him how he maintains such a positive attitude around low intensity and unfocused kids.

"For me, I'm not trying to push kids to the elite level. That's not my main thing. From beginner to intermediate, I just want them to love the game, and I want them to learn that improving is fun. If they get better, then they will love the game and enjoy coming to the rink. I want to set them up for coaches. If they see the little improvements and then realize that with more effort they will improve even more, then they will a lot easier for other coaches to work with."

As I mentioned earlier in this book, I started to feel that I was starting to teach more life values than skills, sometimes to the point of frustration. I asked Jeremy how he dealt with it.

"What I find, and coming back to your core values thing, is that when I first meet kids, before going on the ice with them, I have a quick talk to set some ground rules. The first rule I talk about is that you have to believe; you have to believe that you can be better. If you don't believe in yourself then you won't come focused to each practice. Believe that you can do this because everyone can; it's just a matter of trying over and over until you get it. The more you practice, the better you will get. The second one is focus. If you focus on what I say then you will get better. You're going to take a lot away from this session. We are out here for an hour and if you're focused for the whole time, then you will leave a better player than if you weren't. Don't only just focus on the drill but focus on yourself. When you focus on the feeling within the drill then you know how it feels when you do it correctly. The third thing I ask for is effort. I want to see you guys trying hard when you are out here. I want you guys to own that skill and that takes effort, you're not going to get better if you are coasting around out here."

"That sets the tone and they know what I am looking for. If a kid falls off expectations then I can say, 'Hey, I want to see that effort or that focus'. If a kid says 'I can't' then I can come back at them with, 'Of course you can, and you have to believe you can'. If they start to believe they can then it's easier for them to put in the effort."

"These are great values that they can take home with them as well. In general, they are great life lessons."

At the recreational level, quite often the parent doesn't set any expectation and just drops the player off. This in essence turns a hockey training session into a baby-sitting service, as coaches that have shared this problem, have come to call it. This can be highly disruptive to other players. I asked Jeremy if this happens to him.

"What I find sometimes is that kids just don't want to be on the ice and as a result, they start to be a distraction to everyone else. This causes a major problem for other players that want to get better. I ask the player to take a two-minute break and when they feel that they can participate correctly, they are welcome to join the group. That sets the tone for the other players and usually takes care of any other issues. If the player continues to keep fooling around, then the discussion turns to: 'You don't have to do this session', and 'I don't think that you should be on the ice' and I send them off. I have had the parent come down and, having seen me discipline the player the first time, they understand. They usually see more than I do since their eyes are mostly on their child and I have to watch the whole group."

"The key for me is that I try to understand why they are fooling around. Sometimes it's because they don't want to be there, sometimes it's because it's just their nature and other times it's because they think that they are too good for the session and sometimes, they are just looking for attention. One trick I've found that can work with disruptive players is to give them a job. I might have them demonstrate drills, or ask them to make sure that no one touches the pylons or moves pucks. This can help give them ownership and a leadership role in a positive way. With players that think they are above the session, I have them demonstrate the drills and that seems to bring them back into focus. Now they have to be at their best since the spotlight is on them."

I asked Jeremy what character trait was most lacking in the recreational player. I mentioned to him an interview with Troy Ward, a pro coach in Austria with extensive experience in college and professional hockey, who said that reluctance to change was the one thing that he noticed.

"I think the biggest one is focus, and while perhaps not a core value, it is what I see the most. There are so many things happening in their lives. Sometimes when running a drill, they tell you it's their birthday tomorrow, they tell you their pet hamster's name, stuff like that. There are so many things going on in their head, it's hard for them to maintain focus. The players that have the most focus take the most away from the sessions. A lot of the time, I have to run competition drills such as races or I ask them do an exercise faster, or better than some other kid. The idea is to get them to dial in. Tapping in to their competitive nature helps to increase their focus."

"A lot of the time, the trick is to entertain them through competition. I have to find ways to challenge them to learn by turning what they need to learn into a competition. The idea is that if they do more of, let's say a backward crossover around a circle or, did something faster, they start to improve by effort, by sheer repetition. More focused players can be more detailed, but the challenge is the players that don't have that level of engagement."

"I realize that there are two levels of hockey players." Jeremy continued: *"There is the kid that wants a pro contract; wants to play in the NHL. Then there is the kid that just likes recreational hockey. I try to stress, no matter what level they aspire to, just to try to be the best you can be. There*

is nothing wrong with being a good recreational player. What I hate to see is the player who gets so turned off the game by being pushed that they walk away from it. It is a great game and one that can be played and enjoyed for many years."

Jeremy put together a list of core values that are important to his work; to who he is as a teacher and what he expects from the kids that he coaches.

"Based on the core values we've discussed, I've made a list of the top five I feel are the most important from my position."

1. *Integrity – Since I have the opportunity to reach so many people, my integrity and authenticity are very important to me. I want to help people but also to be a positive influence on anyone who watches my videos or follows me online.*

2. *Respect – Hockey is a team sport, and respect is one of the biggest lessons to be learned from the game. Respect yourself, your team mates, the other team, the officials and the game.*

3. *Work Ethic – For me this is a big one, from the outside what I do may look easy but the reality is a good video takes a lot of time and skill to create.*

4. *Humility – I'm a student of the game, and being humble keeps me open for improvement.*

5. *Discipline – Working from home means I need to keep myself motivated to put in the hours, come up with new ideas, and execute them.*

IAN GALLAGHER

AMATEUR & PROFESSIONAL STRENGTH COACH, FATHER TO BRENDAN GALLAGHER, MONTREAL CANADIANS, NHL

I really had to give it some thought as to how long I have known Ian but it is over ten years. He is one of those guys that once you sit down and talk to him; you feel that you have known him forever. A consummate professional, articulate speaker and full of experience, he has a lot of knowledge to impart on both amateur and professional players. He has been involved in the athletic fitness industry for over twenty-five years, with his most recognizable position being the strength and conditioning coach for the Vancouver Giants of the Western Hockey League (WHL), where he was employed from 2004-16.

He has worn many hats, and has been the Director of the Delta Hockey Academy since its inception in 2004 until the present. It has grown to include seven competitive teams that compete in the Canadian Sport School Hockey League (CSSHL). He is also the father of a professional player, Brendan Gallagher, who worked his way up through junior hockey, playing for the WHL Vancouver Giants and was then drafted by Montreal in the fifth round, 147th overall in the NHL entry draft. He is currently an assistant captain for the team. He is also the father of four children who, he admits, are all completely different. I'm sure that is something that we can all connect with, as parents.

I caught up with Ian for lunch one day at Planet Ice Delta, a four rink complex in North Delta, B.C. that acts as home to the Delta Hockey Academy. We started discussing how his role, not only as a strength coach to many amateur and professional players but the director of an hockey academy, gave him a direct and personal viewpoint on which underlying values were the makeup of elite players.

Ian is the kind of guy who cares deeply about the players he trains. There is a passion and wisdom about how he goes about things. He demands a lot and leads by example. I asked him where this inherent set of values came from.

"When I look at my own evolution, I came from a family of five; Irish Catholic father, three jobs, my mother was a nurse and well-educated. She married a blue collar man. We had a very combative and competitive life but we all felt part of a family. My father did what he could and never complained. He gave us what he could, which wasn't much, but we had all the basic needs of food, shelter and clothing; we were loved and he paid for the first year of university after which we were on our own. In addition to that, we were involved in sports and the coaches that I was fortunate to come across, were pretty important to me. The community also had a role."

"I remember one football coach, in particular, that I worked with in the Edmonton area named Jim GilFillan; he coached for thirty-eight years, and passed away this last January (2018). Not one of the cleanest living souls but he had an articulate humanitarian approach and he could tell the difference between a coach that was all about wins and losses and one that was all about the process. He understood growth. Being a teacher, which I went through and did have that formal training, it has evolved over time. As an athlete, in sports that I was good at, my coaches were significant in modeling and articulating what truly matters. And they had the ability to point us in the right direction and get us to investigate different team success stories such as the All Blacks in rugby around the world. They had a way to engage our inquisitive nature and through that process lead us to better understanding on what it takes to be successful."

"An area that players often have issues with is in the area of criticism. What I have come to understand is that there is some element in truth to what everyone says. We have to respect that. It is their viewpoint on something and to them that is correct. Players have to learn to deal with the fact that the world view is much bigger than theirs of themselves and to be able to take instruction and make changes."

We discussed how the lack of some core values leads to intolerable behavior. The one that really got me engaged when I coached junior hockey was when kids back-stab one of their teammates. It was one of the fastest ways to break up a dressing room and to me it was absolutely unacceptable.

Ian brought up the story of one of his university professors: *"I'll never forget one of my professors who said that in the world there are people that 'tolerate i intolerable'. I didn't want to be one of those people. If it is an intolerable act, I will not tolerate it."*

"One rule that I live by is consistency. I am fairly authoritarian by nature; which is not necessarily a good thing, but I also understand how people respond to authority. One can be perceived as a bully, as arrogant or perceived many different ways. One has to be very consistent in one's hard message or punishments, otherwise it is easy to lose credibility with one's audience. If you are humanitarian in nature, you can be a little more flexible and can be a little more dialed into a child's feelings a little more but consistency in dealing with intolerable actions are critical."

"Accountability is one of the biggest concerns that players needs to understand. Every year at the academy our primary concern is accountability. We make that a strong message and set that theme. We explain to our coaches that when they explain drill objectives, and players don't perform accordingly, it is important that they are held accountable. They have to know that there are consequences to their actions and again consistency from the coaches is critical to building a fair environment."

"Another message that we feel strongly about is resiliency. Ok, you didn't have success but stick with it. You failed so what are you going to do about it. Are you going to quit or get over the hurdle?"

"Another key message is engagement. Keep dialed in. With all of the video games and toys available to kids, they don't have the ability to sustain a ten-to-fifteen minute conversation let alone commit to the start and finish of a drill. Kids today are great at multitasking but horrible at focus. It is a skill set. We teach skills, we teach systems and we teach tactics, but how can they benefit if they can't engage properly?"

CORE VALUES

"I think that there are different levels of engagement and what we try to do is teach up. In other words find the kid that is driving the bus and then tell the rest to catch him. The best leaders I found are the ones that are the most engaged. This year we picked our team captains, not based on skill but based on the rubric of core values. He or she may or may not be the best player, but we felt that it was important to set the tone of leadership."

It has become common knowledge that several NHL teams have suspended players for playing the new video interactive game called 'Fortnite'. For example, the Canucks have banned the players from playing the game. It's all about engagement. There was a saying that I brought up to Ian that I had heard before along the lines of "If something is a distraction, then it is really your passion." The concept was that whatever that distraction was, then *that* was the direction one needed to head in, and not fool oneself and waste time elsewhere. Again, it is all about 'engagement'.

"Being directly involved in fitness training for elite athletes for so many years, do you find much difference in how athletes approach their off ice component compared to their on ice?" I posed.

"In my industry, I get to see the true athleticism of an athlete. That tells me a lot about their commitment to sports and physical activity. Good athletes have an inherent ability to perform compound physical tasks well. That being said, they also have the ability to take ownership of their abilities. They have realized early that how they perform is a direct result of how hard and focused they are on their training, it is how they do and not how others do. This is the core foundation of players that excel within a team environment, accountability.

"I'm a big believer in physical attributes and with the game now changing more to speed and agility, while training regiments are changing, I'm still a big believer in power. Pucks that one competes for at the NHL level are in small areas and this requires power. This takes a commitment to working through the process to get there. With periodization (cycling through the different phases of training from strength through to power), players need to put in the grunt work to get to the point where power becomes beneficial. This "delayed gratification" is difficult for some players who would like immediate results. Developing skill, strength, or power for that matter re-

quires an athlete to put in the time and the work and sometimes the results aren't so noticeable in the short term, but they have to learn to stay with it".

"Going into the gym requires a mindset of personal discipline; showing up to do the work and doing it correctly, accountability; you only get out of it what you put into it and intelligence; knowing that what you are doing is necessary and there are no shortcuts. There is a very long process that one has to go through, to acquire and sustain the physical attributes necessary to play at the highest level. This means that one has to be in the moment and can't look to far ahead since this all takes time."

"On ice performance is more combative with direct one-on-one confrontations taking place, as opposed to off ice training where competition between athletes is subtle and more personal in nature." Ian added.

"During game play, players have to deal with both success and failure. However, it is important to note that along their journey, success is more important than failure. This creates confidence."

"They have to realize early that the confidence and respect of their coach is earned and not given. It is also important they operate well within a team environment. They have to like and work well with people, enjoy a team environment as well as respect the role of the coach. That generally comes from a strong family setting that they are in. The coach is in part a surrogate parent."

I added that I couldn't agree more, explaining that over the past five years, I had spent more of my time teaching core values that were absent in my players than systems. Coaches are very important to a child's development, but the trick for a parent is to find instructors that reinforce important character traits on top of having strong teaching abilities.

"Due the length of the journey, it is important to find coaches that have the ability to put players in both novel and challenging situations." Ian carried on: "Repetitive training can become boring and while personal discipline can carry one through, it always helps to do something that is familiar but with a new twist. Constantly challenging, constantly taking players in a different direction but still arrive at the same place. That benefits the *coach, newness and novelty keep the players energized and engaged in the learning process."*

"Part of the make-up of a player is to understand 'growth'. It is not where I am today but where I could be and what is the process to get there. All along the way they need the core value of work ethic, the core value associated with dealing with failure or 'humility', ability to support others or 'compassion', they need 'wisdom.'

There are so many actual attributes that allow a player not to just stay in the battle but remain in the battle for sustained periods."

"Personal environment is important. For example, one of the words that come to mind is spoiled and to me this word means ruined. Many white-collar parents spoil their kids more as a status symbol than anything else. Parents think that they are doing their children a favor by spoiling them."

Ian added; *"An excuse that I hear often from parents over the course of my coaching career, especially from blue collar workers, is that the road they had when they were young was difficult and they wanted their kids to have a better life. My answer back was they seemed to turn out just fine, so how bad can a little adversity be? Adversity is something that all hockey players at some time have to face and often, how they deal with it will determine how far they go in their career.*

"I think that it is important to also understand family wellness." Ian continued: *"It is important to give them their basic needs; food, clothing and shelter, making sure that they feel secure and are loved. If kids feel well then they are set up to succeed. On one side of the coin, the hardworking blue collar kids often seem to go the furthest and on the other side is the elite white-collar kid, who has had the access to the best training along the way. Sooner or later they meet up and the one with the best set of core values, most often succeeds."*

That was worth a chuckle with me bringing up an old saying I heard around a rink a long time ago: "It's when grunt meets great". I think it pertained to a similar adage of "Hard work beats talent that doesn't work".

We discussed his son, Brendan. At five-foot nine inches tall and 181 pounds, he is by all accounts, a small player in a big man's game. Having watched Brendan play for years, he epitomizes the saying that' "It's not the size of the dog in the fight, it's the size of the fight in the dog." He has excelled at every level he has played, either winning or being nominated for numerous awards including the NHL rookie of the year in 2013, the Calder Trophy, where he placed second in voting. During the 2017-18 season, Brendan recorded thirty-one goals and twenty-three assists during eighty-two, games played for a total of fifty-four points. Where does he get his tenacity and work ethic?

"From a very young age, he loved sports and he played a lot of sports. He loved golf, baseball and hockey. I was an area scout and when I would go watch players, he would come along with me. As opposed to other kids staying at home playing mini sticks or engaged in other activities, he would be right there with me. As a result he became a student of and the game and fell in love with the sport."

"When he played the game, innately, he had an almost unhealthy competitive side. I have four children and they are all competitive but Brendan was at the very top end of the spectrum. When playing street hockey, if the game wasn't going his way, he would grab his ball and go home. He hated losing and was" Ian chuckled: *"A bit of a cry baby. It was the result of his intensity."*

"As he moved up the ladder in hockey, he maintained the same level of competitiveness against older and bigger kids. He was going to play and nothing was going to stop him from impacting the game when he was on the ice. So he had a real core belief in his own abilities, the passion to play the game and had habits consistent in getting better."

Dealing with players of Brendan's work ethic and commitment, were there issues that arose, such as over training? Many players that have that ability to push themselves can do so, often to the point of injury.

"Work ethic and work span can vary from person to person, of course, but the key really is frequency. There are natural physical limits to training. If an athlete is pushing himself or herself hard, after fifty minutes their body is no longer releasing growth hormone. While your training program is a

couple hours long, if one pushes themselves for more than fifty minutes they are in essence over training themselves. All the extra effort becomes a waste and there is no benefit. It then becomes necessary to have a trainer or coach that can take the athletes innate ability and desire to do more, to channel them properly."

"One of the problems with athletes, and even parents for that matter, is a lack of understanding of overtraining. A player will do an intense off ice session and then they go somewhere else and do exactly the same thing, firing the same neurological pathways, which in turn, is detrimental to their development. They need to have a quantifiable plan so as to maximize results."

"As a result, periodization is critical to an athlete. Charlie Francis who was a Canadian Olympic sprinter and track coach to Ben Johnson, wrote a great book called Speed Trap. He was a genius in understanding how periodization worked in training the faster man on earth. He knew the layers on how to move an athlete through from strength to speed. The foundation of that book is what we use in our training."

"One of the best things that has happened to training lately is the inclusion of mobility training; joint functionality and stability, range of motion potential and strength at deep angels and all those things have really accentuated what is taking place in the gym today. This type of functional movement training translates better to the on ice environment. Hockey players have issues with hips, back and shoulders; anything with rotational potential has to be stabilized."

Off ice training is now a critical part of a hockey player's regimen. There was a time when a player would use their training camp to get into shape. Today, every player must be on some form of conditioning program. I asked Ian if he runs into players or parents that have issues with that? I cited the story of a junior hockey that had played for me, and that had a short career in NCAA hockey before moving on to play in the Western Hockey League (WHL) where he completed his career. He was heavily scouted and had what looked like a great NHL opportunity ahead of him. He loved the game and everything about it but hated being in the gym. As a result he moved on and is now a school teacher.

"One of the issues that I have to deal with, when working on mechanics." I explained to Ian: "Was getting players used to being uncomfortable. I use the 'sitting in a chair and then standing' as a visual and physical example of training comfort and discomfort when learning something new. I have them sit in a chair and make themself as comfortable as possible. When they have done so, I then have them stand. I make note of the time difference between the sitting position and the standing one. I then ask them to sit down again but this time, take into consideration that they will have to stand up quickly and have them adjust their seated posture accordingly. Once we do this several times so that they can fine tune the action of 'sit to stand' in the quickest time possible, I now ask them if they are comfortable in the new posture. Their answer is 'no'. What I then explain is that this new posture is called the "Ready Position" and while it is not comfortable, that doesn't make it wrong; just necessary since hockey posture on ice is all about being ready."

Ian then added: *"Don Hay, former head coach of the Vancouver Giants had a great quote that compliments what you said, 'Don't rest on the ice; rest on the bench'. When on the ice, be ready and that is exhausting but totally necessary."*

In closing, I asked Ian what has been the predominant core value aside from hard work that he has noticed in elite level athletes.

"There are a lot of athletes that have the physical attributes to play. Many have exceptional skill but in the end they not only have to be students of the game, but there has to be an innate desire to get better every day. Take Troy Stecher of the NHL Vancouver Canucks for example. He will search and seek out whatever he can to get better. His is driven to make improvements in his game at every opportunity. Another key character trait is possessing the ability to work well with others."

"Every year, players get better, new players arrive on the scene competing for a job and there is no time for players to be complacent. They need to keep to the grind and improve every day. It ultimately comes down to the achievers mentality."

CORE VALUES

"I find that it is the same with teachers. I have been in this business for far too many years and what happens over time, I believe, is that wisdom starts to set in. As trainers, especially when we are young, we tend to try and justify our own existence; pushing the best techniques, our knowledge but as we mature, a more humanitarian side emerges and we start to realize that the athlete is more than just an extension of some technique. If one looks at the Canadian Football League for example, there are a lot of older, wiser coaches. In today's game, knowledge of the teacher cannot be overlooked of course but wisdom and the humanitarian side must be looked at as an integral part of a teacher's makeup."

JOE OLIVER

PLAYER AGENT & SCOUT

I had the privilege of meeting Joe approximately eight years ago and for as long as I have known him; he aggressively pursues the latest in hockey development. He is incredibly passionate about what he does and is driven to provide the best representation possible to the players he works with. He constantly keeps in touch with the WHL, NCAA colleges, and NHL coaches and general managers, so as to better understand league talent objectives, which would also include player and team values.

Joe played amateur hockey up to his midget years, but instead focusing on a career in hockey, he decided to use his knowledge of the game to move up in the ranks of coaching, ultimately landing a job as assistant and then head coach of the successful Vernon Vipers BCHL team. He started coaching at the age of fifteen and continued to do so for the next twenty years, after which he stepped aside to focus on scouting. He is highly respected in the hockey community and is regarded as a premier identifier of hockey talent. Joe's passion for the game and for developing players has provided KO Sports (considered one of the top Boutique Hockey Agencies, and which represents elite NHL talent such as Ryan Kesler, Anaheim Mighty Ducks; Ryan Johansen, Nashville; and Dylan Larkin of the Detroit Red Wings to mention a few) with a unique advantage in representing some of the best young talent in Western Canada.

Joe's brother, David, was a graduate of the University of Michigan and started his NHL career with the Edmonton Oilers in 1994. His NHL playing career included the New York Rangers, Ottawa Senators,

Phoenix Coyotes and the Dallas Stars. In 2007, he joined the Colorado Avalanche organization where he served as Director of Hockey operations for their affiliate AHL team, Lake Erie. He has been Director of Player Development of the Avalanche for the past six seasons. David just recently signed as assistant coach of the New York Rangers, on July 17, 2018.

As a result of having a brother who had, and continues to have, an active NHL career, Joe not only has first-hand knowledge of the journey required to move up the ladder to the NHL, but he knows what teams are currently looking for.

I caught up with him at the BCHL Showcase that was being held in Chilliwack at the Prospera Center, this past weekend (Sept 20-22, 2018). He was checking out some young prospects and we got into discussing hockey talent and how the game is evolving.

I started the conversation with a question regarding his views on what core values he feels strongly when he first identifies and then meets with a young prospect that would perhaps best mirror those of the NHL.

"That's a difficult question." He replied: *"An elite NHL player has many character traits and they are all important: work ethic, accountability, mental toughness, professionalism, etc. When I identify a young prospect the first thing that I do is meet the parents. For example, I'm meeting with the parents of a 2005 forward prospect tonight. I've watched the kid play and I've also done my homework on him. There is a trainer that has experience working with the player and I ask that person, or that source, his opinion on what the kid is like as a person, his work ethic, attitude, and coachability. We share our views on him and I try to dig down on what that player is really like."*

"It's not always that easy to get to a player's character. I may be recruiting a player from Saskatchewan and I don't know whom he works with so it makes it more difficult to identify personality traits. I have to spend more time observing his actions on ice but whenever possible, I track down sources to get more information on the player."

"Another example is a 2003 WHL draft pick whom I have been working with. When I watch him play, I like his work ethic and his skill set on the ice. There are some areas of his game where I feel that he needs to improve. I was able to follow up with the guy that he works with and he told me that 'this kid gets up every morning at six a.m. and goes for a run, regardless of whether he has training or a practice that day. I love hearing that stuff. It tells me that there is something there that one can work with, that he is willing to do the extra to take his game to the next level maybe more than the next guy."

"Parents provide a tangible example of a players make-up and I always meet with a kids parents first to get a feeling for what is going on in their life. I know from meeting the parents of this player that he is the one committed to the process. He is doing this on his own."

"However, as a bantam player, I want to make it clear that this is early in this kid's career and many things happen along his journey. While the player may be putting in the effort, I may recommend some training or tools that he needs to add to his game, I cannot force a player to do those things so, maybe over time he neglects to do them. In my experience I have seen players careers stall and even fail completely because not everyone accepts the advice."

"A lot of players put a list of things in front of themselves and say that they want or need to complete the list to get better, but not every player commits to doing everything on the list that is necessary to be a better player and as a result some of the training that may have become uncomfortable to do is neglected. If this happens the player may tend to pursue training that they are more comfortable with and not push themselves to get the results that are necessary to be a better player. The player may be engaged in the process when they are fourteen and fifteen years old, but maybe when he's sixteen to eighteen the grind or his training might change his mind set and maybe he's not as dedicated. Things change."

"On your core values list you point out eleven different topics: respect, integrity, work ethic, accountability, humility, discipline, teammanship, pride, professionalism, commitment, confidence and leadership. When I watch a game, I don't have such a list in front of me per se, but I watch and try to get as much on their background as possible to identify whether or not they *do all of these things. I do this on a daily basis whether a bantam or midget player or even a professional player. These are all character traits that build a better player."*

I brought up the story of a young recruit for the Detroit Redwings whom I had trained. Just before the draft that year, their Director of Player Development, Shawn Horcoff, called me regarding his character. Teams do their homework and it's not just advisors and agents. One of Joe's recruits, Dylan Larkin plays for the Redwings and we got into discussing the pro mentality and what professional teams look for.

"When I'm discussing a player, say Dylan Larkin, with the Redwings, I'm engaged in the discussion about who he is as a person, his character and his attitude and what that brings to the table. While the team sees his leadership, his skill level and his level of professionalism, they sometimes miss the critical values and it is our job as an agency to sell his other character traits. We brought up the accountability, his work ethic, his drive, commitment and his natural leadership ability. While perhaps he may not always be leading the team statistically, he's driving the team in a lot of different areas. When we negotiate we're not only discussing statistical production but all of the core values that you talk about in your list and they make a difference."

"Everyone in the NHL is concerned with the tangibles, a player's statistics, how they compare to the guy next to him. They put all these stats into a pot, stir them around and then compare them to other players. I try to look at and dissect that information and then get into the deep dive of who that player really is. I can point out that while statistically they look to be the same, the real difference between the two players is their drive, commitment to getting better, their accountability and leadership. Sometimes teams don't care since they are trying to get to a number. But with the Red Wings, we all know that they are in a rebuild. They need to know that they have players that can drive that process and aren't just a statistic. It became an important point that Dylan was a guy that could help drive that process. The question then becomes, when one looks down the bench, whether a player is leading the team in points or is second, third or even fifth, who is driving team's goals and objectives?"

"Core values are critically important but one has to remember that they are intangibles. Teams and the league for that matter are statistically driven. Everyone wants to know who scores and who has the most points. But on a roster of twenty-three guys, the top point guys that have the best leadership, the most accountability, the most professionalism, the best teammanship become far more valuable."

"It is important to note that teams often find it difficult to ignore those highly skilled guys that perhaps don't have the core values that are important to team success. Points matter. Sometimes they look at the supporting structure below that player and hope that they can push the process. There is no question that the first thing teams do when I call to discuss a player at any level is go on the internet and look for his point production. After that, player's intangibles they may be looked at."

"There are layers to the NHL selection process. The first is offensive point production and then they push that aside and move into the second layer, which are a player's intangibles. They work to determine if the guy is a good teammate, if he acts professionally, if he accountable to his coaches and to himself. A problem that often arises when teams are doing their research on a player is that coaches don't want to derail a kid's career so will often dust off their comments and really don't provide answers that teams really want here. If they are concerned about the accuracy of the information, especially during a player's draft year, they will actually call a school and see where Johnny sits in the classroom? They will ask the teachers what type of student Johnny is? I don't know how many teams do this but I know from my experience, that some teams do it for sure."

"One of the main concerns that professional teams have is in the area of mental toughness. With the exception of the top couple percent, everyone else will have to face some degree of adversity during their hockey career. Some good coaching and back coaching, some good general managers and bad general managers, some good teams and some bad teams. They will have to get through it. Those are hurdles and if they can get over those and come out the other side as a good person, a good teammate, and a good attitude they have a greater opportunity at success."

When I was the Technical Director of Next Testing, we were retained as the official tester of the NHL combine in Toronto. I mentioned to

Joe that one of the favorite tests of some of the NHL general managers was the Wingate Test for anaerobic power. They wanted to see how hard players pushed themselves during that test. They felt that this test pushed the player's physical boundaries and wanted to see how they handled the stress.

"Do you find that there are any other concerns that teams have that may stick out in your mind?" I asked.

"It almost goes without saying that hockey has become a very expensive sport. It is expensive to play this game, whether bantam, midget or at the academy level it costs a lot of money to play, even at a league level. I remember one general manager asking me what a player's father did for a living. The father of the player that they were interested in was very wealthy and it was a negative. He was a big guy, strong skater, good shot, thought the game well but the concern was that perhaps he was given a lot in his life. The concern was that he hadn't faced too much adversity, so when he had to grind it out like everyone else, like the kid whose father was a blue collar worker who made his son accountable along the way, he just might not be able to get through it because he might not be mentally tough enough."

"I'm not saying that this is always the case, but this is often a concern. I have seen this happen where a player gets his NHL deal and has to grind it out in the American Hockey League (AHL). I think that the American Hockey League is one of the toughest leagues to play in. Every player is still trying to make it and the coaches down there want to or maybe need to win more than develop. Obviously, NHL coaches want to win too but winning is different in the minor leagues. Winning at the AHL level will help them move up the ladder and that is motivating."

"This player in question couldn't make it. He had all the skills and talent and still couldn't make it. The reason is that it's hard with a capital 'H'. They couldn't get over the fact that they had to beat out other players for a job and they had to do so every day. Every year teams bring in new players to compete for spots and it's a battle. Some players are just not tough enough mentally and it may come down to the fact that they haven't had a certain type of adversity in their life."

In the forty years that I have been coaching I have witnessed a lot of prejudice in other areas, more specifically size and toughness. The NHL went through its phases of size and power, then speed and quickness, and now it's skill and the game that existed ten years ago is being retooled to fit different dynamics. I asked Joe what he has observed over the past five years or so.

"Let's create a scenario. Lets' say that we have ten players that are all at the same high skill level and are five-foot-ten because there is more room in the NHL for smaller players now. We could say that all of them should make it based on their talent level. Then you have the next level; how committed are they at getting better? Then the level after that would be how hard that they continue to work to get better when things get more mentally challenging and it will get more mentally challenging. If we were too look at the same players over time we would see separation maybe even earlier that you would think."

"However" Joe added: *"One intangible that we must consider is 'opportunity'. Let's say that one of these guys has done everything right, done everything to get better, is a great teammate, works hard, he's mentally very strong, but perhaps the coach won't play him as much as another guy who may or may not be the same size and the same skill level. In my opinion this certainly can change the outcome of a player's career. I go back to my experience coaching junior hockey and the guys that drive the team are the eighteen-, nineteen-, and twenty-year-olds. You get two sixteen-year-olds on that roster and in the WHL you may have one or two more but they are not the guys that drive the team. While perhaps they may deserve the opportunity based many factors, the team has to win first and foremost, and teams generally win with older players. The younger players will get some experience in the process but they will have to get a lot tougher mentally until they get their opportunity and unfortunately some players are just not able to do this."*

"In the NHL, the same thing happens. There are contracts that need to be negotiated; there are salary caps and decisions to be made. What sucks is that there may be nothing that the player can do; they just have to wait. So, while there may be fifty players with exactly the same skill level, attitude, mental toughness and size, maybe five will be given an opportunity because

the five teams that drafted them provide an opportunity, based on needs that each team may have and the other guys are on the outside looking in."

"Another thing that happens in this great game of hockey that we love, is a coach at a lower level, say the East Coast Hockey League (ECHL) moves up to the American Hockey League. There is a player on his previous roster that has really impressed him. It may be a player that is great in the dressing room, maybe not as highly skilled, but competes and works hard. The coach will give that player an opportunity because of what he sees and what he believes the player will provide in the next locker room. A player that maybe competing for the same spot will not be given the same opportunity, I have seen this happen at every level of hockey and it is one of the unique things about this game as coaches move up so can the players and vice a versa, loyalty is a great thing in life and a great thing in the locker room."

Another issue that we discussed was the one of training and how teams push players in a certain developmental direction. A player may have all the intangibles; works hard, is mentally tough, wants to get better every day and is committed to the process and yet still doesn't make it.

"Let's take a look at two players that have worked hard on their development and are competing for the same spot in the NHL. The NHL team makes a choice and picks player one to play in the NHL that season player one scores twenty goals and gets thirty assists in the NHL, and player two goes to the AHL and gets thirty goals and fifty assists. A year later both players train hard for the upcoming season, Player two was good before he trained but now he's even better and ready to take the next step. Do you think that the team will move player one and his fifty NHL points and take player two with eighty AHL points? No way; at least not usually. You would think that they would find a spot for player two but remember all the other forwards are on one-way contracts. Player two is waiver eligible and therefore he starts the next season in the AHL. Sometimes it's all about being given the opportunity and some luck as well."

"I evaluate my guys all the time. I'm never negative with my guys but I'm always looking at how they can get better. They have to be better every game, every year, every summer. A lot of players get stuck doing the same move all the time and need to be aware of how the game is changing. One of the guys that I work with made the jump to junior, but ended up getting *released. He always did the same thing; he used the same move all the time, take the defense inside and then take him outside when coming into the offensive zone. I told him to just do a short strong side dump and beat the guy to the puck but he wasn't ready to evolve his game and had to go back to minor hockey and keep working at it. This year he stuck with the team and he's changed his offensive zone entry tactics because he had to. Defensemen today are better than they were five years ago and in general the moves that worked back then don't work today, you have to have a strategy to move your opposition around the ice."*

"Players get stuck in the minor hockey mentality and moves that worked in minor hockey don't work in junior, college or pro because of the way that the game is currently coached at the higher levels. The work with this particular player and every player that I work with doesn't stop, and while we may have helped one issue, we need to keep helping all players to improve in all areas. Players need to objectively look at their game and constantly make improvements. The trick becomes, can the player take advice/constructive criticism and then do something about it."

We both agreed that the game is constantly evolving and as players increase in skill level, then it's the different skills that they start to incorporate into their game play. Players need to be open to change and have to learn to do so quickly. This game waits for no one and those who accept change and push their boundaries, now push those behind them to do so as well.

Coming around full circle, it all becomes quite apparent that there are many player characteristics that need to part of a player's core values. I hope that Joe's valuable contributions here have provided some helpful insights in your own search for excellence.

MIKE JOHNSTON

FORMER NHL HEAD COACH CURRENT WHL HEAD COACH PORTLAND WINTERHAWKS WHL

I met Mike Johnston in the early 1990s, while I was performing skating skill-speed research for a company I had founded called EXCEL Hockey Enterprises. At the time, Mike was one of the associate coaches for the Canadian National team based out of Calgary, Alberta. Dave King was the head coach. We had reached out to the National Team to see if they could contribute to the study by allowing us to time test their roster in twenty-one skating and puck handling tests.

Mike and I have run into each other over the years; he joined the Richmond Sockeyes as a bench coach for our annual alumni game while I was head coach there. I have had the pleasure of chatting with Mike at various hockey seminars where I was either speaking or participating. His hockey knowledge and coaching experience, through all levels of the game, is extensive and I appreciate him taking the time out of his busy schedule to share his thoughts.

He first started coaching at the Camrose Lutheran College in 1982, where he remained until 1987. He then moved to become head coach of the CIAU (Canadian Intercollegiate Athletic-Union) University of Calgary from 1987-1989. He accepted the head coach role of the CIAU University of New Brunswick from 1989-94. While there, he won two McAdam Division titles coupled with three first-place finishes, which resulted in Mike's winning the Telegraph Journal Coach of the Year Award in 1993 and Coach of the Year for the CIAU in 1994. The CIAU is the highest level of ice hockey within the Canadian University Jurisdiction.

He has produced medals for Canada as a head coach in the Spengler Cup Tournament; and won three Gold Medals as well as two World Junior Championships as an associate coach in 1994 and 1995.

Mike worked with Team Canada from 1994-99, serving in the capacity of general manager, associate coach and then finally head coach for the 1998-99 Season. During that time, he was named associate coach for Team Canada at the 1998 Winter Olympic Games in Nagano, Japan.

He left the Canadian National program in 1999, to work as an associate coach for the NHL Vancouver Canucks, where he remained for the next six years. During his tenure there, the Canucks made four consecutive trips to the postseason and won the Northwest Division in 2003-04. After working with the Canucks for five seasons, Mike took an associate coach position with the NHL Los Angeles Kings in 2005 where he remained till 2008.

He took over the head coach and general manager roles of the Portland Winterhawks in 2008, and his coaching success continued. The team won a US Division title and then garnered four consecutive trips to the WHL championship series. In 2013, the Winterhawks posted their greatest season in team history as they won their WHL championship, the third in the history of the franchise.

After his 2014 season, Mike was named as head coach for the NHL Pittsburgh Penguins. He remained there for the next year-and-a-half after which he returned to the WinterHawks' Organization as Vice President, general manager and head coach in 2016.

I caught up with Mike at the start of his 2018 season. Mike is in the unique position of having been an elite coach at many different levels over the years. I thought that he could offer some valuable insights into what teams are looking for in regards to players' character traits. Being the head coach of Portland, the organization, or even the league for that matter, could be considered being in a developmental role. The objective is to both win and develop young players for the pro levels. For example, thirty-three Western Hockey League (WHL) players were selected in the 2017 NHL entry draft.

I asked Mike what qualities he looked for in players and what challenges he saw in players moving up and staying at the professional level.

"I have always appreciated a player's hockey sense. At the NHL level, the players have to be able to think the game at a much higher speed. One needs to have those instincts on support, how to box players out, how to find open ice, when to hold onto the puck and buy time for a teammate. As a result, we recruit players with a good hockey sense. Often players that have a strong hockey sense need to be shown how to compete. In our practices, we incorporate a lot of competition drills and that doesn't mean just in the physical sense. We may run two-on-ones, two-o- twos or small area games where we keep score. The idea is to have players appreciate and understand consequence and learn to compete with each other."

"We also try to have players drive players. This creates a healthy environment of competition. If the forwards are not pushing our defense, then they don't get better. If the defense is not pushing the forwards, they don't get better. Intensity and accountability from within the team itself help push awareness and development."

"In such an environment, one's ability to compete and then be accountable seems to be very important?" I affirmed.

"Agreed. There seems to be a problem today with many players having a sense of entitlement. It wasn't so apparent years ago, but what I see occurring more often today, is that parents coddle their son. When they don't have a good game, it's someone else's fault; they didn't get enough ice time, their teammate didn't get them the puck, line mates weren't good enough, they had an off game. This creates an environment where players never learn to be accountable. At every level, players have a role to play and a job to do. To shift blame away from their own performance limits their ability to deal with issues that ultimately will hold them back."

"In order to make it up through the various levels of hockey and into pro, accountability and dealing with adversity is a necessary part of a player's make-up. Another area where young players need to focus is hard work and getting better every day. Players at the pro level are always working on their game. We look for players that are self-motivated. There is a lot of work that goes into being a pro player and it is not something that takes place

over night. Coaching staff are not a baby sitting service and we want players that take direction but don't have to be constantly supervised to do so."

"Another area we emphasize in Portland, is one of a strong team culture; hard work, teamwork, accountability and development. We have spent the last several years building and defining that culture. Now that the culture is established, we look for players that fit that profile, that are good in the dressing room, are great teammates. We are on the road a lot and as a result, spend a lot of time and energy on team building. We push the team philosophy; work together, support each other and understand each other will lead to success. Our coaching staff stress that the guy next to you, while not someone that perhaps you want to hang out with, is still a critical part of our organization and it is important to the team. Diversity is a part of a team and as such all players need to work together in order to be successful."

We discussed coachability of players today. I was explaining that as a skills coach, it was my job to focus on areas of weakness and, while recognizing areas that needed improvement, I had to be very careful about how much correction I emphasized compared to how many good things I praised them for. If I was too negative, they thought that I didn't like them.

"This is a common issue in junior hockey. A lot of players today seem to struggle with criticism. Again, this comes from what I believe is the sense of entitlement. As a coaching staff, we have to be constantly aware that some players need more emphasis on what they do correctly and limit the amount of criticism we direct toward them. We have other players that can handle a lot of direction; they want to get better and don't let negative feedback affect them. Ultimately, if a player wants to excel at this game, they have to learn to take and accept direction."

"I remember several years ago, when minor hockey players could move from team to team, in the United States. If they didn't like a coach or the way that they were treated, they would go to another team. I see the same happening today in academy hockey. If a player runs into adversity, then they jump ship and go to another one. Unfortunately, these players will never make it to the NHL. Handling criticism and adversity is important and the earlier that a player learns to deal with disappointments and direction, the better."

I raised another point for discussion: "What are other areas of concern that you see developmentally? There seems to be so many more options open to players now than there were years ago."

"Players overall, are much more skilled today than they were years ago. They have access to many skill professionals, but what I think is missing is the development or teaching of game sense. Minor hockey coaches need to focus more on teaching kids the game. While skill training is important, there has to be a balance. I see players that come to our camp that use their skating and their puck skills to try to generate offense but don't use their mind. For example, they have been taught one-on-one skills to beat a defender but forget that it's a team game. They need to know how to move to other areas of the ice to open up team plays and not just focus on trying to slip the puck through a defender's feet. In pro hockey, it's ultimately the mind that drives a player's success, which in turn drives team's success. We emphasize that philosophy every day in practice. I don't want to discredit skill, competitiveness and work ethic, but with the speed of the game today, everyone has to work together."

I reinforced his comments. I often ask players it they watch game highlights on a regular basis and if so, what do they see. The most common answer that I receive focuses on the skill moves and not the team play.

In closing, I asked Mike what attributes he felt contributed to greater player success.

"Accountability and effort. Players need to take ownership of their flaws. It is our job to point them out and to fix them. The road to the NHL is a long one and if a player goes to work every day and takes care of the details, more often than not it works out. At the pro levels, all the top players take ownership and work on getting better."

TROY WARD

PROFESSIONAL HEAD COACH

I had the pleasure of meeting Troy while he was the assistant coach for the NCAA Wisconsin Badgers in 2003. I would either run into him in Vancouver when he was doing prep camps for KO Sports, at the Burnaby Eight Rinks, or in Madison when I was running development camps. In 2005, Mike Valley and I talked him into coming on board Next Testing to act as Vice President of Hockey Operations, a leading international sport research company that we co-founded and that offers comprehensive sport-specific testing. His coaching background is extensive and he was a great addition to the Next Testing Team.

It has been my privilege to engage in many a hockey discussion with Troy. He is a coach that I have a lot of respect for; a consummate professional, well prepared, always on top of the changes within the game and he expects a lot from his players.

His coaching career started in 1985, the year after graduating from the University of Wisconsin-Eau Claire, where he played from 1981-84. He joined the staff there as an assistant coach until 1987, when he took over as head coach. He remained with Wisconsin-Eau Claire until the 1989-90 season, stepping up to the NCAA Division 1 University of Denver in the role of assistant coach the following season.

After three years with Denver, Troy assumed the general manager/head coach role with the Dubuque Fighting Saints of the USHL in 1993 where he remained until 1995.

Never one to miss an opportunity, Troy made the jump to the Indianapolis Ice of the International Hockey League (IHL) acting as Assistant Coach from 1995 to 1997. This pro experience landed him an assistant coaching role with the NHL Pittsburgh Penguins from 1997 to 2000. He then moved to take over the head coaching role for the Trenton Titans of the East Coast Hockey League (ECHL) in 2000-01, winning the John Brophy Award for the ECHL Coach of the Year.

From there, it was a move back to NCAA Division 1 hockey, to assume the assistant coaching role for the University of Wisconsin Badgers from 2002 to 2005. Troy decided to take a break from coaching and this is when Mike and I enticed him to come and work as a consultant for Next Testing.

Troy's love of coaching pulled him back into the fray, and he took over the Victoria Salmon Kings of the ECHL from 2005-2006. Wanting to get back to the American Hockey League (AHL), the following year, he accepted the role of assistant general manager and assistant coach for the Houston Aeros where he remained until 2010. The following season, he accepted a position as assistant coach for the NHL Calgary Flames' affiliate team, the AHL Abbotsford Heat, taking over the head coach responsibilities the ensuing season. His role as head coach was to work closely with the Flames to develop their young drafted players. The team moved from Vancouver in 2014, and did not renew their arena lease with City of Abbotsford, resulting in Troy's moving on to be head coach for the Vancouver Giants of the Western Hockey League (WHL).

A he has his home in Wisconsin, Troy decided to move back to Madison, and took over as head coach for the USHL Madison Capitals for the 2015-16 Season. After that eh got the itch to get back into professional coaching, and accepted the head coaching role for the EHC Linz (Home City) in the Professional Austrian Erste Bank Ice Hockey League (EBEL) at the start of the 2017 and this is where he is currently working.

Aside from his many years of bench coaching, Troy has found the time to give back to the hockey community by founding a very successful hockey school called Hockey and Sons. It provides a unique professional experience for fathers and sons (and also includes Hockey and Daughters) who would like to meet new friends, build that family relationship and learn from knowledgeable videos, skills and tactical coaches. He founded the school twenty-two years ago this summer and it shows no indication of slowing down, maintaining an eighty percent return rate with its clients.

I was fortunate enough to catch up with Troy between practice and coaching and got back to talking hockey.

Through his extensive coaching experience, Troy has had the opportunity to wear both the 'developmental' and the 'must-win' hat. I realize that there is always pressure be successful; however, the importance of developing players for the next level, especially in the ECHL or AHL, must put a strain on winning. The players are constantly being called up and sent back down, so dealing with lineup issues must be quite stressful. I asked Troy what the primary differences were in players' attitudes, relative to such movement.

I also explained to him that I had reached a point of frustration as a coach and skills instructor. I felt that I was spending as much time teaching the core values of life as I was teaching the skills of the game. It seemed that over the past ten years there had been a real shift in parenting, or perhaps something else that I couldn't identify, that had created this anomaly. I was wondering if he had also noticed a difference?

"The biggest shift that I have seen is in the area of accountability; the desire to change their habits. It is no different to what you have to deal with when it comes to fixing stickhandling or shooting habits. The one character trait the players' need to have today is the ability to adapt, to be open to change. The player brings the core value of: 'This is what I do, this is what I want to do and this is what I bring to the table when I'm at my best'. As a coach, our job is to play them at their best and then make them part of a team. So many of the players today aren't really part of a team; they worry about their own identity and what they do and they think that they should be allowed to do it whenever they want, how they want to do it."

"The players that really tend to make it, that make a difference on a team, are open to change; they are willing to adapt and they are open-minded on how they approach the game. Now that I am coaching in Europe and having to go over to over to my North American side, it makes no difference

whether I was coaching in Abbotsford or here. The players that have the ability to adapt and change and fit into the team game are the guys that are more successful. Guys like Joe Pavelski, who is willing to take instruction, and adapt constantly - those are the guys that teams are looking for."

I brought up my conversations with Matthew Barzal and Joe Pavelski. Matt had discussed how he tried to work longer and harder than anyone else did, so that those minutes added up over time. Joe talked about not only work span, but also work quality and quantity, where he would do more perfect reps in more quantity so that it was ingrained as a habit sooner. I asked Troy if that was a common trait in the elite players that he coached?

"For sure, work is a skill set. Back in the day it never seemed like that had to be taught, everyone worked hard. Today, some guys really get it, other guys don't. Some guys have lower pain tolerances so they don't work as hard. Some guys have less focus so they don't train as long. The problem comes back to identity. They don't' see themselves where they need to get to. They just see themselves in the current or past tense. This is what I did in high school so this is what I have to do in the USHL, this is what I did in the USHL so this is how I have to do it in college. This is how I did it in college, so this is how I have to do it in pro. But it never works that way."

It seems that every level has a particular filter that players have to get through, in order to be successful. At the pro level, everyone has skill so then work ethic comes into play, everyone now works hard, then another filter comes into play. I asked Troy what he thought was one of the toughest filters to overcome and what really created separation in players.

"There are a lot of filters with work ethic and as Joe and Matt alluded to, work span, quality and quantity is one of them, but the one that I keep coming back to is adaptability and being open minded. I think that many players today are stuck in their ways in general. It is tougher to find the Joe Pavelskis out there. They just aren't out there. It is one of the core issues that plague players today."

"I have players right now that just won't change for the betterment of their own game or the team game and it is causing us to just be an OK team

right now. Their ability to change, whether it comes from the coaching, their skill coach or their strength coach, they demonstrate an inability to alter their behavior."

"I think that players today take things far too personally. Every coach is different. That's why when I talk about the language of hockey or whether I talk about hockey in general, I think that one has to talk more from a life or personal perspective and then work your way into hockey. It is harder today to just go right after the core issues of an athlete, so if there is a relationship that is built, one of trust and not so much negativity then players will slowly come around. Always hitting guys with their weaknesses, that relationship will burn out over time. If there is a kinship between two men then one can ask more of them. It is the same in other kinds of relationships in life. Form a relationship, build the trust and that opens up communication."

"Junior, college or even professional hockey players get through based on either some form of skill level, their size or speed, some attribute that they have. But ultimately they run into problems. So, you can mask it for a while, say at the USHL WHL or college level. You may be really fast or have some skill that allows you to dominate at a particular level and then you hit pro hockey. They now say that you have to adapt and change the way you play to be successful at this level and they don't want to do. Perhaps they have built themselves up to be such valuable assets at the way they want to play, that they don't see it any other way."

"A great story is Paul Byron. He was on the ice with you and me in Abbotsford. He was always getting beat up by Calgary and struggled and then I would build him back up. I would tell him that he if could adapt and change a couple things he could make the jump. He would come back and say that is was really hard and that it wasn't the way he wanted to play. I would tell him that 'I got that, but you have to start implementing some things into your game'. Slowly, over the two-and-a-half years in Abbotsford, it started to sink in. He started to adapt and change slowly and has just signed an $18.6 million dollar contract with Montreal. He was a little bullheaded at first; was stubborn to change, had to mature and go through the process. On the way, he got the right break and everything seemed to click, but he had to adapt and change over time. That was a real process for him but the good thing was that he had the ability to listen to people *and adapt. He would have been just like any other minor league pro guy, unable to make the jump."*

I brought up the story of Max, a minor league pro player who had moved back and forth but couldn't quite stick with the big club. We talked about taking ownership of his weaknesses at one of the skills sessions we were doing. He took it to heart and now signed a great one-way deal. Was a lack ownership a key issue that he noticed as well?

"Big time. We are going through a massive struggle with my team right now. Ownership is a key issue with any player at any level. Sometimes they meet a guy that causes a shift and they wake up and take the next step. That is the most important change that can happen to a player."

Where do you think that learning ownership comes from?

"There is a general problem with parents today. While they need to support their son or daughter, help them follow their passion and if it's hockey then be thankful that they are good at it. Get them where they need to go, give them support through adversity but don't neglect the lessons along the way. In general, the things that you were frustrated with when we started the conversation, the core values of just life; the please and thank you, the respect, the work ethic, accountability, perseverance, being humble, working together never used to be the coaches job. Now we have to provide the home life, the tutoring, how to raise a kid properly, plus coaching."

That started a great discussion on when this shift in coaching occurred.

"For me, I noticed it in early 2000. The game started to change and the athlete started to change."

I agreed. I had just moved up into junior hockey in 2000 and noticed that there seemed to be a greater sense of entitlement with younger players coming into the league.

"I was associate coach in Wisconsin at the time and had recruited some great talent. The head coach really struggled with some of the players. He tried to change some of them and they basically told him to take off. I thought; 'Wow, really you guys'. I was shocked. I had just run an East Coast League team head office and had taken a year out of coaching after

being in Trenton in the ECHL. There was an issue in Wisconsin with a player and I won't get into details here, but he thought that he was bigger than the head coach. It was the craziest year I've had as a coach. I thought; 'You've got to be kidding me!' That was when I noticed a real sense of entitlement with players, especially at the junior and college levels."

Entitlement seems to be an issue everywhere, even at the pro level now. I had heard that some elite pro players complained to the National Hockey League Players' Association (NHLPA) that what they did outside the team's three-hour window of responsibility was their time to do with what they wanted.

"I can see that, I have been coaching, as you know, in Austria for the past two years. The same thing happens there. Because a lot of these players were never afforded the opportunity to play in a pro league in North America, they view the dressing room differently. For example, the players there speak German or Latvian in the dressing room all the time. That never happens overseas. Coaches respect the European cultures but hockey is an English game. Hockey is not an English game there, we live in Austria, we are Austrian and this is the way we are and this is the way we are as people and if I don't adapt, then I won't be coaching long. That being said, the entitlement thing is more of a cultural issue, it comes down to how they were raised. I would say that entitlement there is more relative to the country, life there not so much hockey related."

"All things considered" I asked: "Would you come back to your earlier comments that a player's ability to adapt and change are the values that most often separate guys at the highest level?"

"I think so. One has to remember that there are filters along the way that we have discussed. Those filters will eliminate most of the players, but the one that I found to be the final discriminating character trait is adaptability. Guys can work hard, they can be accountable and admit mistakes, they can act professional but if they can't change, the game will toss them out."

KURT OVERHARDT

NHL AGENT

Kurt is the founder and CEO of KO Sports, an agency that represents many high level NHL clients, as well as acting as an agent or family advisor to many aspiring amateur Canadian and US players, in a wide range of Bantam and Midget Elite Leagues (also including many NCAA, CHL, BCHL and USHL players). Kurt gained a law degree from the University of Denver's College of Law. KO Sports operates out of Denver, Colorado with satellite offices in select cities throughout North America and has been in business since 1992. Prior to KO Sports and representing professional hockey players, Kurt's career was quite diverse and he ranges in experience from labor employment and intellectual property law to acting intern at the Denver Broncos Football Club. He was the first sports agent to represent professional snowboarders, from 1998 through to 2003, and this included Olympians who participated in the Nagano Olympics in 1998.

KO Sports represents players that include Ryan Kesler, Anaheim Ducks; Jacob Trouba, Winnipeg Jets; Dylan Larkin, Detroit Redwings; Ryan Johansen, Nashville Predators; Andrew Copp, Winnipeg Jets; Travis Zajac, New Jersey Devils and many others.

The KO Sports' team includes NHL Alumni, attorneys and former coaches and has a reputation for treating the players it represents with the highest level of professionalism. I have had the pleasure of working with KO Sports in the area of skills consulting and instruction for the past seven years.

I first met Kurt in Denver, Colorado when I worked with some of KO Sports' star prospects.

Kurt has an intimate working relationships with all of the NHL's general managers and as such I approached him to provide his insights into how the NHL has changed and what the new NHL is looking for in player values and character.

"The traditional core values in the NHL encompass NHL teams' focus on a player's work ethic and personal character, the player's being professional, and what it means to be a professional both on and off the ice. That conversation also includes being a good teammate, and respecting other guys in the league. These core values are still paramount, but there have been adjustments with the new rule changes. The days where players fight for themselves and fight for teammates has changed, and the greatest emphasis is on speed and skill, so the character side of the game has diminished somewhat."

"While I feel it's important to limit my comments on the character of guys in the league to basic observations, clearly players in the league would certainly be better resources regarding that conversation. But with the emphasis now on skill and youth, a lot of younger players are getting an earlier ticket to the NHL."

"One must consider what it means to be a professional on and off the ice. A player that is nineteen, twenty or twenty-one does not have the mental or emotional maturity of a twenty-eight-year-old. They don't have the experiences to draw from and haven't faced that level of compete before. The game is quicker than they are used to so, playing in the American Hockey league for a year or two really helps the maturation process. While the speed is a little off, the compete levels are still there or maybe even more so since at that level, players are still trying to make the jump."

We discussed some of the veteran players in the league that are still driven to get better. With the evolution of the game, increases in skill and speed overall, players today have to be accountable and are held accountable on how they show up at camp and they improve over the season."

"All teams want character guys, guys that are coachable, guys that compete every night, guys that have AA+ hockey sense. But, I think sometimes that the emphasis on skill still wins out and a lot of teams don't take a close enough look under the hood so to speak. The problem is that if the player can't separate himself from others in the elite sense, then the intangibles that enable the work ethic and drive to learn is not there, and the player ultimately fails."

"There are as many of those stories as there are about guys like Thornton, Marleau, and Kesler. Take a guy like Ian Cole, for example, who is a two-time Stanley Cup champion defenceman, how has Ian Cole had such a successful career? You have worked with Ian Cole; he is always looking for ways to get better. He continues to challenge himself as a man and as a hockey player. The player that teams are looking for are like that. Look at Pavelski and Thornton's reputation. They don't sit around during the summer; they look to get better every year. That creates sustainability whether we are talking about hockey players or any other occupational."

KO Sports is an agency that mentors and/or represents young aspiring prospects as well as veteran NHL players. I asked Kurt if there was much emphasis placed on the character and values of each individual, when representing young players who are still finding their way up through the system.

"As an agency, we are always looking for the young player that has the work ethic and drive to get better. Another important factor to consider is sustained effort. Reaching the NHL is delayed gratification and the road is long and filled with many distractions and much adversity. Take guys like Ryan Kesler, Brendan Morrison, Mike Smith, Ryan Johansen, Jacob Trouba, and Dylan Larkin, for example. They have been raised well, all have great parents and they are humble on what they've achieved but they were never satisfied where they were at, they always wanted to achieve more and they want to win. They have constantly strived to be better and realized early that the journey is a marathon and not a sprint."

I asked Kurt if he had any advice that he could offer parents.

"I think that parents need to understand that getting to the NHL is a process; that their kid has to do ninety-nine percent of the work. They also need to understand that being cut from a 'AAA' team or a junior team is not the end of the world and to prop their kids up and cover for their shortcoming or losses, isn't the correct thing to do. Kids need to learn from adversity and failure is one of those. These make for great life lessons that in turn develop character. Everyone needs some failure in their life; it is a necessary part of the growing up or the maturation process. It is important to understand that character is built on how we deal with adversity and rise above it."

'They need to teach their kids to be great teammates, how to be accountable, how to keep learning and how to deal with tough situations."

We discussed sustainability for players that are already in the NHL. What additional advice could he offer?

"I think that players need to think more outside the box. As you know with your research, the game is changing and a player cannot afford to think one-dimensionally. Take a player like Connor McDavid, arguably one of the best if not the best player in the world at this time. Where will he be in five years from now? No one knows for sure. All the great players constantly evaluate their performance and look to get better. No one knows what that will look like, no one can say for sure. They are constantly redefining themselves. It is each player's ability to stay healthy, to learn constantly and to figure out what improvements they need to embrace that which will allow them to continually be the best players."

"I think that Ryan Kesler said it best to me. "It is one thing to play a game in the NHL, it is another thing to make a career of it and its' a whole other thing, once you've established what you are and what your role that you need to play is, to live up to your teams and your own expectations of winning and how the fans expect you to play every night."

"Whether you're a young aspiring player or a professional that has played in the league for many years, the constant really comes down to work ethic, mental toughness, accountability and a drive to get better every day. It goes without saying that one needs to be a good person, respectful, a great teammate and demonstrate leadership"

LIFE EXPERIENCES

RESPECT

My father was a man of riddles and often during my youth, we would sit out on the step looking over our meager front yard and discuss philosophies. He had a riddle for different words and would throw them at me with a gleam in his eye and the promise of an ice cream cone from the corner store if I could come up with the correct answer. Over the years I got better at solving them, but the lessons gleaned from our interactions never seem to leave me.

He had a riddle for RESPECT: *"What is earned over a lifetime but can be lost in a moment; can't be cashed at a bank but is worth more than gold?"*

It is a word that in a way is almost foreign. At times we never seem to know how much respect someone has earned until his or her passing. My father was such a man. I clearly remember standing at his gravesite waiting for the casket to be lowered into its final resting place. The cemetery took place on a hillside overlooking the Alaska Highway, which wound its way to Whitehorse and further north to Alaska. It lay below me and I could follow the gravel road as it wound its way from the south down the hill into the small valley below me and then increased in elevation as it passed below the site where the ceremony was to take place. As far as I could see, were bumper-to-bumper cars, coming to pay their last respects to my father. Fort Nelson was near an Indian reservation and many of the native elders and business men and service workers came to shake my hand, telling me that my father was a great and well-respected man. I had no idea, of course, since I was a foolish youth, but the riddle that he casually mentioned on that warm summer day came bursting back into my consciousness.

Respect is a word associated with a different period of time it seems. When I ask my students about the word, they have difficultly explaining it. Dictionary.com explains it as the following:

"Esteem for, or a sense of, the worth or excellence of a person, a personal quality or ability, or something considered as a manifestation of a personal quality or ability."

The word respect can be a mind-full for sure. We may respect someone for their strength, their speed or even their knowledge. However, what one respects in others may have nothing to do with core values. Respect has a lot to do with how others have shaped our beliefs and while some may respect certain qualities in an individual, others may abhor those same traits.

Obviously, the community that my father lived in had particular values and because he embodied those values, he was deeply respected. Although we live in a larger community as a whole, we are also part of smaller communities: gaming, sports, fitness, health, or family. Each has its own code and expectations and each creates their own definition of respect.

WORK ETHIC

I always found the term, 'Work Ethic' to be vague and too all-encompassing. I try to impress on my students that there is a lot under the surface. For example:

1. Work – Effort. While some players work hard, other players' efforts border on injury. I ask kids to create a scale from one to ten, with ten representing and effort that would make it hard to breathe or where one might even get sick and one representing a warm-up. This helps define the difference in athletes that push the limits of what is possible and those that are afraid to get out of their comfort zones.

2. Work – Span. How long can one work? Depending on the type of training that one is doing; aerobic or anaerobic, there are limitations, of course, but in the earlier part of this book, Matt Barzal and Joe Pavelski explained that they try to work longer than others do. Those extra fifteen or thirty minutes add up over a year.

3. Work – Quality: While one can work hard, how much quality is going into the effort? As the saying, 'Practice makes permanent, ONLY perfect practice makes perfect', explains, it is important to do what is correct.

4. Work – Speed: As explained above in point number three, it is important to perform actions at a speed that can be monitored by one's focal or peripheral vision. Doing it right the every time takes concentration.

5. Work – Focus: This is one that concerns me a lot as a coach. Players often feel that sweat and a feeling of pain or exhaustion in the muscles is what they need to worry about. It is being

aware of how 'CORRECTLY' they are doing the movement that matters.

6. Work – Quantity: Again, Joe Pavelski had a couple great observations here. In the end it is the number of movements that make the difference, provided they are done correctly. If he can get 300 touches of a ball in five minutes, then his skill of tipping puck would improve faster.

That being said, this story is about my father and his interpretation of effort.

My father retired at the age of eighty-years-old and passed away at the age of eighty-one. His work ethic was built on tough times and no excuses. He worked hard through the Great Depression, had to survive the many years where he wandered in the wilderness as a trapper and outdoorsman.

My first lesson on work ethic came from my father during one of our PeeWee hockey practices, one Saturday morning at the local rink. I was enjoying what I thought was a fun practice when I noticed my father walking down from the bleachers towards the players' bench. This was also noticed by my coach who skated over to meet my father, who had tipped his cowboy hat high on his head and was now bending over to discuss what seemed to be a matter of great importance.

The coach nodded his head and then waved me over to meet my father who had asked to speak with me immediately. I could see that my father was concerned about something and I felt a little anxious as I arrived at the bench.

"Everything OK Dad?" I asked.

My father, a man of few words, looked me straight in the eye and in a very serious tone asked me a simple question: "What the heck are you doing out there?"

"Well, practicing Dad" I replied.

He paused for a brief moment, still looking me in the eye to make sure that I was paying attention, and then went to work making his point.

"Son" he exclaimed, "I think that you are floating around out there. I want you to understand clearly that you are a representative of everything your mother and I stand for. We work hard every day and to see you fooling around when you have an obligation to your team and your coach is not acceptable, do you understand?"

I nodded my head in agreement since doing otherwise would most certainly not be a good idea.

"Good" was his response. "Let me be perfectly clear here Son. That if this is how you would like to continue practicing, I will pull you out of hockey immediately and you can find something else to take up your time. I will explain to you one last time that you represent what we stand for and right now you are making a very poor example of that. Don't let this happen again do I make myself clear?"

I again nodded my head. With that he turned to the coach, who was standing off to the side pretending to watch the practice and thanked him for allowing the intrusion. He headed back up into the bleachers where he sat down, cracked open his thermos of coffee and poured himself a fresh cup. As for the coach, I'm sure he heard every word my father said, although it was never mentioned.

COMPETITIVENESS

Competing and playing are two completely different concepts. As a young hockey player, I was very fortunate to work with a gentleman named Carey Klein. He had been a professional player in the Chicago Blackhawks organization and was an incredibly skilled defenceman. He had moved to Ft. Nelson to work, after he suffered an illness and dropped off their radar. I was fortunate to have him as a coach during my midget and juvenile years.

It was an early evening before practice and I had taken up position in front of the concession stand located inside the main lobby. It was operated by a lady who loved feeding kids. Her hamburgers and hot chocolate were second to none. She had a little bowl on her counter full of mini marshmallows and she would always throw a small handful onto the top of her exquisite, steaming hot chocolate. I was looking forward to having a cup. Murray walked into the rink, took up a seat at a picnic table in front of the concession stand and motioned me over to talk to him. He was a great coach and communicator and in years past had kind of taken me under his wing, imparting a lot about the skills and tactics of the game to me.

I could tell that there was something on his mind and I quickly went through the last game and practice wondering if I had possibly done something wrong. We had talked many months ago about the pro game and he knew that my father was a Bruins, or should I say, a Bobby Orr and Phil Esposito fan.

Not holding back, he asked me a very pointed question: "Do you know the difference between a hockey competitor and a hockey player?"

"I think so" I replied. "Isn't competing how hard someone works for the puck in the corners or how hard someone works to win a race to the puck and just playing is someone who takes shifts off?"

"Good answers" he stated but then carried on. "Great hockey players don't play the game, they compete the game. Every time they are on the ice, it is all about the competition; winning battles all over the ice, winning races to the puck, scoring on the goal tender, separating the man from the puck. Players tend to be the guys that love the social life in the dressing room. They're happy to be on the ice but when the going gets tough they tend to step down and don't step up. In order to succeed in this game you have to compete the game every day, not play it".

This taught me to view myself through a different lens. However, while his comments were direct and to the point, one had to look a little deeper.

I think most people naturally associate 'fun' with the word play. We hear it all the time; "Let's go play some hockey and let's have fun." Or, "You have a game to play tonight, make sure you have fun."

Where the confusion arises is in personal philosophical discrepancies between the concept of hard work and that of having fun. Since when is working hard, fun? I think there is a natural progression that creates the best environment for player development and that takes into consideration all the facets of one's training philosophy.

In the following, story provided by Andrew Copp, he describes this as 'cyclic', meaning that hard work in practice leads to better skills, better skills leads to more success, more success means having more fun. Having more fun re-enforces more hard work and so on.

What my coach was describing was the underlying 'caring' of play. Every kid has a competitive nature and when they lose the race to the puck, was it from their lacking effort or their lacking skill? The same goes for a corner battle; did the player lose because of effort or lose because of strength or skill?

Hockey is a game of competition. It pits one player against another in a wide assortment of game skills. As a result, how a player performs during these individual one-on-one competitions will not only determine how much success they have in a game, but how their peers and coaches view them.

This lesson has always stuck in my head and even as a coach I tend to look at players in that light: are they competitors or players?

MENTAL TOUGHNESS

Mental toughness comes in all forms. Look at some of the earlier stories in this book, from Ben Israel and Adam Burish: both players who had to overcome substantial injuries to pursue their dreams of playing hockey. The one that follows is of my father (including a picture of my mother when she was young) and what I call facing your fears.

My Father - Jim Johnson (on horseback)

My father was a cowboy. He was born in 1894, in an era that was completely foreign to me. Aside from his occasional stories about the past, I knew very little about his life. As a young man I was way too self-absorbed in my own life to question what he had accomplished in his. He always wore a cowboy hat and cowboy boots and I just thought that it was who he was.

It was a day like any other. I had arrived home from school and he was sitting at the kitchen table sipping a freshly percolated cup of coffee. He motioned me to join him at the table. I hung up my jacket and sat down next to him. It was then that I noticed a set of spurs on the table. I picked them up and took a closer look. They were made of silver and there were four gold decorations on the side of each one: a spade, a heart, a club and a diamond, as in each suit of a deck of playing cards.

"Wow" I exclaimed. "Where did you get those?"

"I won them Son, at the Calgary Stampede, in 1919"

I had no idea. I knew my father was very familiar with horses and bulls from some of our previous conversations, but had no idea that he had participated in the Stampede.

"How did you win them?" I asked now that he had my complete attention.

"Riding horses and bulls, Son" he replied. "If you stay on them long enough, and ride them hard enough you get awarded points. If you get more points than the next guy, you win."

"Why would you ever get on the back of a bull?" I frowned.

Having been on the farm when I was young, and having been to several rodeos, I was familiar how big and seemingly out of control they were (they weigh between 1,700 and 2,400 pounds). Ft. Nelson used to host a rodeo every summer and I would go with my father and watch the cowboys do their thing. He would talk about the

Jim at the Calgary Stamped in 1919.

horses and the roping, the wagons and the rodeo clowns. I could tell that it was something he had been passionate about.

His reply was a lesson as usual:

"Men define themselves only under greater stress, challenge or adversity, Son. One has to face one's fears and only then does one know who they are. Nothing makes a man more honest about himself than climbing on the back of an animal that wants throw him off stamp him into the ground. The real test is when you do get stamped; do you get back up and try again? One either quits and admits defeat, or tries again, then again, then again until you find a way to win. It's you against the animal and there can only be one winner."

I nodded my head in agreement. "Well, I am glad it was you and not me" I added "I like my body parts intact".

"So, how did you started bull riding? Was it a bunch of guys sitting around a campfire and one guy looked at the other and said, "Hey I have a great idea! And then everyone else chimed in and said, 'whatever it is I'm in?'" I chirped

Yup, I went a little too far there and he gave me the "I think I might reach across the table and smack you look". The he just grinned a little and said. "Yeah something like that. We were young and thought we were invincible. It was a way to compete against each other. Everyone talks big but when it comes to the truth, fear has a way of showing a man's true character. Sometimes it has nothing to do with anyone else; it's just about competing against yourself."

It was his lesson on persevering, competing and facing ones fear all wrapped up into one. In my mind it had a lot to do with mental toughness and courage as well. All I can remember is that after that discussion, when I got rocked into the boards and came home with some aches and pains all he would say was. "Suck it up, get over it and get back on the bull".

The picture below shows the spurs, accented in gold and silver, that my father won in the Calgary Stampede in 1919.

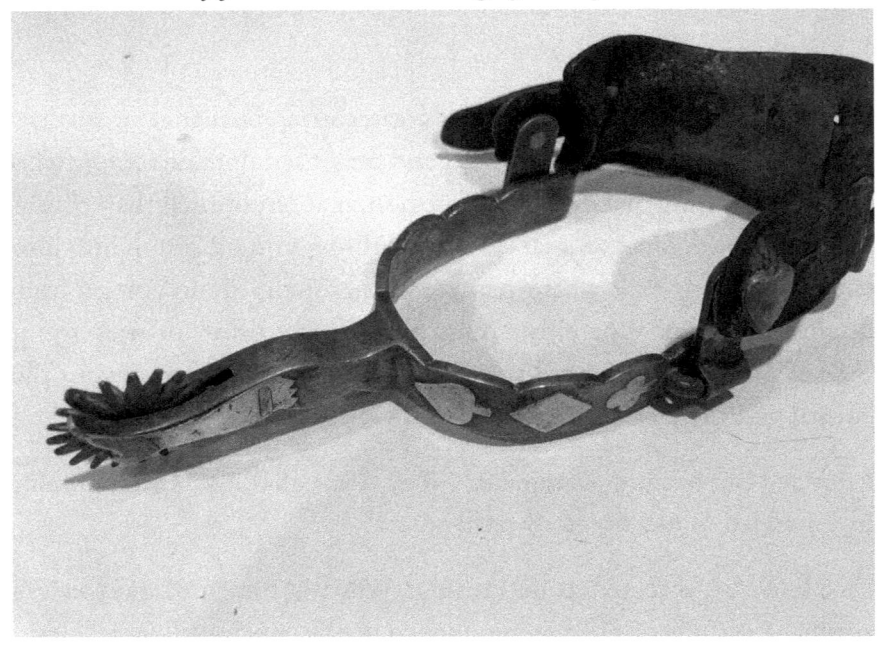

My Mother – Esther Johnson (little girl on the right)

HUMILITY

My father was a humble man. He and Esther, my stepmother, adopted me at six months of age when he was sixty-four years old. As I have aged, I have come to respect who my father was as a man even more. Now, at the ripe age of sixty, I cannot see myself adopting a six-month-old baby. However the fact that they did so has made me eternally grateful. While I only knew him for the first seventeen years of my life, and would have loved more time with him, the stories of his life and the lessons they taught have stayed with me.

He worked five miles out of town, running a large commercial boiler for one of the lumber companies. When I was young, I used to accompany him to work on his midnight shifts, and read Wild West magazines until I was too tired to keep my eyes open. Then, I would climb into a sleeping bag laid out on the backseat of his Ford Custom 500, which he pulled into the large boiler room each night. The roar of the boilers always lulled me to sleep and I woke to the scent of the freshly percolated coffee that he brewed before he went home.

The reserve was located just off the Alaska Highway on the way to town from the boiler plant, and often, on the way to work or on the way home, native Indian elders would be hitchhiking. He would always stop and pick them up; never passing them by.

They would just nod in appreciation when they got into the car and when they exited. My dad would tip his cowboy hat to them in a sign of respect. It was a kind of code with my father and over the years he came to appreciate that there were many people less fortunate than himself. He had lived through the Great Depression and said that hard times tended to ground a person.

He would always say to me: *"No matter their race or color or their stature in life, we are all created equal. No man is above another. All men can feel hunger, loss, pain or love, Son and we all bleed red."*

SACRIFICE

The definition of 'sacrifice' for an athlete might be a lot different than it is to a passive observer. A definition of sacrifice: **"The surrender or destruction of something prized or desirable for the sake of something considered as having a higher or more pressing"** would imply that pursuing one's love of hockey meant that one had to give up something of high value to do so. I remembered reading an interview with Kevin Bieksa, when he was a player for the Vancouver Canucks about sacrifice.

He was asked about the sacrifices that a player had to make over the many years that it takes to become a professional player. His response was that hockey was a passion and as a result, he never sacrificed anything. It was something that he had always wanted to do and there were never any thoughts of having to sacrifice anything.

Sacrifice to a hockey player may mean putting their body on the line to make a play. It may mean push one's body beyond what is reasonable for the sake of training and possibly even forsaking one's health in the future. Each athlete has their own definition, but I have never heard a single professional hockey player state that they had to give up a weekend with their friends or had to give up another sport or hobby for hockey.

I think about sacrifice as being more related to the supporting cast of the player: their parents, siblings and/or friends. Looking back, my mother and father adopted me at the ages of sixty-four and forty-four respectfully. When most people are ready for retirement, my father remained working for the next sixteen years and retired, retiring when I was old enough to take care of myself, and he died dying one year later of a heart attack. He had already raised sons and daughters, who were fully-grown and married by the time I came along. He worked shift work to pay the bills, and when I was a lot older and had worked twenty-two years of night shift myself, I truly came to understand and respect what he had sacrificed in order to keep me clothed and fed.

The beauty of sacrifice is that anyone, anywhere, is capable of giving up something in pursuit of a greater good. One of my favorite stories begins with a summer hockey camp that I was running when I was in my twenties. I had formed a wonderful relationship with a coach named Gary Napper, who asked me to help him with a Bantam Rep team in North Delta. The season had come and gone and we decided to run a late summer hockey school at the North Delta Recreation Center, to prepare kids for the upcoming season. He would look after the business side and I would look after the instructional side.

I eagerly put together some camp flyers and hung them up at various businesses and rinks in the area. Summer was moving along far too quickly and there were lots of preparations still to be made. I put together a teaching plan, met with junior instructors and prepped them for the camp. I checked on registration numbers, checked on flyers and replenished them when they were low.

Finally registration day arrived. There was a lot of excitement in the air, both from the kids and the instructors. A table was erected inside the lobby of the rink and parents and kids were lining up to sign in. I was checking players off the list when I noticed a woman motioning to me off to the side. With her was a portly young man with a very anxious look on his face, and she appeared quite nervous.

I passed my sheets off to an assistant and walked over to greet her and to see what the problem was. She quickly shook my hand and after a brief pause jumped right into her concerns.

"This is my son, Billy, and this is the first camp he has ever attended", she stated. "While he has a big heart, he has little hockey talent but he loves the game more than anything. We registered for the camp but as I was standing here I saw some of the players coming in and know that they are very talented. Billy is a beginner and I don't want him to hold anyone back."

I turned to look at Billy who was standing there fully dressed in brand new gear and sporting what were obviously a brand new hockey bag and a new freshly but awkwardly taped stick. He was a sight to behold, barely holding back his excitement at maybe being allowed to participate in the camp and yet apprehensive about being rejected.

I quickly assured her that all would be fine and that I would assign one of the junior instructors to guide him for the week. With that she let out a huge sigh, a wide grin blossomed on Billy's face and they moved back into the lineup.

One of the instructors at the camp was a young lad named Bryce. He had thick blonde hair, piercing blue eyes and an athletic build. He was a real character and the guys that had played with him the past season affectionately called him the 'Ruskie'. While not one of the top players on the team, he had tons of attitude and always an eager smile.

He was standing off to the side chatting with the rest of the junior instructors. Getting his attention, I called him over and introduced him. I brought up Billy's mothers concern and asked if he wouldn't mind being Billy's personal instructor over the course of the week. Never one to back down from a challenge, Bryce nodded in agreement and put his hand on Billy's shoulder, directing him towards the dressing room. His mother watched him disappear down the sidelines of the rink and with an apologetic sigh turned to me and said,

"Thank you so much, this means the world to him!"

The first day always begins with the instructors hitting the ice first, taking a couple laps to get their legs and then coming back to the player's gate to welcome the kids onto the ice one by one. Bets had been made in the instructor's room on how many newcomers would forget to take off their skate guards before stepping out onto the ice. All who had witnessed or participated in hockey camps before knew from experience, what could happen. The skate guards offered no resistance to the ice, and their first step onto the surface would result in wildly flailing arms as their feet went out from underneath them and they ended up on their backsides. It was always good for some chuckles and this year didn't disappoint with several players taking the plunge. Thankfully,

Billy wasn't one of them and with new confidence they headed out on the freshly-cleaned ice.

The week went by as all hockey schools do with focus on skills and drills, then repeat over and over until I'm sure the kids were sick of them. During this time, Bryce had done a great job tutoring Billy and he had improved immensely. Every day he exuded more confidence.

The most important day of the week was Friday where a scrimmage would be held and players would be able to show off their newly acquired skills. Over the course of the week, the players on the ice had become familiar with Billy's story and had offered him support and encouragement. There were some very talented players participating in the camp and were eagerly awaiting Friday. They knew they would be divided up into equal groups, and while they were good friends, they were also competitors and they would be lined up opposite each other to see who would win the showdown.

Billy was apprehensive about the game and did not want to let anyone down. He had never scored a goal before and he admitted that it was the most important thing that he desired. Bryce and the other players told him not to worry. All would work itself out.

Friday finally arrived and there was certainly a new level of excitement in the air. Jerseys and players were divided up and a couple of the junior instructors were going to ref the game. Challenges were thrown back and forth with players razzing each other about who would win, who would score, and all of the other things that crazy friends could say to each other.

During the week, a young goalie, named Mike, had quickly become a clinic favorite. He was quick-witted, always smiling and always chirping the shooters when they couldn't score. He was a talented young man; almost as wide as he was tall, so he could back up his comments and threats.

He was calling for the win and as the game went on, it was apparent that he meant business, diving side-to-side, snatching shots out of the air and stopping almost all of the shots he faced. The game clock was counting down the third period and the score was tied. Billy had hardly touched the puck but worked as hard as he could to contribute to the play.

I was on the ice supervising, and offering support to him and others. With only a few minutes left on the clock, I overheard a conversation between a couple of the very talented boys on Billy's team.

"Hey guys, why don't we get Billy that goal?"

"Geez, really? The game is tied and we can win this!'

"It's just a scrimmage, not the Stanley Cup. Come on. Let's see what we can do for him."

Billy was on the ice at the time and was completely unaware of the conversation. At the next stoppage of play I saw one of the guys go up and talk to one of the defensemen on the other team. A quick couple blasts of the whistle got everyone back into position and the game was back on. I looked up at the clock when the whistle blew to signal the next stoppage of play and there was under a minute left. One of the players came up to me and asked if they could have a time out. Having heard the discussion between them earlier, I figured that they needed an opportunity to organize their plan.

Both teams went to their benches to discuss their strategy. I headed over to Billy's bench to hear what crazy plan they were concocting.

"Ok Billy, listen. We want you to go and stand at the far blue line right after the puck drops. We will get you the puck and all you have to do is skate hard to the net. Give it your best shot OK?"

Billy: "You want me to just skate to the other blue line and not help you out in our end?"

"Yes, yes, just do it okay!"

All the boys were staring at him as he mustered a weak reply "OK."

The best four boys on the team went out on the ice with Billy following behind not quite sure of what was going to happen. He didn't want to disappoint the guys and realized that with the clock down so low his chances of scoring were low. What I didn't realize was that the players on the other team were also in on it and agreed to help if they could. Mikey, our crazy little goalie on the other hand was having a tough go of it. His was a winner and hated giving up any goal no matter the cause.

Players lined up, the puck was dropped and Billy skated hard to the other blue line with his feet chopping into the ice and his arms flailing. The faceoff was won and with a quick flip in the air over the blue line, the puck was on its way to the other end. Just as Billy turned to look back, the puck arrived beside him and with new determination he took off heading for the goal. The defenceman, responsible for his side of the ice, conveniently lost an edge and this gave Billy a breakaway.

The only thing between Billy and his dream goal was now Mikey who had pushed out from his crease and was staring him down. It was a sight to behold, Billy out of control, the players yelling "Skate Billy Skate!" What typically happens when one is empowered with common sense is a time comes when one must make a judgment call. I looked at Billy and he looked out of control and coming in fast on the net. Mike was now considering his safety knowing from the week of practice that Billy's stopping technique left much to be desired.

At the last possible second, common sense kicked in and Mike bailed out of the net. The puck that Billy was pushed aggressively now slid into the opening and Billy, realizing he had scored, threw his arms in the arm in excitement almost at the same time as he realized that he would now have to stop. The resulting action of his arms sailing upwards, threw him off his feet and he crashed straight into the goal post with his feet split apart.

As all males know, the impact of a metal hockey post on a plastic jock strap and cup is no contest and there was a resounding "OOOOHH-HHH". Billy lay back on the ice with his arms over his head. I was following the play and when I arrived he had tears streaming down his face crying "My nuts, my nuts, my nuts!"

Mikey, being the smart ass that we knew him to be, was now bending over, thankful to be alive, and with his goal mask tilted up high on his head. He stated matter-of-factly: "Come on Billy you have to admit that was the funniest thing we have ever seen!"

By this time, all the kids were crowded around and grinning ear to ear.

I can confidently say, watching a young boy cry and laugh was worth every hour spent at the camp. The kids hoisted Billy to his feet cheering, "You got your goal Billy!" He had this grin on his face and while tears still ran down his face, we helped escort him over the players' gate where his mother was anxiously waiting to see if he was okay.

All he could muster was, "I scored Mom, I scored."

I looked back at the kids who had so graciously planned the event and they were slapping their sticks on the ice. All had grins on their faces and I'm sure that after all these many years that have passed, they still remember, as I have, the day when they sacrificed their goal of winning for something far more important.

DISCIPLINE

Simply put, we could define Discipline by the following: *"Do what needs to be done, the way it needs to be done, when it has to be done, every single time!"*

Discipline can bound many actions. It could be the foundation of how we act, how we train or how we play. I associate discipline with the saying: "Only perfect practice makes perfect!" Discipline is really what builds our core values. We are taught a certain behavior; why we do it, when we do it, how we do it and where we do it. Only through disciplined repetition can one make massive changes in behavior or skills. However, one needs to become aware of a disciplined action to truly appreciate how in grows and manifests in the other actions that one performs.

This story begins in my early twenties. I had decided that I wanted to learn a martial art and as luck would have it, a class opened up just a short distance from where I was working. It was a Japanese style called Shorei-kan and was being taught by a senior student from Japan, Sensei Koyabu, who had been chosen to bring the style to Canada. It was my first real foray into martial arts. I had taken a judo class at the local elementary school in Ft. Nelson when I was young but I didn't stick with it.

It was during the Bruce Lee era and stars of that period, such as Super Foot Wallace and Chuck Norris, had sparked my interest in the eastern arts. I can still remember the first day of class. The class entrance was at the back of a local school and as I walked inside I noticed that everyone's shoes were laid out against the back wall. A student was using a dust mop to sweep the floor, which looked perfectly clean already.

CORE VALUES

There was a small dressing area, where the boys and men changed into their training clothes, known as a Gi. The class was a blur after that. I was a white belt and was introduced to the various forms of punching and kicking. Technique was very important and we were informed that there were things to learn which we would be tested, when we were deemed ready to take the test for the next belt level.

The class finished and this time a different student grabbed the dust mop and proceeded to go over the floor again. Imagine my surprise. I worked in an ice rink where cleaning up the dressing room destruction was part of my everyday routine. Players and coaches were constantly using the dressing room walls for either target practice or backdrops for their practice plans. The floors and showers of the changing area were always used as their garbage dumping ground.

My everyday routine was a tedious cycle of cleaning the dressing rooms, letting the teams in, doing the ice, cleaning the dressing rooms, letting the teams, doing the ice. For twenty-eight years it was like ground hog day. Several times a year, out came the can of latex paint and all the walls would be refinished and away we would go again.

I even tried an experiment, I welded up several broom and shovel racks and placed them outside each dressing room to see if they would get used. While it made my job easier by not having to carry the darn things around from one end of the building to the other, it made little difference in the actions of players and coaches.

The philosophy behind the cleaning of the dojo was quite simple: respect the area that you train in, for without it, you can't get better. You had to bow to your partner before and after he kicked your butt. For without him, you would never know your weaknesses.

This disciplined approach developed good habits that carried on to your life. You ALWAYS, cleaned the floor before and after. You ALWAYS put your shoes to the side of the door. You ALWAYS bowed to you opponent both before and after training. Pressure to perform your techniques correctly was ever-present and reinforced without fail. We would stand in our basic stance and throw hundreds of kicks and punches and if they were sloppy, we did them over and over again.

It was a code developed over many hundreds of years. When compared with martial arts, hockey was, and still is, a new sport with little history of this kind of discipline and respect. I can't remember ever skating onto an outdoor rink where, after we were finished a game, we picked up a shovel and took the snow off for the next guy. It seemed that we would have to shovel before every time we wanted to play. I don't ever remember bowing or shaking the hand of the guy that just ran me over in open ice teaching me to play with my head up. Or how about a goaltender skating up to a player after a game and saying; "Thanks for scoring three goals over my glove, now I know that I have a weakness there".

My father believed in the discipline of training good habits, especially the polite ones. ALWAYS say please and thank you, ALWAYS hold the door open for people when proper to do so. ALWAYS use Mr. and Mrs. when greeting an adult. ALWAYS have a firm handshake because it was representative of your word.

I still remember the iceman in the old military hangar where we played when I was young. If you wanted to get on the ice early, you ALWAYS helped sweep the dressing rooms. He never faltered in his demands and it became second nature to grab a broom and shovel before we laced up our skates.

DISCIPLINE - TRAINING

Many of the examples that I have already written about in this book could fall under this category as well, but several memories stand out in my life, that sum up this concept better than others do. This is one of them.

The martial arts, of which there are many, are ancient disciplines dealing with self-defense. We could add a multitude of other benefits such as fitness, health, confidence, etc., but in the true sense of the meaning, "martial" means war, therefore the 'war arts' are really about living and not dying. The word, martial, was derived from Mars, the Roman god of war and one of the most important gods of Ancient Rome. He was responsible for everything military, from warriors to weapons. According to the Merriam-Webster Dictionary, it describes three meanings: 1. *"Of, relating to, or suited for war or a warrior"*, 2. *"Relating to an army or to military life"* and 3. *"Experienced in or inclined to war"*.

I was familiar with both Chinese and Japanese styles of marital arts, having studied Tai-Chi (Chinese), Shorei-Kan, and Judo (Japanese). Japanese martial arts also include weapons styles such as Kendo (way of the sword) and Kyudo (Way of the Bow). Chinese martial arts such as Kung fu also use hand-to-hand techniques as well as weapons.

The whole concept of disciplined training was a natural extension of perfecting technique. In early China for example, during the Battle of Changping, in 260 BC, the state of Qin drafted all males over fifteen years of age and they were sent into battle.

This meant that mastery of their techniques was critical to living or dying.

Many rules were developed as guidelines to follow, which were the underlying building blocks for good training habits. The following story deals with the philosophy of training.

Going back to my martial arts training days, as a brown or black belt, we were often invited over to our sensei's home for a cup of tea and some great conversation. During one of these informal gatherings, while we were kneeling around a large wooden table in the living room, he brought out a large bowl of pennies.

Our sensei never missed opportunities to teach lessons in technique or philosophy, and he had a great way of presenting a learning situation to his students that always burned the lesson into our minds. I assumed that this was going to be one of those teaching moments.

Setting it down in the middle of the table, he asked us to take a handful of pennies each, and by stacking them on top of each other, to build a tower as high as we could. We did as he requested, reaching into the bowl and grabbing a handful, before setting them down in front of us and beginning to build. Taking a quick look around, I could see that each one of us had a slightly different philosophy on how to go about this. While we all took care, some would carefully stack the pennies on top of each other one by one and others would throw on three of four in a row and then make slight adjustments as the tower increased in height. I was one of the 'place one, line it up the best I could, add another one' types.

Everyone was eager to do a good job; however, it only took a couple of minutes before stacks some started falling over with the rest to follow a short time later.

Sensei sat there sipping his tea, watching this all unfold and after the last stack had collapsed, he stood up and explained the purpose of the exercise.

"In your quest for achieving the highest possible tower, did you take the time to plan how you would go about doing that?" He paused and then continued; "Not planning to succeed means that you are already planning to fail."

CORE VALUES

"In your journey to become the best you can be, your foundation must be perfect." He stated: "In this test, the journey was represented by the tower of pennies. So therefore we must ask ourselves, which penny was the most important?"

He paused for a second to let the question have its full effect. "It's the bottom one of course, since all of the pennies need a strong base on which to stand. If we were to consider that each penny represents your skills in training, all must be built on the best base possible. How many of you took the time to select the perfect penny?"

I knew that I hadn't and as I had taken a quick look at others while building mine, I didn't notice anyone being so selective. No one else spoke up. Continuing on he added: "Which penny is the next most important?"

Now we grasped the concept, several chimed in: "The second one of course!"

He nodded his head in agreement then carried on. "Selecting the first penny is the most difficult part. This is because we have to view many to figure out which qualities we are looking for in a perfect penny. Does it have a flat surface? Are there any marks on it? Are the edges worn? After setting the standard for what is acceptable in the base penny, each penny that comes after, becomes easier, thereafter taking less and less time. We know that the height of the tower is dependent on the base and every penny after that. While we could always go back if the tower is not too high and replace a penny with a better one, we would find that if a time restriction was placed on the exercise, sooner or later we would be unable to go back if the tower got too high."

Again, we all nodded our understanding. He carried on with the second part of the lesson.

"While selecting pennies is important to the tower, we are missing something else." Again a deep pause: "Did any of you ask for assistance from the person next to or across from you?"

I knew that I hadn't and while building mine, I didn't hear anyone else talking. All agreed that they had not.

"Remember that from your view point, it is just that. The tower may look straight from your perspective, but from a different point of view, perhaps it is not. It is important to ask others' opinion on how your tower is aligned vertically. This is the same with our training. Without guidance in our training or along our life's journey, if we are afraid to ask questions about our technique, or who we are as individuals, we can only see from a selfish single viewpoint. We must not be afraid to ask others' opinion and take criticism."

"Would you like to try again?" He asked.

The exercise was much more careful and interactive this time. Everyone's tower reached greater heights and the person with the newest pennies had greater success. We all engaged those around us to ask their advice. It became clear that while we thought we were doing a great job, counsel from others demonstrated that we could make some more adjustments and improve our success.

That lesson has had a great impact on me. It has been one example that I have used many times over the years. I have used the creation of a puck tower to demonstrate, visually, the principles of building a strong foundation.

The highest tower that I have seen built in my studio was sixty-three pucks. I called that the NHL pile. Fifty-eight was the AHL pile, fifty-two was the next level below and so on. Each student understood that without careful selection and execution, coupled with advice from an objective observer, there was no way their career or, 'Puck Tower' would achieve full its potential.

The visual and philosophical lesson taught that day that has lived with me for all of these years.

ACCOUNTABILITY

This core value has probably received more print space than most of the others. Both coaches and players stress that being aware of your mistakes allows you to fix them faster. However, being accountable to oneself is different from being accountable to someone else. It is hard to admit a mistake out loud. It invites criticism and shows other that maybe you are not as good as they think you are.

I had to learn that being accountable to myself was a matter of pride, and being accountable to someone else meant that I was man enough to admit my mistakes. I was willing to do the job better next time and if I didn't know how, then I wouldn't be afraid to ask.

It was one of my first real summer jobs. One summer when I was sixteen, I was hired under a student-work creation program to provide career training for local youth. The job description was specific to commercial painting and while I had done some minor brush and roller work around my home, this was my first experience of doing so in a commercial setting. I was instructed to show up at a business address and meet the boss. He seemed like a great guy, greeting me with a warm smile, and a firm handshake. He took me through the job site, showed me where he wanted me to start, told me how he wanted the job done and then pointed me to where the paint, brushes and rollers were kept. He asked if I had any questions? Shaking my head I answered that I couldn't think of any and that he had explained himself very well. With that, he again shook my hand, welcomed me aboard the team and walked away.

It was a tedious job with lots of cutting in. That means that one has to use a lot of brushwork to paint around things before one could use the roller and pan. Several hours later, I felt that I had completed the first room to his standard and walked outside to see if he was available to check my work. He was discussing another job with who appeared to be the job foreman, and seeing me at the front door, he paused his conversation and walked to greet me.

"Would you mind coming and taking a look at how I've done? I asked.

"Sure, let's go take a look", he stated and walked into the area where I had been working. He took his time looking around the fixtures and after standing back to look for any roller streaks, walked over to me with a serious look on his face. "Looks not too bad for your first try, but I'm going to ask you to do it again."

I hurriedly agreed and apologized for not doing a good enough job. With that he smiled and walked out of the room. It was back to work. I started all over again, taking extreme care in making sure that I didn't miss any spots. I couldn't see that I had missed very much since at home my father was a stickler for doing things right, but after all I was just a rookie and what did I know. I just wanted to make a good impression on my first day.

It was easier this time of course but I made sure that everything was perfect on all the cuts and roller work, at least to my expectations.

Finishing, I again walked out the front door to see if I could find him. The job foreman was smoking a cigarette and I asked if he knew where the boss was. "Yeah, just around back," he replied.

As I was about to walk around the corner of the building to find him, he appeared abruptly in front of me as if he had somehow anticipated that I would be finished and had come back to check.

As he walked through the front door with me trailing behind, he questioned over his shoulder, "How do you feel about the job you did this time?"

I told him that I really took care and tried to get everything the way he wanted.

"Good!" he replied and with that, he again set about checking on my work. After some very tense moments on my part he turned and said: "Close but not good enough, please do it again".

My shoulders slumped, because I didn't want to disappoint my boss on the first day of my job and secondly, it was tedious work. I wanted to be further ahead and didn't want to get stuck in the same room all day.

He looked at me and then broke into a smile. "Hey look, I'm kidding Son, the job looks very good, but I just wanted to make a point. Remember that this is my business and your work and attitude towards your work impact what people think of me. If your works sucks, then my reputation as a painting contractor sucks. I need to know that your work is done very well and that you need to be accountable for that." He paused and then added "Any time you do something new, it's going to take a while before you can speed through things without compromising the job quality. Take your time and set your standards high. Before long you'll be whipping through these jobs in no time. Any questions?"

"No", I replied and inside I was thinking; "Does he know my dad?", since I seemed to remember a similar lesson at a hockey practice years earlier.

With that, he asked me to carry on in the next room and left. He only checked my work one more time after that. Three years later I was hired to lead a painting crew of eight employees, commissioned to complete the painting of a well-head for an oil and gas company.

It was a lesson that stuck with me for many years and it was one that I used often, but in different guises.

Lessons in accountability come in many forms and the one that follows will be familiar to most coaches and players.

I had taken on the task of coaching a youth spring team of thirteen-year-olds. We had been together for approximately a month before we agreed we'd enter a tournament in South Surrey, B.C. They were a great group of kids who worked hard every practice and the coaching staff all agreed that it would be a great opportunity to test what they had learned.

I arrived at the rink early to scout one of the other games. I checked the dressing room assignments and after standing at the end of the rink to catch a couple shifts of our possible competition, I decided to head down and check the change room.

It was a complete disaster with Gatorade bottles, tape balls and other litter all over the floor and shower. I exited, walked down to the end of the dressing room hallway hoping that the iceman would have left a broom and shovel close by. I wasn't disappointed. Grabbing them, I headed back into the room and proceeded to sweep the floors and shower area. I was halfway through when a of couple players walked in and saw me sweeping up the garbage.

"Why are you cleaning the dressing room, Coach? It isn't our mess." One asked.

I paused, and of course made the obvious comments:

"First of all," I started, "would you like to get changed in this? Secondly," I continued, "Our team will be the last to leave and with this mess all over the floor, who do you think the next team, coming in, will think is responsible?"

"Third and final comment, don't you have a standard that you want people to remember you by?"

They stood there thinking for a moment, grinned and then nodded in agreement with what I had to say. With that they placed their bags on top of the benches and proceeded to help. Needless to say, after the game, they all pitched in and made sure that the room was spotless for the next team.

It's always easy for a coach to state the case and then supervise to make sure that the players follow suit. It really matters when a supervisor or coach is not there and they perform above expectations. This was the case weeks later in a different tournament that I couldn't attend. Tim, one of the associate-coaches, called me after the tournament. He commented that I would be very proud of the boys explaining that he had walked into the dressing room and the boys were picking up garbage and sweeping the floors. When he asked what they were doing, their comments were the same as tournament before. "We don't want to change in this garbage and who do you think they'll blame for the mess?"

"Accountability is possessing the ability to answer to, and be responsible for, one's actions".

Lessons learned and lessons passed on.

CONFIDENCE

There is story in this book from Randall Johansen - the father of two professional hockey players. In the story he explained his feelings on how instilling confidence in his older son, Ryan, led him through some tough times in junior, enabling him to make the NHL. Jeremy Rupke, the founder of How to Hockey had some great comments as well. It is so important for coaches and parents to instill confidence in their children: confidence that they can both perform what is expected and the confidence to overcome obstacles.

This story had its humble beginnings about eight years ago, inside my training studio in North Delta. Earlier in the day, I had received a call from a woman who was looking for some shooting training for her son, wondering if I could squeeze him in later that afternoon. I replied that indeed I could, since I had just received a cancelation, opening up a six p.m. slot.

When she arrived, it was quite apparent that she was a professional of some sort, dressed in expensive grey slacks, a fashionable top and a dress jacket. Her son looked very nervous and trying to put him at ease, I walked over to the studio entrance with my hand extended, to welcome him to his first class. He introduced himself as "James" as did his mother, saying "Mary" with an extended hand.

We proceeded with some small talk as is customary at the first introduction class. Where did he play? What position? What shooting skills was he trying to improve? I asked him age and he responded; "I'm twelve".

I asked him to take a couple of warm-up shots, more to get him comfortable and to take a quick look to see what mistakes may show up.

His mother took a seat on the couch located at the front of the class, watching in earnest as he nervously approached the shooting area.

I had recently taken out the hockey net that was positioned at the end of the studio, because it posed an injury liability. A couple days before, a Midget player had taken a shot that had caromed off the cross bar directly back towards the front of the class, zipping over the head of his mother as she bent forward to put her coffee mug on the table. It certainly woke everyone up and there was no question that I had to remove it. As a result, I had positioned a specially designed shooting tarp with the customary goaltender and the front face of the posts behind him where the net used to be.

His first couple of shots hit the tarp with barely a sound, the puck not having much velocity, and spinning end over end as he released it. I heard his mother sigh and watched his shoulders drop. It was evident that she expected a lot out of him and he was quite aware that he was disappointing her.

I have always found it interesting viewing, to observe the interactions between parents and their children in a learning environment where the techniques are challenging. I could immediately see that this relationship was strained and that it would be a long hour for the young lad.

I walked over to where he was slowly readying another puck for delivery. I had a smile on my face as I spoke. "Look, everyone feels nervous in the first class. The important point to remember is that my job is to make small simple adjustments to help you. If you're worried about making a mistake, then how can you ever learn something new? Relax, trust me. Improving your shot is quite simple. Why don't you start again and let's take it one step at a time."

This certainly helped and his face lightened up, eager to fix his technique. The one-hour class went by quickly. Aside from the occasional sigh from his mother when it took him too long to execute a technique, or a shot seemed insignificant, he said he felt better when I asked.

We put away the pucks, readying the studio for the next student, and did a quick review. The, I sent them on their way with a firm handshake and a brief; "I look forward to seeing you again."

Later in the week, I received another call from Mary questioning whether I had room the following week to squeeze him in. She felt that he had improved and James had mentioned that he would like to come and see me again.

The day arrived and they both entered promptly on the hour. He greeted me with his hand extended and after shaking hands, proclaimed that he had done some practicing since I saw him last. He was hoping that I would notice the improvements. His mother, again dressed quite professionally, walked over and took up residence on the studio couch.

The class started similarly to the first one, a quick warm-up then down to business. I could see that Mary was watching each shot intently. When James struggled for a few, she would again sigh and tense visibly. His technique had improved but he was struggling with his wrist action. After five or six attempts with little success she blurted out: "Come on James, you can do better than that. Focus!"

Again, James shoulders sagged and it was as if someone had knocked the wind out of him. From his reaction I could tell that this interaction was common. I put my hand on his shoulder and quietly asked if he would do me a favor.

"Would you mind stepping outside of the studio for a moment? I would like have a quick chat with your mother."

He nodded, and laying down his stick and gloves he quickly exited the room. Mary had an inquisitive look on her face as I approached.

"I usually don't ask personal questions but would you mind telling me your occupation?"

"No problem" she responded. "I'm a lawyer for a firm down town."

"Would you mind if I asked you a couple questions?"

"Of course not" she answered with a smile. "How can I help you?"

CORE VALUES

"Correct me if I'm wrong but I'm assuming that your occupation has very high expectations with the most important being to win cases?"

"Yes, that is the expectation of our clients." she agreed then added. "But I'm not sure I get your point?"

"Well, it's quite simple actually. I'm sure that when you were studying to be a lawyer you made mistakes. It was called learning and only through that process did you arrive at where you are today: great case study habits, very precise case presentation and cross examination habits."

"Yes, I can agree with that" she stated.

"Then let's look at your son. I have done this for many years and I can easily see that he suffers from a lack of confidence. Would you agree?"

"Yes, he's always had that problem. We have been working on that but it is a slow process."

"Did you ever think that you were helping to create the problem?" I asked "Every time he makes a mistake, I hear you sigh and when he takes a little too long to learn a technique, you get quite anxious."

I quickly carried on. "He is young and like you in the beginning of your career, he needs the type of encouragement that helps push one through those tough times when struggling with a case or him a technique. Learning new things can be quite challenging and if one is always confronted with negativity, one's enthusiasm for the activity disappears and one either quits or rebels."

"Of course this is just my opinion." I continued: "I understand that sometimes one needs to refocus, but what I don't see is your response to the positive things that he does. Sometimes those improvements are very small and the observer is the one who needs to focus and see those minute changes. It is my job to criticize and then to encourage. You're actually making my job a lot harder and I can see that his excitement to learn is starting to fade. Would you mind encouraging a little more often? I'll provide a quick wink as a clue if you need one."

With that, she thanked me for my feedback, just as James came back into the room. He had an inquisitive look on his face.

"All good James, your mother and I were just discussing your hockey career and how much you were looking forward to having a rocket shot."

With that he smiled, recovered his equipment from where he had left them and the class began anew.

His mother observed the rest of the class quietly, much to her son's surprise I think, but it was a refreshing change. She actually complimented him on a cue from me: "Well done James," she exclaimed with a smile.

He seemed to attack the new techniques with a little more conviction. Time flew by with the class ending with the usual cleanup, summary and goodbyes and off they went.

I wasn't sure whether they would return for more sessions but a couple days later I received another request from Mary. Apparently James was excited after the last class since he felt like he had overcome some of the tougher obstacles.

They showed up as expected and this time Mary asked James if she could speak with me alone for a minute. "Sure," he responded and turned and left the room.

"I did a lot of thinking after our conversation. In my business, failure is not well received and we have to work incredibly hard to prepare for cases and try to eliminate any chance of error. It is a tough business if one wants to be successful. I had forgotten all the work that I had put in and it was something that I was passionate about. I wanted to be a lawyer and make a difference. I loved the research, the debating, but had forgotten that I had to learn and learn from my mistakes. I just wanted to thank for you bringing me back to my senses."

She extended her hand, turned and exited the room to retrieve James from the entranceway.

The class was different that time. She assumed her usual position on the couch, but this time she had brought in a book. James, feeling the improvements from last time excelled a little faster. Occasionally, she would look up, smile and voice encouragement and then return to her reading. I saw them several times after that. I saw an eagerness return to James' actions. He walked into the room with more confidence, recognizing his newfound skills and eager to learn new ones.

Parents, teachers and coaches have such a powerful influence over children and I often see the negative effects of over-criticizing. I can see how the ability to learn and the enjoyment of learning are directly related to confidence. There is so much to learn and so little time to do so. It is important to provide a positive environment that instills confidence and doesn't destroy it.

TEAMWORK

Team work has been a major theme among the contributors to this book. Shawn Horcoff, Mike Johnston, Adam Burish all explained how strongly connected teams win championships. Teamwork within families also builds a strong, healthy home environment. This was mentioned by Patrick Marleau, where teamwork on the farm is critical to its success.

My father tried to instill the values of teamwork in me around the home. I was expected to do little chores to earn my keep as he used to say. This is one of the many lessons he threw my way.

My father was a man who never yelled. He could raise his voice, give you that stern look and make his voice increase a couple of decibels but he would never yell.

One Sunday morning he had made my favorite pancakes and syrup. He used to take a bottle of bland Bees syrup, add some brown sugar and some cinnamon, bring it to a boil and whip up a concoction that made everything taste that much better.

I was an avid comic book reader. On this particular day, I was enjoying a full stomach of pancakes and syrup, sipping on a fresh cup of hot chocolate and half-way through my favorite Batman comic when my father asked me to take out the garbage.

"Okay Dad, just one minute okay" I replied, it was getting interesting and I didn't want to lose the train of thought the comic was heading in.

A couple minutes later, my father asked again; "Son, please take out the garbage now."

"Okay Dad, just one minute okay," I answered, my concentration completely on the pictures and not on the task I was given.

"Ron, TAKE OUT THE GARBAGE NOW!" he yelled. The volume of his voice scared the heck out of me. The comic flew out of my hand, I almost fell out of my chair and I jumped to my feet. I had never heard my father yell like that and it really startled me. I ran over, grabbed the garbage from beside the kitchen counter and raced outside. I dropped it in the metal garbage just outside and raced back into the house.

My father was sitting in his favorite La-Z-Boy recliner in the living room about eight feet from the kitchen table. To his left was our couch, which was positioned under the picture window looking out into our front yard.

He motioned for me to join him, pointing at the couch.

I sat down, and turned slightly to face him.

"Did that shock you Son?" he asked as he gave me that steely look of his.

"Yes Dad," I answered: "You have never yelled at me like that before. It kind of scared me."

"How did it make you feel?" he continued.

"I don't like it when you yell Dad. It makes me feel bad."

"It's not nice when people yell at you is it?" He continued. "I would like you to remember that I asked you three times to take out the garbage and all you had to do was put your comic down the first time, take it out and all would have been done."

"What did it take, one minute of your time, if that? People will always ask you to do things and sometimes it's not your time that matters, it's theirs. When you're asked to do something, just get it done. Be the guy that gets work done when asked to do so. It may be an inconvenience to you when it's asked, but in the time it takes to complain about it, the work could have been done. Do you understand?"

"Yes, sorry Dad. I won't do that again." I replied

"Good," was his answer and with that motioned that it was OK to go and finish my comic book. I came to realize that simple requests that are acted upon quickly make people happy. This is especially the case when coaches ask players to perform simple tasks such as: "Keep pucks deep", "Put pucks on net", "Clear pucks off the glass and out", or "Pick up your check coming into the zone".

Of all the lessons on teamwork that my father taught me, this was perhaps the harshest. While having nothing to do with hockey, it made me realize the importance of working together to accomplish a goal. It was in the early spring and I had just turned twelve years old. It was at a time and I was at an age where I was certainly more interested in my own self-indulgence than the petty responsibilities around the home. The snow had barely left after the winter thaw when I had my eyes opened wide.

I had come home one day from school and when I walked into the porch I noticed that there was a suitcase just inside the door. I continued on inside the house, where my father was seated in his favorite chair smoking a cigarette.

"Are you or Mom going on a trip?" I asked.

"Not us, but you are" was his reply.

I was shocked at his answer and couldn't grasp what he was saying. I had no plans to travel and no one in the extended family had asked me to go anywhere that I knew of.

"Excuse me?" I pressed. "What do you mean I'm going on a trip?"

"Let me explain" he offered and with that he got up and walked to where the suitcase was. He picked it up, walked it outside and sat it down on the step.

"Well Son" he exclaimed, "It seems to me over the past month or two that you've figured things out; you've become a man. You've taken it upon yourself to go about your own business and let the chores around the house and yard slide. Apparently you're ready to do your own thing now. I had to go to work when I was ten and you're past that age so I think you're ready to move on now. So which direction will it be?"

With that he pointed south "Fort St. John" and then he pointed north "Whitehorse?" "One can always find work there. You're a capable young man and I'm sure that you will find a job".

With that he turned to look at me. "Well Son, what do you have to say about that?"

I was in shock and disbelief that my father would pack my clothes, put the suitcase outside and then wish me a great future, especially at twelve years old.

"I don't want to go Dad." I answered

"Well, we had better have a chat and then, I'll let you decide what you want to do," he started "You see, Son, this is a family and as a family we all work together. Your mother goes to work as do I and we put food on the table and clothes on your back. All we ask is that you contribute. We know that you have school, but you need to share in the family responsibilities. You don't do your chores, you come home and read all day, you take off with your friends and that's not how we work together. I tell you what" then he paused. "We will keep this suitcase packed for a couple days and then you can tell me what you want to do, agreed?"

With that he instructed me that I could take the suitcase back into the house.

I was more than happy to comply and with that, went to my room to think about what had just happened. Of course my father was right. I had become a little too self-absorbed and had neglected my tasks in the yard and around the house. After that I didn't need to be told. If my father was out in the yard, after I got home from school, I picked up a shovel if he was working in the garden or just assisted in whatever he was doing. After a while he would turn, give me a smile, thank me for my help and tell me to run along and see my friends.

My mother never found out about the incident that I know of. It was never mentioned again. It was a lesson that hit hard but was a valuable lesson nonetheless.

This lesson stuck with me for the rest of my life. However, while it made me realize the importance of team responsibilities, it never really taught me the value of how shared responsibilities, during times of grueling competition, create bonds of friendship.

That lesson happened while I was coaching the Richmond Sockeyes, who played in the Pacific Junior Hockey League (PJHL). They were a hardworking group of players that we had assembled with the objective of winning a championship. Some of the players had played for me on the Bantam AAA North Delta team that won the National title in 1999. They had matured another four years and had brought their great leadership and experience to the team.

Others were very young; fifteen years of age and they had played for a winning organization, the Burnaby Winter Club. Together we had a collection of mature talent with championship experience, younger players that had experience in winning, and a collection of players that hated losing since the Sockeyes had not won a major championship in several years.

This set the stage for an interesting year. The owner at that time, Mr. Ken Kirby, was a businessman who loved a challenge, had impeccable character and treated all the players with the outmost respect. It was a first-class organization from the trainers to the team staff. All the players had to do was compete since everything else was well taken care of.

It was a long, hard-fought season with the league being very tight. I was trying to make a last minute trade with the team that was in first place. At that time we were ranked as fifth in a league filled with older players. I was trying to make a trade for a rookie forward who was a former member of the Delta championship team in exchange for my team captain. He had asked to be traded and we were willing to comply with his request. It was his final season as a senior vet and, as is customary in junior hockey, if a team is not in a position to win a championship, trades would be made to accommodate so that they could finish their career on a winning note.

Our captain was also our top defenceman. We had a forward on the team named Jason Garrison, a skilled left hand power forward whom I had used several times back on the point. He was very poised under pressure and it was apparent that he could handle the position if need be. The general manager and I met with him prior to the trade being finalized and discussed the options that were before us. We needed a quality defenceman to make up for losing our captain. He had played all year on the left side but I guaranteed him that if he would go back and anchor up the team's backend, he would get a lot of ice time, probably more than as a winger. It was stressed that the trade would not go through unless he made the decision and we were in no way forcing him to go back, if he didn't want to. The general manager and I gave him a couple days to make his decision.

Luckily for us Jason agreed to play on the back end, our captain was traded and David joined our team roster.

That year we pulled off an upset, going through several overtime rounds to end up facing the team that we had traded our captain to, the Delta Ice Hawks. It was a very tough, gritty series and after the dust settled, we managed to pull off a victory, winning the league playoff championship. Jason proved to be an invaluable addition to our defensive corps and David anchored the specialty team department being our number one penalty killer.

That year, we had to travel to Vancouver Island to play the winner of both the interior and the Island divisions for the provincial championship (Cyclone Taylor Cup). The round robin was everything that it was billed to be, a tough head-to-head dogfight. Our character guys came through, battling hard through the round robin to end up in second place. This meant that we would have to play the Campbell River Storm in the final. They had won the Island Championship and were a highly skilled and capable team with a great coaching staff.

Mr. Kirby arranged a team supper the night before the final. Parents and players were socializing with the usual antics taking place; the 'shoe check', and chirping back and forth. For those unfamiliar with hockey, the 'shoe check' is where a team member will crawl around under the tables and put something disgusting on the top of someone's shoe. The Captain will call out 'shoe check' and then everyone looks to see who got nailed. It's all in good fun and is great for taking the edge off the nerves before a championship game.

At the end of the supper, when everything had calmed down and the plates had been cleared, I stood up to address the team. After a few words of thanks to the ownership and staff that helped get us there, I got down to the main topic: teamwork.

"Boys, we have come a long way and it has not been easy season." I started: "We have battled through a lot of adversity together and this has brought us closer together as a team. I'm not going to preach to you guys about hard work and sacrificing your body to make a play in the final tomorrow. You have already been doing that. However, instead I would like to focus on the guy next to you. If you look around, you can see great teammates and great friends that have battled together. I am proud to stand here with you and applaud your accomplishments. However, there is work to do ahead of us. I would like you to consider what losing the game tomorrow means. You guys have fought together side-by-side for a season. No one expected us to be here and yet here we are.

"Battling together has built a bond of friendship between all of you and if we lose tomorrow, this bond of friendship will be over. You will all go your separate ways. However, if we win tomorrow we get a chance to practice, play and be together for three more weeks. I don't care if we win, I'm proud of our accomplishment and with our effort; there is no shame in losing. I would like you to look around and see if the bond of friendship that you guys share is worth fighting for. I think it is, but in the end it's up to you."

We toasted the tournament success so far and then headed off to catch some much-needed rest and prepare for the game the next day.

We ended up winning that game by one goal. The Storm was pushing hard in the last half of the third period. We were hanging on more with determination and effort than with skill. In the final seconds of the game, a great sacrificial play by Johnny Crang, one of our gritty, hardworking defensemen, killed off the clock. He went down on both knees to block a slap shot, staring the shooter down face-to-face, and taking the rocket shot into his stomach. The Storm pressed hard, we regained possession, and cleared the puck out of the zone ensuring the win.

After all of the cheering and celebrations, the players collected all of their equipment and reported to the dressing room. Reporters came in to talk to the players about what they had accomplished. When asked how they managed to pull off the win, their answers were, "We actually didn't care about winning, and we just wanted to stay together as a team for another month".

The season ended three weeks later with a Silver Medal at the Western Canadian Junior B Championships. It was a hard-fought game that we lost in overtime. It was one of the finest junior hockey playoff games that I had been a part of. The score changed hands back and forth, no quarter was given, and no one quit on either team. Finally, a rimmed puck went off a referee's skate, out into the slot and was hammered home. It was a shocking end to a great hockey game that players on both teams were proud to have been a part of.

I will always remember the potential of a true team and the adage that describes them; "One that fights together, stays together". Many of them have become lifelong friends and still get together to catch up and talk about life and their hockey conquests.

POLITENESS

I am sure that every mother and father makes sure that their sons and daughters say their 'please and thank you'. My father was big on; 'Excuse me, Pardon me, I'm sorry, and Hello Mr......,' I was constantly reminded that to act in any other way was totally unacceptable. I tell the players that I coach that when they act this way; they are working on being professional. It seems sometimes that the word 'polite' is almost viewed as a weakness around young kids today. This way, I give them the out to mimic the players that have been gracious enough to help me with this book. This story is a reminder to me that my father's values are never too far behind me.

With the weekly grocery list in my father's hand, we jumped into his old Ford Custom 500 and headed up to the local IGA. As a ten-year-old, I didn't want to miss this opportunity to walk around and add some much needed things to the list such as chocolate ice cream, orange popsicles, marshmallows for roasting on the natural gas stove we had, and perhaps a box of Kellogg's Captain Crunch. I didn't often get what I wanted but I figured that if I were not along for the ride, then there would be no way possible that I would even stand a chance of getting some of my favorites.

We pulled into the parking lot and I don't think that the car had come to a full stop before I leapt out and headed for the front door. By the time I reached the entrance, my father was in hot pursuit having just exited the car. I grabbed the handle, whipped the door open and was skipping through when I heard a loud whistle behind me. That could only be one person and I stopped in my tracks, turning to see what my father wanted. A woman was just coming through the door and he was right behind her.

"Get over here right now!" He demanded: "What the heck were you thinking?"

The woman was just inside the door now and she seemed a little embarrassed by what my father was saying.

I was obviously unaware of what had happened and as a result, I had a puzzled look on my face. "You closed the door in Mrs. Thompson's face. Apologize young man!" He exclaimed.

"It's alright Jim, he's just a boy." She said.

"No it's not and it's totally unacceptable. He should know better." With that he gave me that look and asked one more time: "Apologize, Son."

Being hell-bent on getting to the ice cream aisle, I had neglected to see anyone around me and as such had opened the door and let it close on Mrs. Thompson, who was just behind me.

"I'm really sorry Mrs. Thompson, I was very rude."

With that she answered: "Thank you very much for your apology, young man," and she headed on into the store after giving my father an approving nod.

"Don't ever let that happen again, Son," was all that he said, giving me one more stern look before he reached into his pocket for the grocery list, heading over to where the grocery buggies where kept.

HONESTY

In an earlier part of this book, Bill Fordy expounded on the virtues of honesty in policing. Being honest is a big part of accountability.

My father, as you will have noticed by now, was never one to let a lesson slip through his fingers.

Back when I was young, the corner store used to sell nickel bags of candy, a tantalizing treat after a hard day at school. My father used to give me an allowance here and there for doing chores around the yard. It might have been a couple of quarters or even a dollar if I was lucky. Inevitably, it always went to my favor comic book, ice cream or a nickel bag of my favorite treats.

One day, I was poking around in my pockets looking for a nickel so that I could head up to the corner store. After some thorough digging, I found a couple deep in my jacket pocket. As I came of my bedroom after retrieving my jacket, I noticed a couple of quarters and a dime, sitting on the corner of the bookshelf that separated our kitchen from our living room. I couldn't believe my luck. I had enough money for a couple of nickel bags, with these coins I could buy my favorite comic book as well.

Thinking nothing of it, I threw them into my pocket and off I went.

Late in the afternoon, I was sitting at the kitchen table when my father returned home from work. He gave me a pat on the head and a "Hello" as he walked by to take a seat in his favorite recliner. I answered a muted "Hello" back. I was too engaged in the story that I was reading to give him my full attention.

CORE VALUES

A couple minutes later, I heard my father call out my name, asking me if I had seen the coins that he had left on the shelf.

"Yes, Dad": I replied, "I used them to buy my comic book this afternoon."

"Hmmmm" Was all that came out, and then he was quiet for a few minutes. "Son, would you mind coming over here and sitting beside me on the couch?"

Remembering the 'Take out the garbage lesson', I was eager to comply.

The lecture started in his usual methodical way.

"Were they your coins?" He asked.

"No." I replied.

"Hmmmmm" Again: "Did you know where they came from?"

"No, I just saw them there."

"Hmmmm" Again and this time he nodded his head a little with a slight frown.

"Okay, so they weren't yours and yet you felt that you could take them, correct?"

"Well actually, I didn't really think of that, Dad." I got the sense now that I had screwed up and it was certainly the coins.

"I know that you weren't thinking about it but perhaps you should have. They didn't belong to you so why did you feel that you could take them?"

Yup, I was in trouble; how much I wasn't sure but there I was caught red-handed not thinking. But I thought that maybe I could angle my way out of the situation.

"Well Dad, you guys weren't home so I thought that you or Mom wouldn't mind"

"Makes sense doesn't it, Son." He rationalized along with me, or so I thought. "No one is around so you take it now and ask later. Was that the plan?"

"I guess so. I just forgot when you came home." I answered.

"Well that's how it all starts, Son, one coin at a time."

Now I was puzzled; was I right or wrong? Not sure where Dad was going with this one, I decided to keep my mouth shut.

"You see," He continued: "Let's say that a couple of hours went by and your mother or I hadn't said anything and you forgot to tell us. A little more time goes by and now you notice that nothing has been said. You've seen us walk by the bookshelf several times and we must have noticed that they weren't there. Then you start to think that too much time has gone by and now you feel awkward saying something and then you start to rationalize that it's OK because we didn't say anything. Because we didn't say anything, we are okay with it. You following me, Son?"

I hadn't been saying anything and he wanted to make sure that I was getting the full message.

"I think so."

"Okay, let me continue, then. So a couple of days from now, you find yourself in the same situation, you look over and you see more coins on the shelf, maybe instead of sixty cents (hey, how did he know it was sixty cents? My brain suddenly woke up), it's one dollar. Same thing happens, you put it in your pocket because now you think that we left it there for you on purpose since we didn't say anything about the sixty cents (there is that darn sixty cents thing again I thought, now realizing that something was fishy). A week goes by and now there's two dollars on the shelf, what do you think starts to happen?"

I had this dumbfounded look on my face and I think that he realized I had figured something out.

"Not sure, Dad." I replied. I figured that it was easier to stay neutral on this one.

"OK, let's look at this from another angle then. Let's say that I didn't say anything about it this time, but a couple of days go by and there are more coins left, which you take. This time I notice and I ask you where the money went. You reply, 'Well I borrowed it, Dad' and I get upset so you apologize and everything is okay with that and nothing more was said."

I just nodded since the story was getting deep.

"Well Son, it gets bigger and bigger and before you know it, you start taking other things that you want and then you sit back and see what happens. There's an old saying, Son that I'd like you to remember; 'It's easier to ask for forgiveness than to ask for permission'. Understand what that means?"

I was thinking about what he had just said and started to make the connection.

"So, I will make myself very clear. Taking something that isn't yours is stealing – plain and simple. You knew that the coins were not yours, so what makes you think that it's okay to take them? Take now and maybe apologize later and all will be forgotten is not the road I think you need to start going down. Do I make myself clear?" He took a deep look into my eyes and then added:

"Don't EVER let that happen again, unless you ask first. Do you understand?"

"Yes, Dad I understand clearly."

"Okay, well since you spent the money already, you can go out and cut the grass and we will call it even this time."

I just nodded my head. As I went outside to get the lawn mower I marveled at how he'd planned that. I was set up, there was no question, but I got the message and it was very clear. To this day, I couldn't take a penny that wasn't mine. It stays on the counter.

During the many years that I have been coaching, the one thing that I stress is honesty from my players. I have met with parents many times and have expressed the following to them.

"Kids tend to explain their actions in a way that makes them feel comfortable around you. I can guarantee that most of the time, the discussions that I have with them on why they are not getting ice time, or why they are not playing on special teams, will be completely different from what they tell you. If you confront me about this as a parent, then you had better be ready to deal with the truth and this is how that works. I will call a meeting that includes your child, since I believe that players must learn to be accountable for their actions. You will explain your side of the story that they have given to you and then I will look them directly in the eye. If what you say to me is different than from I have told your child, then they will be sat, cut or traded immediately. "

I had one season where I decided to go back to minor hockey, after retiring in 1999 to coach Junior. I wanted to give back to younger players and had brought on board several of my junior hockey players to act as assistants.

The season tryouts started with a bizarre occurrence, which should have forewarned me about the year ahead. It was during the Atom AAA tryouts for this same team.

I was running the ice session when I looked over towards the corner where the drill had started and there was a player, and this is not an exaggeration, lying on his back moving his arms up and down. I quickly skated over and asked him if he was OK? Looking up replied that he was okay and he was making a snow angel. I have to admit that it was the first time in my life, at a rep tryout, that I had witnessed such a thing. I asked him to get up and to point out his parent in the stands to which he eagerly complied. The father, just witnessing what his son had done, shook his head in bewilderment and then walked down to talk to me at the bench.

"You obviously saw what I saw." I stated: "Was there any reason for him doing that? You know that this ice session is a rep tryout meaning 'representation' of the association at the highest level and of course he is representing you."

The father, obviously embarrassed at what had just occurred said that his son hadn't done much training during the summer and he thought that he would pay the tryout fee for the extra ice, just to get him going. He never really expected his son to make the team.

I have pondered this many times over the years. Knowing my father and how he demanded hard work and respect and what would have happened to me if I ever attempted such an act, I was truly baffled.

Once the team was selected, I met with the parents prior to the start of the season and explained the philosophy of hard work, attitude and attendance. "We will NOT play favorites and if a player is being sat, it is either due to his conduct on the ice, on the bench, or his lack of effort. All we care about is accountability and effort. Winning is NOT important here, it is about working hard, being a good teammate and getting better every day."

Of course all parents nodded in agreement with the commitment to explain what was discussed with their son. We had several talented hockey players on the team and as with ten-year-olds, there are different views on what hard work is and what is not. We also talked to the players in the dressing room, sharing what was explained to their parents about what was acceptable, and what was not, both on and off the ice.

Before practices, which were held after school, parents would drop off their kids and then head down to the local pub, which was one block away from the rink. Kids and coaches would hurriedly get ready and try to get out on the ice a few minutes early to get some extra practice time in. This usually meant shooting pucks and chasing each other around. After ten minutes or so of chaos, the structured practice would start with some warm-up stickhandling and passing drills. It became evident early in the season that several players had a different concept about what working hard actually was.

The coaching staff all agreed that talk was cheap and that several of kids didn't understand that putting in an effort was important. It was discussed that perhaps they didn't understand, conceptually, what hard work was. We took time to explain that if they were close to the puck when the opposition had control, they had to skate hard and put pressure on the puck carrier. If they were caught deep in the zone and the other team broke out, they had to skate as hard as they could back to their positions of support. When they changed lines between whistles, they had to skate hard to the bench.

After explaining what we wanted and expected, we then decided we would sit a player for a shift or two that didn't do as we had instructed. All of the players had acknowledged that they knew what was expected of them and knew what the consequences would be. We initiated this disciplinary action and it wasn't long before our team manager started to hear grumblings from some parents. I asked the manager to call a meeting with the parents to discuss what was happening.

I still clearly remember standing in front of the parents and asking; "I hear that some of you feel that the coaches are playing favorites?" No one replied. "I do remember talking to you all at the start of the season and explaining what was going to happen. If the kids didn't work hard in practice or games there would be consequences. This is a team game and everyone has responsibilities to their teammates."

"This was explained in detail with them both at practice and in the dressing room before games. I realize that most of you don't stay around and watch the practices first hand, so you don't get to see your son take a drill off or see the lack of effort. However, you all watch the games and I'm curious to know your philosophy on effort. Since when is it acceptable to float around and not put in any effort? Is there something that I'm missing perhaps? We explained in depth to each child how we defined hard work, which we kept simple, citing only three examples that they would be judged by. I assume, then, that they never explained this to you, as we asked them to do."

"This meeting was called so that you could express your concerns. I have explained what we have been doing and why, so if you have any questions please feel to bring them up now. Thank you."

No one had anything to say. It was a very strange exchange. What I came to realize in that moment was a very important concept. Most parents assumed that the more skilled players were just that, skilled, and this meant that while they were more skilled, they did not see the effort that each was putting in. What I have found in my life is that the harder I work the more success I achieve. Skill is exactly the same. The weaker kids, due in part to a lack of effort, do not excel as the others do, and instead of attacking the principle of "Hard work beats talent that doesn't work", they sit back and spectate. The parents hadn't even noticed when we actually sat the better kids.

This lack of honesty between the player and the parent drove me crazy. This past year of coaching has posed the same issues. These players were thirteen and fourteen years of age and not ten or eleven. I had assumed that they understood the value of hard work and commitment, of playing as a team and being accountable.

One player on the team had a poor work ethic. While having some skill, he had difficulty applying it and when things didn't go well, his effort dropped off considerably. It became almost a pattern, where a lack of effort would result in distraction. This would then lend itself to a very poor practice performance, which in turn would screw up almost every drill he participated in. Practice after practice this went on, with talk after talk occurring to try and figure out what was happening. It became so frustrating that one practice I pulled him aside. I explained that he had to make a decision on whether he wanted to stay on the team or not, since his attitude and effort were so poor. I then walked off the ice and met with his father in the lobby, explaining how frustrated both coaches were with his consistently bad performance, practice after practice. His father's comment was that sometimes his son just couldn't get going at home and even he had difficulty getting him off the couch.

He wasn't the only player on the team that had the same work ethic issues but he was by far the worst.

I met with his former coaches and the comments were the same. "Yes there's some talent there but as the season progresses, he takes more shifts off both in games and in practices."

To me, this attitude was unfathomable. I won't go into more detail here, but suffice it to say that the end of the year did not go well with the parent making a lot of noise behind the scenes. What frustrated me was the complete lack of parenting that many neglect. They have an inability to tighten the reigns on their children for reprehensible behavior. This lack of honesty creates issues down the road.

Questions that I have always posed to parents: "You have brought me on board to teach your sons and daughters the game of hockey, its skills and teamwork. However, do you think it fair to have me teach core values to your children and then attack me for doing so when it is so obvious in what they are missing? How difficult is it to assess whether or not you child is working hard? How hard is to recognize when your son lacks discipline? How hard is it to recognize selfish play? How hard is it to recognize a lack of commitment or accountability?"

The real question becomes, if the parent can't teach these values, who will?

I remember another incident of honesty and lack of accountability. I was coaching the Richmond Sockeyes of the PJHL at the time and we were playing the Grandview Steelers, a top, well-coached team in our league. We had a rookie defenceman on the team that had made a great play from the point, taking several quick steps laterally along the blue line and then delivering a well-timed slap shot through a screen, and scoring a goal.

One should then assume, that in junior hockey, the opposition would adjust and the chances that this happening the same way again would be slim. Well that is exactly what happened. The wingers playing his side of the ice now played him a little tighter and for the next three slap shot attempts, all rebounded off the defender's shin pads and out of the zone. One such rebound led directly to a goal. After the first shot off the pad, he was instructed to wrist the puck and not bury his head. This instruction was totally ignored and he took another one. He was again warned not to do it again. This time it led to an opposition goal. After the third warning to try something different and another shot going off a shin pad, he was benched for the remainder of the period.

His father, frustrated with the benching of his son, marched up to the owner and asked for a trade saying that it was unacceptable for his son to be sat. Didn't the owner see the goal he scored? The owner came down to the dressing room between the second and third to discuss what the parent had done with me. I explained to the owner the steps that were taken before the player was benched, with the comment: "I told him to make a new mistake and don't make the same mistake again."

I discussed with the owner that if this was going to be this player's conduct, the best thing to do was to cut him loose and to make a trade. We both agreed and he returned to the stands to meet with the parent. After the game the owner discussed what transpired during his interaction with the parent, with me.

He told the parent what I had said about his decision-making during the game, what we had asked him to do, and that there had been no change. He then pointed out that he knew of several general managers and owners who were in the stands watching the game and, before the third period was over, he was sure that he could organize a trade. He also stated that the head coach had agreed to a trade and that maybe it was in the best interest of the player to be moved, since perhaps what was being asked of him might be too difficult.

At this point the parent was shocked that things had progressed so quickly, and backed down, saying that all was good.

Again, a complete lack of honesty about what was transpiring before everybody's eyes. The player continued with the team and became a valuable contributor for the rest of the season. He learned that making mistakes was a part of learning and as a result, it was important to make them; just don't make the same mistake over and over again. After all, isn't there that famous quote "To keep doing the same thing over and over again expecting a different result is the definition of insanity?"

I could bring up many such stories but in the end, I came to realize that in most cases, it comes down to the supporting cast of each player. Whether a parent, a close friend, a teacher or a mentor, we all have to add to the collection of values that each player possesses. However, the player has to want to learn and change. They need the ability to take a closer look at who they are, how they are performing and then realize that they need to improve. If not, then somewhere in their hockey career a coach, general manager, owner or even teammate will make them accountable and by then it may be too late.

ADDITIONAL LIFE LESSONS

THE MIRROR

After an early season junior hockey game I received a phone call from one of my former students. He asked if he could drop by and talk to me about how his season was going and get some advice. I agreed to meet and set up a time to get together later that evening at the local Tim Horton's, just a quick one-minute drive from my training studio.

I was sitting inside enjoying a hot cup of coffee when he arrived. After the usual greetings and handshake, we sat down to discuss his concerns.

"*Coach,*" he began, "*we are eight games into our season and I don't think I'm playing well. I started on the second line and now I'm down to the fourth line. I'm worried about not getting a chance to move back up the line-up or even getting cut.*"

"Fill me in on why you think that you aren't playing well?" I asked.

"*I'm not getting the puck very often and when I do, I'm not scoring. It seems as if when I make a mistake, I get sat and when some of the vets do the same thing, it's OK. I'm working hard in games and practices but can't quite figure out what he wants me to do?*"

"When does he complain the most?" I asked, trying to get to the bottom of the situation.

"*He wants me to engage more physically, I guess. He is always talking about putting pucks in deep and finishing our checks. I see myself as more of a play-making guy and we have some guys that play that way already but I wouldn't call them great with the puck.*"

"Well, let me approach this issue from the coach's perspective first." I had coached junior hockey for over twelve years at this point and had put players in the same situation myself.

"I like to call it the 'coach's mirror'," I explained. "The coach was hired to direct the team. As a result he gets up every day with the confidence that he was hired to do a job. He looks in the mirror and likes what he sees. He dries his hands and face and heads out to go about his day. He does this every day. He has to look in the mirror and like what he sees. This image represents how he acts, what he thinks, how he coaches, what he believes and how he goes about winning."

"Every day you get up and you look in the mirror. The image that stares back at you is what you believe in. It is both how and why you play hockey. It is how you act as a person and is what you believe. You dry your hands and face and you head out the door to go about your day."

"When you both look at each other, you each need to see a representation of yourself in the other person. For example, perhaps the coach likes his players to demonstrate a strong physical presence when on the ice, so when he looks at you he needs to be reminded of what he likes. You like to play a skill puck possession game, so when you look at him you need to see your philosophy in how he coaches the game. The problem arises when the image of what he sees in you doesn't match the image that he sees in the mirror and visa-versa. The exact opposite rings true as well. The coach looks in the mirror and there are things that he doesn't like. The same is true for you. He doesn't like players that are skilled but soft and you don't like coaches that play a dump and chase."

"Unfortunately, he is the boss. This means that the owner has looked in his mirror and likes what he sees. He decides that the coach he just hired fits his profile. They can shake hands knowing that each see a lot of common ground when they look at each other."

"Getting back to you now," I continued. "You are in essence an employee, meaning, the coach has a plan that he is implementing in order to win, and you have a job to do. You show up to work and the boss, or the coach in this instance, wants you to do a particular job. You may have your own interpretation of what he asks you to do but he still wants it done to his standards, and on time. This earns you what I call 'wiggle room'. Say a problem arises, you have to go to a dentist one day and the appointment is during the afternoon. You have been a great employee and done everything he has asked, worked hard, never complained, showed up on time. He gives you the green light to take the afternoon off to go. That 'wiggle room' is earned."

The player had listened in earnest and was nodding his head slowly in understanding.

"Have you ever had a summer job?" I asked.

"I did some work on a construction site as a laborer."

"Was there an interview for the job?"

"Yes, I guess. My buddy got me the job. He told the boss that I played hockey and worked out. When I met the boss, he looked happy to see me and gave me the job."

"OK, so the boss had his own mirror and he needed someone that wasn't afraid of physical work. You show up, he checks you out and you're hired. Seems simple enough. So what was the trade off?" I continued.

"I guess getting paid for the work," he answered.

"OK, so let's follow a plan of logic here. Were you forced to do the job?" I questioned.

"No," he responded. *"It was physical work but I'm OK with that."*

"What were the demands of the job?"

"Well, I had to show up on time, take equipment and supplies to the trade guys, clean up the job site, stuff like that."

"Were there any parts of the job that you didn't like?

"Well, some days it rained hard and that sucked. Other days they had me running around trying to do a hundred things at once."

"And in turn you received a paycheck for doing that correct?"

"Yes."

"OK, so in junior hockey there is no paycheck but there is a reward for your work and that is ice time. Agreed?"

"I guess so."

"So think of hockey like a job, you can love it and work hard at it but there are days when you have to do things that you don't like, or sometimes you have to work in conditions that aren't so favorable?"

"Yeah, I can agree with that."

"Well, here is what I advise then. Essentially you only have two choices. Stay with the employer that you have or change jobs by asking for a trade. I would recommend that you think hard about what the coach is asking of you and see if that is beyond your capability to perform. After all, he is trying to win and I assume that he was hired because he wins and not because he loses correct?"

"Well, he has won before so I can see your point."

I told the player one last story about something that had happened to me when I played. The coach I had at the time wanted simple plays at certain times of the game. That meant putting the puck off the glass and out of the zone. I was playing defense and I preferred a more puck possession game. I got the point but at times I could see a great passing opportunity and would make it. The result would be that I would get yelled at. I was a rookie at the time. I went home after the game and gave it some thought. I tried to look at it from his standpoint instead of mine.

After the next practice, I took a bucket of pucks and dumped them out around the bottom of the defensive zone circle. I would pick one up, figure out the best shooting angle to get the puck off the glass and out, both forehand and backhand. I hated icing the puck and after twenty minutes or so, I started to figure out the best angles and how much speed to put on the puck. Because of my focus, I hadn't noticed that the coach had stood and watched me for a while, seeing what I was up to.

The next game he brought it up to me saying he was impressed by my attitude. That game, I talked to my weak side winger and told him that if he saw me get the puck in the corner, to break into the neutral zone and I would get it to him. Sure enough, an opportunity presented itself and I set him up for a breakaway, which resulted in a goal.

Coach gave me an approving nod on the assist and that earned me wiggle room. I called it compromise. He wanted something done; I didn't have to like it. It wasn't how I liked to play, but I adapted and found a way to get the job done in a way that fit me, while satisfying him. He would have been happy if I had simply iced the puck.

What I learned from the experience was that he wanted a player that could follow instructions when told to do so. He had been around the game much longer than I had and had a little more game wisdom than I did. I compromised. The funny thing that happened is that my ice time went way up as a result of what I did, because he knew that he could depend on me to get the simple job done right.

"I get it," He responded.

We engaged in some more small talk about life and hockey finally shaking hands and parting ways.

When I reached out him a couple weeks later to see how things were going, he was a lot happier. He explained that he had listened to what I said and decided to give it a try for a couple games and as a result, he was back in the coach's favor. He had been moved up to the second line, and was getting some power play time as well. He found that when he played more physically and simplified his game, he actually got more offensive opportunities from the pressure and turnovers.

THE EMPTY CUP

This story happened when I was in my twenties. I had decided to take a Tai-Chi Chuan class that was being held in downtown Vancouver in a little corner studio one block off East Hasting street. One could drop by every day and join the group practicing in Jackson Park, which was just across the corner, or could sign up for scheduled lessons a couple times a week. This was my best option, since driving from North Delta to the classes during the week was difficult, so I signed up for the Saturday class held in the early afternoon.

For those who have taken Tai-Chi classes, especially as a rookie, a substantial amount of concentration is required. The moves are quite precise and follow each other in a chronological sequence.

I had taken the class for several weeks and felt that I was lagging behind a little. It was easy to see that some of the people who were in the class had been doing it for many years and they moved with a grace and fluidity that I couldn't duplicate. I had taken several styles of martial arts by this time, but the moves that I was used to, were more powerful and explosive. Getting used to the very slow precise moves took a little getting used to.

It was after one of the classes that I decided to take a little walk around the area and have a cup of Chinese tea in one of the local shops several blocks away. Sitting at one of the tables was an older Chinese gentleman that I had seen at one of the classes with whom I had engaged in some small talk. I asked him if I could join him.

"Of course," He responded and motioned for me to sit down across from him.

CORE VALUES

After we had engaged in some chat about the day, he asked me how I liked talking the class.

"I love the training although I find it a little frustrating. I am kind of a perfectionist and the techniques move from one to the other, albeit fairly slowly but fast enough that I feel like I'm missing the exact technique. I'm used to a small variety of punches and blocks and even fewer kicks from other styles that I have taken. There seem to be so many moves: Grasp the bird's tail, single whip, crane spreads its wing, hand strums the lute and so many more. It seems overwhelming at times.

"Yes, you are correct." He answered: *"But there is no hurry to learn them. The idea is to come with an open mind and each time progress a little further. I have taken it for over thirty years. It is not something that one learns overnight."*

"I can certainly see that. I drive quite a distance and it's hard to get here more than twice a week. By the time I show up again, I feel that I've forgotten what I've learned. I work midnight shift so I get time to practice but I hate practicing the moves wrong."

"I can understand your frustration. Even if you only practice two or three moves that is fine and over time, you will learn them all. We name them so that they are easier to remember. The names that you remember provide some visual understanding of what the move feels like."

With that he paused and took hold of an extra empty cup that was positioned on the table. The server had come by and filled up both of our cups with tea. He positioned both of them in front of me.

"What do you see when you look at these cups?" He asked.

"I see one that is almost full and one that is empty." I replied feeling that my answer was a little too obvious.

"Correct. But, let's look at these cups in a different way. Let's say that the cups represent our minds. The cup that is almost full would represent very little room for knowledge. Our mind could be full of other philosophies, ideas, doubts or even frustration. The second cup is empty which means there are none of the worries that fill the other cup. This means that it can

receive more information or more knowledge. The problem that you are facing is that you expect too much from yourself, which is not necessarily a bad thing, but your frustration has filled up your cup or your capacity to learn. I would encourage you to come each time with an empty cup. This way you can accept more knowledge and not worry about so many things. The important thing to remember that there is no race here; it is about the breathing and the movements, not the pressure to complete all movements in a month's time."

This lesson stuck with me for the rest of my life. I think that there are different phases of understanding one's knowledge. In the first stage, I thought at nineteen years of age, I knew it all. I wanted to take on the world and then in my twenties, the world slapped me back down and I came to realize that while I knew some things, my knowledge was minimal at best. As one matures, there is a realization that even though one's knowledge is growing, the little bits of information that one may overlook may be the most important piece. Each day, I try to wake up with an empty cup. While I have been around this wonderful game most of my life; playing, coaching, practicing and researching, I have come to realize that there is always a new angle or a new twist. The empty cup allows me to be open to new ideas, to see new possibilities. It is when we admit that we truly know very little, is the time when new discoveries come to us.

THE SENSEI AND THE MASTER

What is the difference between a sensei (teacher) and a grand master (master teacher)? That was the question I had posed myself on many occasions while taking one form of martial art or another. To meet a true master in any form is a rare and prestigious event and one I have been fortunate to have on several occasions.

When it comes to meeting a true master teacher of ice hockey, it is a much more difficult task. One of the problems with hockey is that the instructional part of the game, the true skills and mastery of the details of the sport, are in most part, a well-kept secret.

Skill coaches keep their knowledge to themselves, carefully guarding their secrets. This is mostly because the competition to teach the next great one and take credit for it is fierce. They also have an incredible advantage in that parents, unless they have played at the highest level of hockey, really don't understand the scope and technical excellence of the skills required to be successful at that level. Simply put, they don't know what they don't know. In all of the forty-plus years of hockey that I have coached, I have only experienced a curious parent, who took the time to sit down with me and ask the tough questions, three times.

In one example, the father of a twelve-year-old boy whom I coached, approached me and asked; "*I got to thinking about your forty-plus years of experience and what that could mean in just simple knowledge. I'm thirty-nine years old and to think that you were coaching before I was born was a little mind-boggling. Would you mind if I sat down and ask you some questions?*"

Often times, our thirst for knowledge and our inexperience creates its own issues and, as is often said, 'BS baffles brains' becomes a pretty relevant saying.

However, being respectful is an important part of a student's character and sometimes, watching, listening, doing and feeling are enough to create an understanding of the knowledge of our teacher.

As I mentioned in an earlier story, I took an interest in a Japanese martial arts style. I studied and trained hard and acquired my brown belt. My teacher, Sensei Koyaku, was an amazingly skilled martial artist and his movements had a grace and power that I found incredible. I had witnessed him performing some of the attacks with the more advanced students and there was no doubt in my mind that he was the real deal. It was indeed an honor and a privilege to train with and be taught by such skill.

It was during my brown belt training that the student body was informed by Sensei Koyabu that his master, Seikich Toguchi (1917-1998) and the founder of Shorei-Kan, would be coming to Canada to train with us.

It was an exciting time. How often does one get to meet a founder of a martial arts style that was recognized all over Japan? It was an easy leap for my imagination to make that perhaps, I would have the opportunity to meet a very well respected and revered grand master.

He was to come to Canada and stay for several months, to work closely with the senior instructors, making sure that the style was being taught correctly. We were informed that Sensei Koyabu would host an evening with the grand master and only the senior students; brown and black belts, would be allowed to ask him one and only ONE question.

We set about raising money for his journey and accommodation. Time seemed to drag on and everyone was excited about meeting him. Training was extra hard and our techniques were pushed and critiqued more severely. No one wanted to disappoint him.

During this time, I pondered a hundred questions; "How did he come up with the style?" "Why did he come up with the style?" "When did he start training?" "Who was his instructor?" "'How did he choose Sensei Koyabu?"

The questions were a constantly changing stream flowing through my head daily. I couldn't decide what to ask. I was in horrible torment. The months slowly rolled by and we were all getting impatient, we had heard so much about him.

The day came when he finally arrived. We were told that we would meet him after one of our evening classes since he had to visit another dojo (training center) in another location first. I had no idea what to expect since I had never seen a picture of him before. Sensei Koyabu was fairly tall, not quite six-foot and was very slim, toned and very fit. I assumed of course that they must look alike, perhaps just an older version of our sensei? Curiosity combined with the single question problem was taking its toll on me.

The day finally arrived and we were introduced to him at an evening class. He was not what I expected in stature. He was short and what stood out in an abstract way, was his incredibly bowed legs. He moved with the familiar grace and power. It was very evident from the confidence and control that he exuded, that he was a man to be greatly respected.

It was during the warm up exercises that my life was changed forever. We were performing punching exercises on a beat count and both Sensei Koyabu and Master Taguchi were walking around the perimeter of the class watching the students with a keen eye. I was on the edge of the brown belt line and when Sensei Koyabu walked by, he gave he a nod of approval. I had trained hard over the months and wanted my punches and kicks to demonstrate power and speed.

He continued his walk down past the belt lines and then as he turned the corner to circle around the back side of the class, Master Taguchi came into view on my side of the dojo. He took a look at me; watched for a moment then approached me grabbing my wrist and re-adjusted it ever so slightly. He quietly commented as he held my wrist, "*Much better and more power*".

With that he walked away to view the other students behind me. I was completely frozen and did not want to move. My hand and wrist were frozen still. I was completely focused on what it looked like and what he had said. I did not want to lose the moment! Two things raced through my mind. The first was that an incredible teacher and martial artist had just walked by and nodded that I was doing OK, and the grand master had walked by stating that I wasn't quite good enough. The second thing that entered my mind was; "What would happen if I forgot such a tiny thing?"

I continued staring at my wrist and then very carefully punched with my other hand and then froze, trying to duplicate exactly what had been corrected in my first punch. The class was continuing on, with the senior student at the head of class counting out numbers in Japanese to which all were punching or kicking in cadence to. A fellow student beside me had this puzzled look on his face, frowning at me in distaste, feeling that I was disrespecting the class and the instructor.

Sensei Koyabu had moved to the front of the class after his circle by me and had not noticed what I was doing. Master Taguchi on the other hand continued walking the perimeter of the class and as he came by where I was standing, he just smiled and nodded his approval. The rest of the class was a blur. We moved on to blocks and other strikes, kicks and stances and I was left with this weird feeling that something amazing had just happened.

Several days later, we were informed that Sensei Koyabu would be hosting the informal get together and that we should be prepared having our question ready.

I was a confused mess before but this time something seemed much clearer in my mind. I couldn't forget the incident and it had burned its way into my consciousness.

I was far too eager to pose my question, and to this day I can't remember what the other senior students, who went before and after me, asked. I know that seems incredibly disrespectful but something had changed inside me. I had to focus and make sure that I worded my question wisely; I only had one opportunity.

CORE VALUES

It seemed like forever but finally my opportunity came. I took a big sigh and then asked; "Master Taguchi, remember when you stopped me in class and made that very small adjustment in my wrist?"

"*Yes*" he answered with a gleam in his eyes.

"Is success in our techniques or even success in everything we do in life all dependent on the smallest of details like you showed me with my wrist?"

It was as if I had hit every one of the students in the room with a baseball bat. They looked at me as if it was the craziest question that anyone could ever ask.

He then replied: "*It is the smallest of things that we do that demonstrate who we are; saying please and thank you, bowing to your opponent or making sure that your technique or even how you act is the very best that it or you can be, not settling for anything less*".

While I have tried, I freely admit that I have failed miserably at being the very best that I can be. However, his comments and his correction that day put me on a path that I have so frequently traveled since. It has been my objective ever since to seek out solutions, no matter small, to questions on skill development or game play. I was a kid with a dream and it was through genuine acts of kindness in the simple things that people such as Bud McNabb, Dick Doyle, Carey Klein, Bob Erickson did that impacted my life when I was alone after my father's death, that provided some guidance and compassion.

In the end I have come to realize that mastery is really a depth of knowledge that comes from thousands of hours of dedicated practice. It is about only accepting the correct way and then having the courage and mental fortitude to go and look for it. It is about being the best that we can be every minute and while we fail greatly, we can still strive to do so since ultimately it is the search for such answers that truly define us.

THE HANDSHAKE

There comes a time in a child's life that certain greeting rituals must be taught. My first introduction to this was when I was asked to address adults as "Hello Mr. Jones" or "Hello Mrs. Simpson" whenever I met them. The second lesson came in the form of the handshake.

I had noticed that my father would greet his friends with a kind hello and then they would shake hands. We were sitting at the breakfast table one day and I asked my father about why he did this. While I greeted his acquaintances with a "Hello Mr...." he would extend his hand. I notice that adults never extended their hand to me.

"*Well*", He started: "*The handshake is an old ritual which I was introduced to as a young man many, many years ago by my father. Many of the men and women that we knew in my youth couldn't read or write. The handshake was kind of a contract that when a person gave their word that they would do something, the handshake was their way of saying that their word was their commitment.*"

"*You are a young man and haven't really learned the value of what giving your word really means. In the adult world, the handshake is used to represent honesty, sincerity, character and commitment.*"

"*It is also used as a sign of respect. If a man or woman can give you their word and use their handshake as a commitment to keep it, they deserve your respect. When I greet my friends, it is used a sign of respect.*"

"*Come here and let me show you,*" he added.

My father had large hands, with strong, thick, powerful fingers from years of roping and hard labor. I remember very clearly when he put my hand in his, how seemingly small and insignificant my hand was.

He positioned my hand properly and then showed me how to squeeze properly explaining that one wanted a firm grip, not a crushing grip or a loose 'dishrag grip' as he called it. He showed me how to give a quick grip and a slight pump; up and down motion. This was to act as a confirmation of what the handshake meant to the person giving it.

"Why the difference in how hard a person squeezes?" I questioned.

"In my day, the right amount of 'squeeze', as you put it, was respectful. Too much meant that the person was being disrespectful and maybe trying be a little above you and if too soft, it meant that their word perhaps couldn't be trusted."

As he was demonstrating it with me he continued: *"And you always look the person in the eye, Son. That is the final step in showing that you are sincere."*

"Go ahead now, you try a couple with me"

We practiced shaking hands several times and then he commented; *"I think you've got it, Son. Now the next time you are with me and meet one of my friends, extend your hand and see what happens. As a matter of fact I'm meeting Ken in an hour, why don't you come with me?"*

It was the first time that I had greeted an adult with a handshake. It was an awkward moment and once I saw the smile, the sparkle in Mr. Jenkins eyes and the *"Good to see you"* response, I felt that I had in some way grown up just a little bit more.

It is important to mention here that different cultures have different views on and presentations of the handshake and as such need to be respected. My father came from a frontier time and that was how it was explained to him in the early 1900s.

RIDDLE A DAY

Hopefully, by now you have come to appreciate that my father was a man of wisdom and this came at quite an expense. He was a cowboy and an adventurer for much of his life; he did the rodeo circuit, played cards, drank heavily, smoked and fought too much. He lived in the bush as a trapper and hunter, traveling throughout the Nahinni Valley National Park of the Mackenzie Mountain region approximately 500 km (300 miles) west of Yellowknife, in the Northwest Territories. It had earned the dubious nickname as 'The Valley of Headless Men'. It was not just a scary nickname for a remote mysterious northern Canadian wilderness, for the area has long been known for people disappearing and then turning up without their heads. He explored and traveled extensively through northern British Columbia and as a result, he knew many native Indian elders and had old, rough and grey-bearded mountain men as friends.

When he adopted me, he was sixty-four years old. He had seen the errors of his ways both as a man and as a father. My stepbrother, Ernest, had died of cirrhosis of the liver from excessive drinking, after following in my father's footsteps and my oldest stepbrother, Mark, whom I met the one time at my father's funeral, would never talk to him.

He found that he had a new beginning with me and tried his best to steer me in the right direction. One of his favorite pastimes was to hit me with riddles.

One Saturday afternoon, my father and I were sitting out on the new lawn swing that he had erected in our front yard, overlooking the Alaska Highway. His cowboy hat was tilted back on his head and a cigarette was smoldering in his fingers, when he turned, looked at me and said.

CORE VALUES

"*Here's a riddle for you, Son.*" This immediately got my attention since there was usually some small prize, like an ice cream cone, if I could solve it.

He took a long drag on his cigarette, exhaled and after a short pause asked:

"*What is freely given, seldom taken, enriches those that use it and impoverishes no one?*"

"*Take a moment to think about it and at supper tonight, see if you can come up with the answer. If you do, (I was waiting for it), I'll treat you to an ice cream cone from the corner store.*"

With that he headed off to tend to his favorite pastime, the garden in our backyard that was full of strawberries, beans, peas, tomatoes, carrots, green onions, lettuce and potatoes.

I was left to contemplate his message.

I sat there for a couple minutes thinking but wanting that ice cream cone sooner rather than later, I got up and headed to where he was tending to his strawberries, his removing weeds from the stringers.

"OK Dad, I think I have the answer." I started.

With that he straightened up, rested his elbow on the hoe and turned to face me with a smile growing on his face. "*I take it that you want that ice cream?*" He chuckled.

With that I blurted out what I thought was a great answer. Laughing, he just shook his head. "*Look, Son, give it some more thought and let's see what you come up with at the supper table.*"

Frustrated, I turned and headed to the garage to get my bike. Maybe a good ride would help.

The afternoon came and went and it was all I could do to wait for our evening meal. I had it in my mind that I would solve this, claim my prize and then walk up to the corner store a block away and get that ice cream cone.

The meal was an agonizing affair, twisting and turning in my chair wanting so desperately get the answer that I knew had to be right, out of my head.

After supper, as mother was clearing away the dishes, my father took the cue to ask me if I had come up with the answer yet.

"I think that I have the answer, Dad." I said confidently and told him what I was thinking.

"*Nope*" he answered with that darn devilish grin on his face. "*Have to give it a little more thought.*"

I couldn't believe my ears. I was so sure that I had the answer. I voiced another.

"*Nope*"

And another.

"*Nope*"

I was sitting there puzzled and had run out of options. He had left the table and went to sit in his favorite recliner to read a newspaper. Apparently our conversation was over. He turned and saw my disappointment and frustration. "*You'll think of it soon enough.*"

Being a little mischievous, I thought that I would solicit some assistance from my mother, so when Dad wasn't around, I threw the riddle back at her. She obviously knew what my father was up to but wanting to have a little fun on my behalf, gave me that half pause and that deep inhale where it looked like she was going to give me the answer and then said: "*No, sorry, can't help. This is between you and your father.*" Then, that darn fiendish smile."

I was done, hook, line and sinker. My friends had no clue and I had given my best shot two days previous.

Sunday came and went, Monday came and went and finally on Tuesday I had given up completely. I had exhausted all the options that a young boy could think of.

CORE VALUES

That evening at the supper table, in complete frustration I turned to my father.

"Come on Dad. I can't figure it out. I've thought of a lot of things but I just can't get this one."

'It's OK, Son. I'm glad you put the time in to think about it." He took a sip of his freshly percolated coffee and with a stern look on his face, looked me in the eye and said.

"It's advice of course."

The light bulb went off in my head. Darn it, how come I didn't think of that? I guess that being so young, I had no advice to give of real importance, leaving that train of thought so far removed from my mind that conceptually I couldn't connect.

Of course my next concern was the ice cream issue. I hadn't solved the problem and therefore, I wasn't entitled to the prize.

My father watching the emotions ran rampant over my face as I moved from one thought process to the other, let out a deep chuckle.

"After my cup of coffee we can walk up to the corner store and I'll buy you that ice cream I promised. I know that you didn't solve the riddle but you did put in the time thinking about it, that's good enough for me."

Both my mother and father had an amazing way of engaging me as a child, trying to teach me old values that were so important to them.

LAST STORY – SPECIAL FORCES

I have saved this story till last, in part because it summarizes most of the values that have been talked about in this book. I will use the pseudo-name, 'Jim', in this story because of the nature of his occupation. Jim was an elite operator within the Special Missions Unit of the United States Joint Special Operations Command, more commonly referred to simply as JSOC. These are elite special operations force units that perform highly classified activities. I had the pleasure of meeting him and his son, whom I'll call Eric (again a pseudo name), a couple of years ago during a training session where I was instructing a hockey shooting skills class.

When meeting him, I had no idea what his occupation was. I am not of the mindset to question parents about their choice of employment, focusing my attentions instead on their son or daughter.

His son was a disciplined student, who listened intently and worked hard on the new skills he was learning. During the hour-long class, he never got distracted. This is an anomaly for a child of four-years old. I found this rather intriguing and during a later informal meeting, I questioned Jim about why he would start Eric in mechanics at such a young age.

"I think that it is important to build the correct skills at a young age so that they learn to do things right." He replied: *"I feel that it is important to have a strong base on which to build the rest of his hockey fundamentals."*

I mentioned to him that I was very impressed by his ability to focus, his work ethic and how polite he was

CORE VALUES

Over the next couple of years, we shared an equal opinion that the youth of today seemed to be missing some of the basic core values. We engaged in conversation about the importance of strong values such as respect, hard work, discipline, integrity, honesty, commitment, teamwork, accountability and being polite, all of which were things in which he and his wife were very strong believers.

It was during that time that I initiated the discussion on his background. While my father was from a different time, born in 1894 and passing away in 1975 at eighty-one years of age, I was curious to know where his values came from.

"My father was old school like yours." He commented: *"While not from that era, he was a firm believer in hard work, respect and keeping your word. If you said that you would do something, then get it done and when doing it, do it the very best you could."*

"My father passed away when I was young" He carried on when I pressed him further on his values: *"My brother and I are completely opposite. While raised by the same mother and father, we turned out different. It's hard to explain how that happens. For some reason, I was a kid that was very aware of myself and knew inside what was right and wrong. I knew that every day I had to get up and look in the mirror. I had to be happy about how I treated those around me and had to be proud of my actions."*

"What was the path to you took to get to there?" I questioned.

"I graduated high school and then spent four years in college acquiring a BSc. in economics. However, when I graduated, I decided that there was no way that I would enjoy that for the rest of my life and decided to join the army. I had no idea what I wanted to be when I grew up" he chuckled pausing and then added *"I thought that maybe somewhere inside that world I could figure stuff out."*

"I immediately realized that this was the world I wanted to be in. You were rewarded for your hard work, there were many like myself with the same attitude. Basic training was difficult but that didn't bother me. I have always worked hard in my life and I knew that with my belief system I could get through it. Upon completion, I wanted to be challenged and looked at different careers in the military where I could excel."

"After my basic training, and after counsel from one of the instructors, I decided to venture into the JSOC part of the US Military. I had come to realize early in life that there are people who know what they are talking about. The problem with many young people is that they think that they know it all. I came to realize early that I knew absolutely nothing and because of that, I was ready to listen to those around me with vastly more knowledge and experience. Such was the case with this instructor, he gave me his advice and I took it. He knew who I was and stated that I needed to be in a role that both challenged me yet allowed me the flexibility to think on my feet."

"It was very rigorous training and yet I knew that I could overcome any obstacle."

It was when I asked him about what value he thought was the most important in achieving his goal, he quickly reinforced his previous statement; *"Believing in oneself! Life is full of challenges and one has to know without question that you can conquer them."*

"But belief in oneself has to come from somewhere?" I questioned. Trying to create an analogy to his expand on his thoughts, I used the skills of building a house. "Belief that one can first learn, then one can apply what they learn and then possess the work ethic and pride to get the job done on time and to standard. Those qualities allow one to take on any challenge even building a house. Would those be a precursor to creating the belief in oneself?"

"I suppose so" He agreed; *"A very strong work ethic, ability to learn, a high level of accountability and the not-worrying-about-failure, means that no matter what the challenge one could ultimately make it through. This was the approach that I had through my life and even through college. I can't say that I like economics but I still scored at the top of my classes."*

He added; *"After I joined the military, I saw that there were many people with the same attitude and I looked up to these men. They had impeccable character and they helped to define who I wanted to be. They lived by a very strong code or set of values and held everyone accountable to those standards. I wanted to be like them. I wanted to believe in a higher cause, something bigger than myself and then be accountable to that cause."*

CORE VALUES

"In JSOC, we all come to depend on the guy next to you. In essence they become your teammates. In our line of work, its life or death and the guy next you has to depend on you and you on him. There is no room for questioning one's ability to act and one needs to know in a fire fight that they are trying to keep you alive as much as you are keeping them".

I asked him what experiences in his life had locked in his character and which ones had the greatest impact.

"I have been on many missions that were very dangerous and we knew going in that there was a chance that we wouldn't be coming back. When you believe in a higher cause and you're responsible for your teammate, you don't look back; you have a job to do."

"The most honest lesson that one can learn is that of life and death. I have held teammates in my arms and watched them die. The same with close friends, guys that I trained and lived with every day. Those guys became your family. Watching them die in your arms changes you. You knew that they depended on you and while you didn't let them down, you always feel that you have to be better, you have to work hard at every one of your skills so that you don't ever come up short."

"In twenty years I never took a holiday. When we were given time off, I would use that time to work on my diving, shooting or whatever was a part of our craft to make sure that I was always prepared to get my job done. The guys around me depended on me. I had to look in the mirror every day and know that I wouldn't let them down, knew that I honed my skills and was always prepared for the worst."

"A dying man is an honest man. He looks back on his life and realizes that he could have lived his life differently, could have done more; could have been a better father, a better husband. In all the times I held them and listened intently to each word, they never talked about the future; it was all about the past and what they could have done better."

"I have had to deliver their caskets to their families and see what loss does to their wives, their children and their friends. It is the most somber of moments and makes a man realize what responsibility really is, what accountability really is. I knew that every day I had to be better. There could be no excuses and taking time off. There was always work and a commitment to getting better."

"I came to realize that the world is full of pretenders, those that talk the talk but never walk the walk. These are most often the people that offer up criticism. I have seen grown men that tout their accomplishments, that brag about their achievements and yet when the bullets start flying and all hell breaks loose, they are the guys that hide."

"I have never cared about what people think of me as a result. Ninety-nine percent of people have never experienced much adversity so who are they to judge me. I am my own worst judge and critic. I have to look in the mirror every day and see who I am. I have to live by a code that makes me proud of who I am and who I stand for."

Jim paused in his commentary, I think more to let me absorb all that was said. Adversity in life for me was being bullied, having experienced the death of my father in my teenage years and subsequently having to fend for myself or having close nephews commit suicide. If these are the worst things that I have experienced, I was by no means even capable of understanding the depth and breadth of the lessons he had learned.

I asked him about his son, Eric, and how the lessons in his life have impacted on his role as a father.

"My son loves hockey, it is a passion that has engulfed him and we let him run with it. We are here to support him but every day we tell him that he has a responsibility to his teammates. He must train hard and when the going gets tough, he can't quit, he has to find that next level. I also explain to him that he can't have external goals like; I want to play in the NHL. While it is an admirable goal, it does not define him as a person. He desires to be the best that he can be every day, is the most important goal. If he strives to be the best then he will achieve that through hard work, commitment, discipline resulting him achieving that goal. It is how he acts in this regard that lets him know that he can attain anything."

"We also tell him that you can't worry about what people think, your values or belief in yourself allow you to look honestly in the mirror and then you can live with yourself. I stressed to him that we didn't care if he won a game and scored five goals or lost a game and caused five goals. We need to see that 'put-it-behind-you attitude', be humble and get back to work. It is important that he doesn't lose focus that every day is a new day, put the past behind you. There will be great days and bad days but it's the desire to move forward and get better that is important".

"Every day he trains at something. He is six years old now and has learned that if you want something badly enough, then there are no excuses and only a commitment to getting the job done. Work on the skills that make you successful, the ones that your teammates need you to be the best at. But most importantly, be able to look yourself in the mirror and be able to say that you've done all you could and left nothing to chance."

As they say, the apple doesn't fall far from the tree. It is easy to see that Eric, under his father and mother's guidance, will make the most of himself. If it is the current path of ice hockey that he continues to pursue, then he will arrive where and when he wants to. If it is another path that he travels, he will undoubtedly achieve that.

Jim sent me an email about a year ago that really affected me. I have shared this with others and would like to share it with you now.

"The only battlefield that matters, at all, is the one in your mind. You lay down with it, you get up with it. You win the fight in your own mind, in your own head. And the only thing that should matter to any of us, it is what we have to say to ourselves, during that fight. The

fear, the failure. The conversation with ourselves; what we are willing to accept from oneself determines whether or not we win or lose on that battlefield.

Fear is a great motivator. But not fear for the sake of it, but fear that we have not been honest with ourselves about what we are willing to give in order to achieve. The worst lie in the world is the one you tell yourself."

SYNOPSIS

I hope that you find value in the stories that we have shared with you. The acceptance of change is an interesting phenomenon as I have discovered in my life, both as a member of society and as a coach. Sometimes, the quick shock of a hard lesson changes us forever, or it is the slow percolation of an idea that appears at the right time. It can be the result of a thirty second conversation or a two-hour grueling test. Whatever the case, we change.

I remember a lesson my martial arts instructor told me about how quickly change can take place.

"You trust me," he stated to which I nodded in agreement. *"Yet you have no real reason that you can explain as to why you trust me. Maybe it's my actions or how I speak to you. Let's say one day that I walked up to you and quickly slapped you in the face. Your thoughts of me would change instantly. In a one-second action, I created an irreversible consequence. I can never recover the trust that you gave me and in that same second you will view me differently. Sometimes an action can alter a person's perspective quickly and decisively. Remember that your actions and your words have an impact on others."*

While the story above demonstrates change, it may not be the kind of change that we desire.

What we must remember is that the growth of an individual is a slow, evolving process. There are many events that transpire on our journey and it's how we view them that really matters. It has been said that nothing is ever negative; it is how we view it. That may be a hard statement to swallow but when such events transpire, change occurs albeit sometimes slowly but change does occur. A young player gets cut from a team; his world has been turned upside down and now he has to make a choice: deal with the reality and get back to work or move on to something else. Whatever the case, change occurs.

Many of the stories in this book talk about mental toughness; having the ability to deal with such adversity. Other stories deal with accountability; owning one's actions and then doing something about it. Teamwork is another constant; working with others and getting along, being a part of something bigger than oneself. Ever apparent is one's effort or leadership: be an example.

We are not born with these values but are taught to use them. It has been said that it takes a community to raise a child and as such, we need to pick the people that we associate with well.

In my life, I have come to learn that two things are important: what we do with our time and with whom we spend our time.

I would like to add a closing story.

As I explained earlier in this book, my father passed away when I was seventeen. My mother remarried several years later to a wonderful man, Wilfred Leduc. I realized that I really knew little of my father and while he imparted many wonderful life lessons to me, I never really sat down with him and talked about his life journey. Yes, there were fragments that were shared with me over seventeen years but the real deep dive never took place. He was a man of wisdom gleaned from many harsh experiences.

With Wilfred, I had a new opportunity to learn and to ask the important questions that I had neglected the first time around. We spent many moments together over the years talking about life, playing pool together, going for walks, or having tea. I learned so much more about life the second time around.

The most important lesson came at the end of his life. Wilf had been diagnosed with cancer when he was eighty. It was the result of drinking heavily and chewing tobacco when he was young. As a result the surgeon had to remove the whole left side of his lower jaw and install a metal support piece as a framework to build the rest of his mouth.

They took tissue from his arm and implanted it inside so that he could live a somewhat normal life.

He died at the age of ninety-three and over the remaining years he never complained about the discomfort of eating, or the pain that it caused him. He was never angry about his life, or about the cancer but was just grateful at the long life he had been granted.

The cancer slowly spread through his bones and in the last couple months, I could see that he was in discomfort but again, he never showed it. I would sit by his side and when he awoke we would talk about life and the lessons he had learned along the way.

I could tell that he was close to the end and during one of his waking moments I asked him a question that I felt was the most important to me. It was like the question that I was allowed to ask the Grand Master Taguchi.

"Dad", I paused: "Would you mind if I asked you a question? I have had much time to think about it and it has become very important to me. You have experienced much in your life and through it all, at least from my observations over the past twenty-two years, you never complain. What belief inside you has allowed you to deal with adversity as you have?"

"It is quite simple actually, Life is full of challenges, some brought on by ourselves, some by others and sometimes life just throws something at you. I came to realize that I could only worry about the things that I could control. I cannot worry about the things I could not and I just needed to learn how to recognize the difference."

"Time teaches you that and the faster you learn the better. What you can control you have to be accountable for, and what you can't control you have to find courage, mental toughness and perseverance to overcome. Knowing the difference is just looking deep within oneself and being truthful, not blaming others."

He passed away in his sleep a day later with family members and my mother by his side. His words still reverberate with me to this day. That was almost ten years ago.

CORE VALUES

What I have come to realize is that those that rise above and exemplify what it means to be a good person, a good teammate, or a great leader are the kind of people that I truly enjoy knowing. It has been a privilege to engage them in the conversations that are demonstrated within these pages.

I hope you have enjoyed and learned from them as much as I have.

Thank you for reading.

Ron Johnson, BSC. MSc.

REFERENCES

Ethan Wolthers - www.eliteprospects.com/player/294559/ethan-wolthers, carubberhockey.com/whether-hes-on-the-dirt-or-on-the-ice-wolthers-excels/

Ben Israel - www.eliteprospects.com/player/196934/benjamin-israel, www.collegehockeynews.com/reports/roster/Colorado-College/16

Chris Connor - www.eliteprospects.com/player/10995/chris-conner, www.hockeydb.com/ihdb/stats/pdisplay.php?pid=71411, www.gnghockey.com/2017/07/06/phantoms-re-sign-chris-conner-sign-4-players-a

Kaleigh Fratkin - en.wikipedia.org/wiki/Kaleigh_Fratkin, www.eliteprospects.com/player/59978/kaleigh-fratkin, www.nwhl.zone/roster_players/13721061

Matt Barzal - www.nhl.com/player/mathew-barzal-8478445, www.eliteprospects.com/player/186310/mathew-barzal, en.wikipedia.org/wiki/Mathew_Barzal

Andrew Copp - www.eliteprospects.com/player/101962/andrew-copp, www.hockey-reference.com/players/c/coppan01.html, en.wikipedia.org/wiki/Andrew_Copp

Dylan Larkin - en.wikipedia.org/wiki/Dylan_Larkin, www.eliteprospects.com/player/177693/dylan-larkin, www.espn.com/nhl/player/_/id/3114755/dylan-larkin

Hockey - In Search of Excellence

Brenden Dillon - www.nhl.com/player/brenden-dillon-8475455, en.wikipedia.org/wiki/Brenden_Dillon, www.eliteprospects.com/player/23790/brenden-dillon

Joe Pavelski, - en.wikipedia.org/wiki/Joe_Pavelski, www.eliteprospects.com/player/10372/joe-pavelski, www.foxsports.com/nhl/joe-pavelski-player-stats

Ryan Kesler - en.wikipedia.org/wiki/Ryan_Kesler, www.eliteprospects.com/player/9014/ryan-kesler

Patrick Marleau - en.wikipedia.org/wiki/Patrick_Marleau, www.eliteprospects.com/player/3671/patrick-marleau, sports.yahoo.com/nhl/players/1644/

Garry Toor - www.eliteprospects.com/player/92060/garry-toor, www.parkviewsurgery.ca/meet-us/meet-dr-garry-toor/

Steve Wicklum - www.hockeydb.com/ihdb/stats/pdisplay.php?pid=8934, ca.linkedin.com/in/steve-wicklum-3b876a96, www.nytimes.com/2016/09/20/sports/hockey/private-coaches-adam-oates.html

Cam Stewart - kosportsinc.com/team-members/cam-stewart/, en.wikipedia.org/wiki/Cam_Stewart, www.hhof.com/LegendsOfHockey/jsp/SearchPlayer.jsp?player=11571, www.hockeydb.com/ihdb/stats/pdisplay.php?pid=5188

Mike Valley - www.hockeydb.com/ihdb/stats/pdisplay.php?pid=30804, www.eliteprospects.com/player/8/mike-valley, www.elitegoalies.com/team

Peter Harrold - en.wikipedia.org/wiki/Peter_Harrold, www.eliteprospects.com/player/9043/peter-harrold

Adam Burish - en.wikipedia.org/wiki/Adam_Burish, www.eliteprospects.com/player/10196/adam-burish, www.espn.com/nhl/player/_/id/3395/adam-burish

CORE VALUES

Shawn Horcoff - en.wikipedia.org/wiki/Shawn_Horcoff, www.nhl.com/redwings/team/shawn-horcoff, www.eliteprospects.com/player/4375/shawn-horcoff

Randall Johansen - www.tricitynews.com/sports/charity-golf-tourney-gets-star-power-1.23161937, twitter.com/sportsguynorth?lang=en, www.facebook.com/nashvillepredators/posts/randall-and-rosalind-johansen-made-

Jeremy Rupke - howtohockey.com/about/jeremy-rupke/, ca.linkedin.com/in/howtohockey

Ian Gallagher - deltahockeyacademy.com/coaches/, www.nhl.com/canadiens/news/ian-gallagher-looked-after-his-sons-physical-training-, www.nytimes.com/2014/01/30/sports/hockey/trainer-finds-himself-on-both-sides-of-c

Joe Oliver - kosportsinc.com/team-members/joe-oliver/, www.nhlpa.com/the-pa/certified-agents?range=O-P

Mike Johnston - en.wikipedia.org/wiki/Mike_Johnston_(ice_hockey), www.hockeydb.com/ihdb/stats/pdisplay.php?pid=29039, winterhawks.com/hockeystaff/

Troy Ward - www.eliteprospects.com/player/105704/troy-ward, www.hockeyandsons.com/troy-ward,en.wikipedia.org/wiki/Troy_G._Ward

Kurt Overhardt - kosportsinc.com/team-members/kurt-overhardt/, www.forbes.com/profile/kurt-overhardt/, www.nhlpa.com/the-pa/certified-agents?range=O-P

TESTIMONIALS

"Ron's training has taken my skill development to a new level. The detail and direct correlations to game situations has helped me dramatically."

Max McCormick NHL -Ottawa Senators

"His knowledge of the game is exceptional. He has a deep understanding of skills and how they apply to game situations. This allows him to think outside the box."

Ryan Kesler – NHL Anaheim Ducks

"Ron is one of the most innovative and hardworking people that I've ever met. Additionally, his ability to tell it like it is and hold people accountable is second to none."

Andrew Copp – NHL Winnipeg Jets

"Ron's advanced knowledge of hockey combined with his expertise in biomechanics makes him an incredibly valuable coach and mentor. Whether it's skating, individual skill development or offensive concepts, Ron's experience and background make him one of the best hockey minds in the world."

Ben Street – NHL Anaheim Ducks

"What separates Ron from others is his deep knowledge of the game. I truly believe what he teaches is next level. He is and always has been three steps ahead of the other guys in the industry. Ron takes the required time to work with each individual and because of this he gives you that crystal clear understanding of how and why things are done through every process."

Randall Johansen - father of Lucas Johansen, Hershey Bears AHL (Washington Draft pick), and Ryan Johansen, NHL Nashville Predators.

"I still remember as a teenager having my very first shooting clinic session with Ron. I thought at that time I had already mastered my snap shot. Within three sessions, radar demonstrated that I had added about fifteen mph to it."

Ryan Johansen NHL Nashville Predators

"Ron is a transformational teacher and a stand out human being who had profoundly impacted the lives of our two sons. Ron is extraordinarily insightful, dedicated, hardworking and loyal. He is will to give valuable and direct feedback and is not afraid to push boundaries. Our boys have matured tremendously with Ron's guidance because he has taught them countless rudimentary lessons that are applicable both on and off the ice. If is for these reasons why our family goes to extraordinary lengths to work with Ron and why you should read his book!"

John Ross – father of Tyler and Austin Ross, New York.

BIOGRAPHY

Ron Johnson is considered one of the top technical, bio-mechanical, and tactical hockey advisors in the world according to the New York Times. He has a Bachelor of Sport Science (BSc.) and a Master of Sport Science (MSc.).

His pioneering research studies have led to the creation of Elite Hockey Science (EHS), a comprehensive skills development company based on his applied learning system called STEP (Sequential Training for Elite Performance). EHS has analyzed over 30,000 NHL goals in the last ten years to track mechanical, behavioral, and tactical trends in professional hockey in order to advise professionals and improve individual and team development at every level.

Ron also served as a technical director on the movie "Miracle", as well as being the co-founder and technical director of Next Testing, an international hockey advisory company pioneering on ice performance assessment and working with the NHL, Central Scouting and many NCAA and junior hockey programs.

International players from Australia, Japan, South Korea, China, Czechoslovakia, Russia, Germany and the United States travel to train with Ron. He currently serves as a personal coach to many NHL players, as well as spending a good portion of his time, locally, working with youth hockey players. Ron currently resides in Langley, BC, Canada, with his wife Catherine.

CLOSING COMMENTS

This book is the first in a series that will try to uncover the mysteries of the game. The second book will be entitled; *"ICE HOCKEY – IN SEARCH OF EXCELLENCE: THE LEARNING GAME"*

I often use school learning as an example of the shortcomings of our thinking. If one were to follow a chronological process, learning in public or private school would follow a certain pattern:

1. The first stage would be one's ability to 'read and listen'. This would of course take into consideration, reading and listening comprehension.

2. The second stage would be memory. Can we accurately remember what we read or heard?

3. The third stage would be to regurgitate what we learned, either verbally or in writing that makes sense to others.

If we were to translate this into athleticism, we could make the following associations.

1. The first stage would be one's ability to 'look at and see specifics' in what the instructor or person of our attention is physically doing. This is done either focally or peripherally. The student would need to comprehend the feeling of the physical action.

2. The second stage would again be memory; could one accurately remember physically what was demonstrated?

3. The third stage would be physical memory; the ability to 'mimic' or duplicate exactly what the instructor did.

If we think of highly skilled or professional players, they have the ability to acquire and perfect more skills than others. In essence, it is predominantly one's ability to learn new skills and then execute them, successfully, in game situations that leads to success.

The next book in this series will focus on one's ability to learn and then to apply hockey skills in the most efficient and expedient way possible. Please look for it online or at your preferred book retailer.

Thank you,

Ron Johnson, BSc. MSc.

CPSIA information can be obtained
at www.ICGtesting.com
Printed in the USA
LVHW050305141218
600366LV00027B/680

9 780228 809456